DEVELOPING
NUCLEAR IDEAS

Chris Gamer
225 252 1735

NEW INTERNATIONAL LIBRARY OF GROUP ANALYSIS

Series Editor: Earl Hopper

Other titles in the Series

DEVELOPING NUCLEAR IDEAS

Relational Group Psychotherapy

Richard M. Billow

KARNAC

First published in 2015 by
Karnac Books Ltd
118 Finchley Road, London NW3 5HT

British Library Cataloguing in Publication Data

A C.I.P. for this book is available from the British Library

ISBN 978 1 78220 089 5 (hbk)
ISBN 978 1 78220 205 9 (pbk)

Edited, designed and produced by The Studio Publishing Services Ltd
www.publishingservicesuk.co.uk
e-mail: studio@publishingservicesuk.co.uk

www.karnacbooks.com

CONTENTS

ACKNOWLEDGEMENTS

"Every writer needs a Charles Raps," replied my friend, Earl Hopper, when I requested he hold off a final read-through of this manuscript for one more edit. He does not know Charlie, but I did not need to tell him who and what would be involved. Friends know our habits, our limitations, and strengths, and, therefore, of my reliance on Charles for a first, second . . . and final examination of my work. As with my companion volumes, *Relational Group Psychotherapy: From Basic Assumptions to Passion*, and *Resistance, Rebellion, and Refusal: The 3 Rs*, *Developing Nuclear Ideas: Relational Group Psychotherapy* benefits greatly from Charles' dedication to my needs, writerly and otherwise. He and his wife, Rosemarie, have hosted my bi-weekly winter visits to their home in Salt Lake City, Utah, and provided spiritual and material comforts, delicious food, and a quiet study and computer. On and off the ski slopes, Charlie insists on well-executed turns—thankfully. He has discussed, clarified, and contributed his originality to each volume's central theses, ideas, and cogency of the clinical examples. I minimally reciprocate his unsparing dedication by dedicating this volume to him.

Joining (in season) our subgroup, and weighing in with his valuable philosophical and psychoanalytic insights, Bionic and otherwise, James Poulton, PhD has been a trusted resource and ski buddy.

It is unlikely that anyone is, or could be, more interested in group, ideas about group, and people who are involved in the study and practice of group than Earl Hopper, PhD. His leadership in the group movement is worldwide. Group people know Earl through his erudite writings, organisational guidance, and as a star presenter, discussant, and courageous "taker" of conference groups, large, median, and small. Earl does not suffer what he considers the foolish or pompous—and is not known for holding back such opinions. So I am complimented by his interest in, and understanding of, my writings and in me, personally. Earl oversaw my efforts and provided interesting directions to take some of my ideas. He is an enthusiastic travel companion and makes any conference or time together a special event. As the Editor of the New International Library of Group Analysis, he perused the final manuscript and shepherded its publication.

Oliver Rathbone, of Karnac Books, has been the ideal publisher, welcoming and responsive to my concerns, and upfront with his own opinions. As with my previous volume on the 3 Rs, he and the entire Karnac staff have been reassuring presences, easing me through the publication process. Rod Tweedy has served as sensitive and responsive desk editor.

Les R. Greene, PhD, the current president of the American Group Psychotherapy Association, has been an ongoing source of support and guidance. I will miss his editorship of the *International Journal of Group Psychotherapy*. He oversaw the submissions and revisions of my *Journal* articles, many of which I have rethought, reconfigured, and redeveloped for this volume. I thank him for his good spirits, and for supplying first-rate reviewers for my submissions, organising their helpful and often lengthy evaluations, and, most especially, for his own.

The following organisers and organisations provided opportunity to sharpen my work, by inviting me to present to colleagues and students from different subcultures and cultures. Maria Ammon, Erwin Lebner, and Nikolaj G. Neznanov, the World Association for Dynamic Psychiatry and the German Academy for Psychoanalysis, Munich, Germany; Lars Bo Jørgensen, Helle Østerby Andersen, and Per Sørensen Group Analytic Society and the Institute of Group Analysis, Copenhagen, Denmark. Charles Huffstadt, Dutch Society of Group Psychotherapy and Group Dynamics (in Dutch, NVGP); Mike Teplitz, Israeli Association for Group Psychotherapy, John Chebultz, Eddie Hunt, and Karen Shore, Group Psychotherapy Association of

Los Angeles, Daisy Reese and Haim Weinberg, Northern California Group Psychotherapy Society, Ronnie Levine and Dominick Grundy, The Eastern Group Psychotherapy Society, Dale C. Godby, University of Texas, Southwestern Medical Center (Dallas), Jay Erwin-Grotsky and Jan Morris, Austin Group Psychotherapy Society, Cecil Rice, Gaea Logan, and Julie Anderson, Northestern Society for Group Psychotherapy, and Chris Garner and Rudy Troyer, Louisiana Group Psychotherapy Society. My special thanks to our friends, Drs Sabar and Piloo Rustomjee, who were wonderful hosts and tour guides during a visit to Melbourne, Australia, and supported my presentation to the International Organization of Group Analytic Psychotherapy.

I appreciate the collaboration of respected colleagues who have worked with me and have invited my contribution to their publications and conferences, and have responded to my writing. These include Victor Schermer, Christine Kieffer, Fred Wright, Joe Shay, Robert Grossmark, Malcolm Pines, Andy Eig, Dominick Grundy, Jerome Gans, John Schlapobersky, Haim Weinberg, Jeffrey L. Kleinberg, James S. Grotstein, Lise Motherwell, Juan Tubert-Oklander, Arnout ter Haar, Ben Roth, Esther Stone, Leyla Navaro, Cecil Rice, Robert H. Klein, Robi Friedman, Sharan Schwartzberg, David Scharff, Martha Gilmore, Lisa Stern, Robert Farrell, Eleanor Couselman, Ed Neukrug, Nina W. Brown, and Steven L. Van Wagoner.

The American Group Psychotherapy Association, under the attentive eyes of Marsha S. Block and Angela Stevens, the Eastern Group Psychotherapy Society, and the International Association for Group Psychotherapy and Group Processes have been durable host organisations, providing a community of receptive colleagues, stimulating meetings, and scholarly publications.

The Derner Institute of Advanced Psychological Studies of Adelphi University has been an intellectual and emotional home for over forty-five years. Directing our Postgraduate Group Program has given me access to an especially creative and vocal population of candidates who have provided rich material from their own practices as well as participated creatively in experiential learning. I am grateful for the support from the Director of the Postgraduate Programs, Dr Mary Beth Cresci and our program directors, Mike Zentman, Steve Hyman, Elaine Seitz, Andy Karpf, and Jack Herkovits, and from our recently retired Administrative Assistant, Mrs Marge Burgard.

I thank the inspirational sources of my thinking, and writing: the sensitive and articulate individuals I have been privileged to work with in my clinical combined practice. The knowledge that I write books on groups has entered in our culture, but I believe it affects me far more than anyone else. I have an ongoing supervisor—the reader—whom I imagine overlooks my efforts, and kindly, but not always.

Finally, to my wife, Elyse, who devotedly supports my efforts, and me. I love her especially for maintaining the faith in, as well as for tolerating the grumpy lows of, the creative process. Our children, Jennifer, David, and Brette, and son-in-law, Bryon, our grandchildren, Jordyn, Jaxon, and Mason, and our niece, Olivia Billow, spur generative impulses that lift spirits and put scholarly and clinical ambitions in their proper perspective.

Revised material

Revised, reworked, and excerpted material from the following journal articles and book chapters I authored appears in the following chapters.

Chapter One: (2013). Developing nuclear ideas. *International Journal of Group Psychotherapy*, *63*: 544–570.

Chapter Two: (2013). On scrutiny: a nuclear idea. *International Journal of Group Psychotherapy*, *63*: 1–22.

Chapter Three: (2013). Sense and sensibility in group psychotherapy. *International Journal of Group Psychotherapy*, *63*.

Chapter Four: (2012). On hostage taking (A psychoanalytic object). *International Journal of Group Psychotherapy*, *62*: 45–68.

Chapter Five: (2012). Facebook as "social fact". *Group*, *33*: 213–222.

Chapter Six: (2012). Bullying: the gang inside and outside. *Group Analysis*, *45*: 189–202; (2013) The bully inside us: the gang in the mind. *Psychoanalytic Inquiry*, *33*: 130–143.

Chapter Seven: (2013). On inveiglement. *International Journal of Group Psychotherapy*, *63*: 274–300.

Chapter Eight: (2011). It's all about "me": on the group leader's psychology. *Group Analysis, 44*: 296–314; (2012) It's all about me: introduction to relational group psychotherapy. In: J. L. Kleinberg (Ed.), *The Wiley–Blackwell Handbook of Group Psychotherapy* (pp. 169–185). Chichester: John Wiley.

Chapter Nine: (2012). It's all about "me" (behold the leader). *International Journal of Group Psychotherapy, 62*: 531–556.

Chapter Ten: (2013). The invited presenter: outrageousness and outrage. *International Journal of Group Psychotherapy, 63*: 317–345.

Chapter Eleven: (2013). Appreciating "Le Non/Nom". *Group Analysis, 46*: 33–47.

*To Charles S. Raps, PhD—my multidimensional and
most singular reference group*

ABOUT THE AUTHOR

Richard M. Billow, PhD, is Board Certified in group psychotherapy, a clinical psychologist and psychoanalyst, and an active contributor to the psychoanalytic and group literature. He is Clinical Professor and Director of the Group Program of the Derner Institute of Advanced Psychological Studies, Adelphi University, New York, with a private practice in Great Neck, New York.

Very few psychoanalysts have yet realised the theoretical and clinical implications of the shift and development from a one individual organism psychology, based on a theory of drives and instincts, to a two-person psychology, based on a theory of asymmetrical interactions between mother and infant, let alone to a multi-person social psychology, based on a field theory of relationships within a transgenerational socio–cultural–political context. If social systems, on the one hand, and their individual members, on the other, are each polarised abstractions from the magna of the universe, then surely the social sciences and psychoanalysis are also polarised abstractions, based more on the administration of knowledge in institutions of higher learning than on attempts to understand the dynamics of human entities. Such abstractions have heuristic and management value, but they are false and misleading in our attempts to understand persons and their groupings.

It is axiomatic in group analysis that clinical theory should be expressed in terms of persons in relationships within their families, organisations, groupings of various kinds, and their contextual societies (Hopper & Weinberg, 2011). Of course, very few of us are able, or even inclined, to work with each and all of these entities.

Certainly, very few of us are trained in their pertinent explanatory and treatment modalities, which range from intensive psychoanalysis within the clinical dyad to political action within parties and interest groups. None the less, we are all obliged to be aware of these entities and their interpenetrating and overlapping constraints and restraints, and to be informed by the ideas and data that characterise their respective modes of enquiry, which range from biology and neuro-physiology to the social sciences in general (Hopper, 2013).

The most mature and, perhaps, even the most ethical attitude of the contemporary psychoanalytical and group analytical clinician is, therefore, independent and eclectic, but also integrative and relational. Above all, the clinician must be truth seeking and truth bearing. At the same time, however, he must be wise and compassionate concerning the psychic pain and suffering, as well as the emotional and intellectual freedom, that are likely to emerge from hard-won insights into the non-conscious, unconscious, and pre-conscious mind, which is always a changing collective mind, virtually by definition. The epistemology of the understanding of living human systems will always be coloured by political and philosophical—if not religious—assumptions.

Dr Richard Billow is one of a small band of colleagues who appreciate such concerns. After studying Modern English Literature at graduate level, Dr Billow worked in fiction and non-fiction trade publishing in New York. He then completed the Derner Doctoral Program in Clinical Psychology at Adelphi University, concentrating on cognitive–developmental psychology. His dissertation was supervised by Dr Sonia Osler, a noted Piagetian scholar. In fact, he published three very well received articles on metaphor and their comprehension by children (Billow, 1975, 1977, 1981). Having interned at the Massachusetts Mental Health Center in Boston, Richard immediately joined the Doctoral Faculty at the Derner Institute in Adelphi, and then obtained postdoctoral certificates in psychoanalysis and group psychotherapy. From the beginning of his training, he experienced individual and group psychoanalytical psychotherapy, as well as both clinical modalities combined. He was influenced by such pioneers as Elizabeth Zetzel, Harold Searles, and, more recently, James Grotstein in the USA. He had several supervisory consultations with W. R. Bion. Billow immersed himself in the work of early Object Relations psychoanalysts, such as Klein, Winnicott, and Fairbairn in the UK, Jacobson, Kernberg, and Kohut in the USA, and Racker in Argentina, each of whom has contributed to laying the foundations of what has come to be called "Relational Psychoanalysis". Dr Billow was influenced especially by mining the mother-lode of Melanie Klein, and has developed a particular identification with the late New World work of Bion. However, I have no doubt that in the context of psychoanalysis in the UK, Richard would be regarded as an Independent, and would be pleased to accept this "location".

Billow is much appreciated as a teacher, supervisor, and professional colleague. He is a longstanding member of the Postdoctoral Faculty of the Derner Institute of Adelphi University, and the Director of the Postgraduate Group Program. He has served in the Governance of the American Group Psychotherapy Association and other professional organisations. He presents his work in many local, national, and international conferences and workshops.

In his own view, Billow's living contribution to the relational perspective can be traced to his deep involvement in his own family life. His interest in groups was forged in his relations with his maternal and paternal cousins, and his early, perhaps even precocious, leadership of these overlapping kinship groupings. His wife, Elyse, is not only his companion, but also a colleague, and they share their ideas about theory and clinical work. Richard is a father and grandfather, and clearly has a personal sense of connection to transgenerational and transnational processes.

Although his personal and professional roots are in Europe, he is very American in his way of life and work. His clinical language is down to earth and experience-near. He is antiauthoritarian and almost instinctively egalitarian and democratic. He needs to make his own discoveries in the context of diverse traditions of thought. This is manifest in his interest in modern art, currently in Latin-American painting and sculpture. It must at least be mentioned that "Rich" spends almost as much time skiing and exploring the slopes of several mountain ranges as he does thinking about psychoanalysis, group analysis, and the human condition.

Richard Billow has helped to lay the foundations of "Relational Group Analysis". If unconscious phantasy, innate malign envy, and projective identification are the key elements in the Kleinian and early Bionian project, then the primacy of helplessness, the complementarity of introjective identification, and the importance of preconscious symbolism and communication in general are the key elements of the meta-psychology of "relational group analysis". Implicit in this new book of extensively reworked and revised peer reviewed articles are questions such as: what are the key elements in a meta-social psychology of groups as living human systems? How can this emerging perspective be applied to experience-near clinical work? Only a few of us have risked the leaps of thinking that answers to such questions require. Each of us has acknowledged the influence of the great social psychologists and sociologists of the nineteenth and twentieth centuries, although not always directly. Each of us has also struggled with the vicissitudes of dire mastery, which involves knowing one's own forms of resistance, rebellion, and refusal, the "3-Rs" of one of the "nuclear ideas" that inform and structure Billow's work. The structures, functions, and vicissitudes of nuclear ideas are explored and clinical examples presented. The study of his own countertransference processes is central to Billow's project.

It is not surprising that Dr Richard Billow has discovered the work of S. H. Foulkes, who defined group analysis as ". . . a form of psychotherapy by the group, of the group, including its conductor" (1975, p. 3). I suspect that in one way or another, the next step in Billow's passionate study of authenticity in the clinical relationship will be a return to the work of existentialist psychoanalysts. I also anticipate a further exploration of Lacanian ideas concerning the nature of pleasure, desire, and satisfaction. I suspect that this will lead to a deeper engagement with ideas about the social unconscious.

I readily recommend this book to colleagues and students on both sides of the pond, and on both sides of the Equator. It is astute, enabling, and positive. It has many zones of excitement, interest, and enquiry.

Earl Hopper, PhD
Series Editor

Introduction: relational group psychotherapy and the nuclear idea

"Relational"—a word of the *zeitgeist*—is commonly understood to refer to what goes on between people, including inner representations and phenomena. It must also refer, then, to the relationships people and groups have with their individual and collective ideas. Relational theory builds on neo-Freudian, Kleinian Middle School, interpersonal, intersubjective, and self-theory constructs (for recent reviews, see Poulton, 2013; Schermer & Rice, 2012; Schwartz, 2012). The common denominator is the emphasis on relationships, internal and external, and their dynamic, life-supporting qualities, rather than primarily on metapsychological entities such as drives, defences, ego structure, or an archaeological unconscious.

The need for "truth", that is, to think about and digest intersubjective experience to make it meaningful, is a central motivator and organiser of the self and group.

However, individuals remain in conflict over discovering truth, since it might cause pain, and all group members (including the therapist) struggle with a limited ability and willingness to pursue the infinite potentials of the meaning-making process. As well, certain truths, and certain modes of truth seeking, might be experienced as destructive to the self or to the other, and so not beneficial. Even when factual, truth may be challenged as misleading, irrelevant, or inappropriate, a buffer against genuine mental interaction, and so, in some sense, false. Individuals and groups resist, and also rebel against or refuse to participate in truth-seeking for all sorts of motives, including some that are reasonable and wise.

In my previous book, *Resistance, Rebellion, and Refusal in Groups: The 3 Rs*, I presented a model of group organisation and activity as a series of pathways—each with moves and countermoves—directed to express, redirect, modify, or block the search for emotional truth. In leading the search for truth, the group therapist grapples with the 3 Rs—strategies our patients (and ourselves) use for intrapsychic and psychosocial purposes. Since I believe that the psychology of the therapist remains central in all phases of group life, I continue in this volume to emphasise personal and professional factors that the therapist needs to struggle with. However, as a relational practitioner, I remain wary of reliance on any model, theory, or specific perspective on truth and truth-seeking, including my own.

I try to enter a group session with an open mind and without expectations, except the expectation that something unexpected will emerge, and that it will be challenging to me personally. I know that I might not be able, or even willing, to adequately understand the truth that is emerging—to have the skill or fortitude to address the situation successfully. I take comfort that I am not the only person struggling to think and make sense out of experience. In most groups, someone, several, or all will work with me—even when we might seem to be at odds—and in due course, provide material for collaboration and mutual growth. I approach each session with a sense of newness, excitement, and some dread.

Therapeutic relationships, sometimes conceived in terms of ongoing, inevitable, transference–countertransference "enactments" (see Ivey, 2008 for a recent review), reveal the currency as well as the history of interpersonal affiliative patterns. Explorations of the past—retrospections—are useful in understanding the present, and in releasing the individual and group from old allegiances, allowing for increased vitality, change, and growth.

I depend on introjective–projective processes, precursors and accompaniments to empathy and bonding. Initial and ongoing verbal and non-verbal exchanges give me a sense of each member and the group mood: "them", "me", and "us". Frames of mind—internal, subgroup, and group—shift, from the moment of greeting and reunion (the new session), yet there is continuity, too. Every group begins with some tentativeness, for, however familiar, the group, as an evolving, exploratory entity, faces the unknown.

Most often, I sit quietly and see where others take us. But I monitor the proceedings and feel free to intercede diplomatically (Chapter Four), that is, to negotiate the nature and boundaries of interpersonal exchange, and work towards therapeutic goals. Being diplomatic might be as simple as suggesting that we stay "in the room" or attend to what is going on "now". However, sometimes my diplomatic manoeuvres—how I go about bringing people together, and structure relationships, rules, and mediums of exchange—do not chime with the mood, beliefs, or intentions, of another, or many others (see Chapter Ten, in particular). If resistance is implicated, as classically understood, I consider its valence in the immediacy of our co-creation, whether it resides primarily in the speaker, the target (often me), their interaction, or also, in the socio-political context of the professional relationship.

The group process might shift from interest in intrapsychic and interpersonal levels of meaning, to strategies of rebellion: questioning or challenging how I lead, the structures I wish to set up and maintain, and the truth-goals I work for. Not infrequently, certain phases and exploratory foci of the work are met with refusal. Although group processes of rebellion and refusal might be personally difficult for the therapist, they need to be respected as possibly raising legitimate and thought-provoking issues.

The best hope I have of leading a successful group is to relax, give people a sense of who I am by relating to them in a thoughtful, sometimes playful manner, and conveying that I am thinking about and trying to make sense of the here-and-now group experience. As we know, the emotional and cognitive tasks of the group therapist are multiple and complex. I engage in and attempt to absorb the emotional experience of being in the group and responding to other members, all the while subject to my associations and cohering thoughts at various levels of personal awareness. Ongoing narratives unfold in my mind, connected to, or even, seemingly, disconnected from, anything else that is taking place or had taken place in group.

At some point, I realise that my thinking is converging on what I will be referring to as a nuclear idea, which might have been vague and unformulated, suppressed from consciousness or from public expression, or surprising and unforeseen. Probably, I will share my experience about this thought that has captured my attention, linking it to occurrences that could serve as a common group reference, such as an explicit or submerged interactional pattern, or a recurrent theme or metaphor. Usually, I leave the nuclear idea as a tentative formulation, and see how and if others respond and develop it further.

The nuclear idea emerges out of a discourse between the therapist's mind and the mind of each member of the group, separately and together—all minds being influenced by the others, and the immediate and historical context of the group, non-conscious processes,[1] outside events, personal, cultural, and societal. Still, as in my previous volumes (Billow, 2003a, 2010a), I confer on the therapist's experience as a thinking subject a primary influence on the formation and evolution of the group structure, culture, and process. The therapist comes to formulate and reflect on nuclear ideas, which may be about other individuals, him or herself, or about the group.

My intention in this volume is to define and illustrate the utility of thinking about and developing nuclear ideas, and becoming aware of thought-limiting, action-orientated polemic ideas, without suggesting certainty or finality in assessing self, other, and the group interactions. In making distinctions and introducing complexity, the therapist calls attention to the ambiguous, multi-faceted nature of intersubjective group experience. People are drawn to a type of multi-level, multi-relational (psycho)analysis in developing nuclear ideas, which investigates and also stimulates intense emotional reactions, but without being unduly confrontational or threatening. The emotional–intellectual, truth-seeking venture comes to characterise the culture and process of our groups.

A good and well-timed idea serves holding and containing functions: modifying excessive tensions and aggression, reaffirming bonding, and setting boundaries around feelings and fantasies—providing the scaffolding of appropriate safety and risk for thought. Nuclear ideas contribute to the therapist's essential task, which is to establish an environment to utilise the self, others, and whole group as "transformational objects" (Bollas, 1989)—to foster meaning making, growth, and development.

I attempt to discover something fresh in my sense of my own psychology, as I participate in, think about, and review the groups I lead. During and afterwards, I attempt to identify blind spots and unresolved conflicts, manage anxiety, and push forward towards new areas of emotional growth and technical finesse. We cannot reach the unobtainable Freudian ideal of post-analytic inoculation purification, but we can be different to ourselves and in our interpersonal relations.

Each and every group meeting should be a learning experience, and that involves the growth of ideas that link up to the group and also become personally relevant. Core ideas might first dwell in the imagistic and unformulated, in dreams, individual and group enactments, and in the stream of verbalisations, associations, and themes. Developed as nuclear ideas, they may soothe or stimulate interpersonal tensions (or accomplish both simultaneously): they strengthen mutual interest and respect, curiosity, faith in the group process, and positive expectations.

Groups are commonly understood through various lenses: whole group, interpersonal, and intrapsychic. The nuclear idea integrates these three views, and so provides a unified basis for leader interventions. I now introduce the reader to the organisation of this volume and supply brief chapter descriptions.

Part I: "The nuclear idea: concept and technique" approaches my topic from different viewpoints. Chapter One, "Developing nuclear ideas", provides the framework for how the therapist—and the group itself—might go about the task of containing and making sense of the perceptions, conceptions, affects, and enactments of the dynamic group process.

The chapter puts forward and defines what I believe to be an essence of relationally orientated group psychotherapy. Evolving from the verbalisations and enactments through which the group symbolises and becomes known—a nuclear idea takes shape. It emerges from the nucleus of the group process: co-created from intersubjective forces and locations that cannot be fully specified, yet might be possible to observe, name, and utilise clinically.

Chapter Two, "The four dimensions of a nuclear idea", calls attention to the experiential, symbolic, affective, and metapsychological dimensions of a nuclear idea, via an investigation of "scrutiny". In effect, the intersubjective metapsychology of the group comes about through the very process of self–other scrutiny. A series of group psychotherapy sessions describe how each member's mental relationship to the prospect or experience of scrutinising or being scrutinised contributed to a prominent and productive nuclear idea.

In Chapter Three, "Grounding the nuclear idea: sense and clinical sensibility", I emphasise how the domain of sense functions as a crucial reference point. Each member asserts influence in taking a role as the perceiver and the perceived, the senser and the sensed, and reference to sense brings experience near and grounds group discussion. The leader utilises his or her particular clinical sensibility to reach the group and focus attention: to link sense to psychic qualities, to the personality of the members, to the group culture and process, and to the live clinical interaction that grounds the nuclear idea, and ultimately, energises its metapsychology.

Chapter Four, "Processing nuclear ideas via four communicative modes", employs the four modes of leadership paradigm introduced in my previous volume (Billow, 2010a). Diplomacy, integrity, sincerity, and authenticity call upon different aspects of the therapist's (inter)subjectivity. All were brought into play as I developed with the group the idea of "hostage taking", in reference to a dramatic enactment that gripped us all.

Chapter Five, "When the group refuses a nuclear idea", considers the common occurrence of a group's overt disavowal of interest in the leader's ideas. In one therapy group, members decided to connect via Facebook, which I attempted to approach as nuclear idea in order to make explicit and explore some of the purposes it served, in fantasy and in the intersubjective context of our group. A significant interval of time passed before the group seemed ready to consider the factors behind Facebook's importance to so many members.

Part II: "The influence of polemic ideas" introduces the concept of the polemic idea, which functions in tension to creative thinking, and has a goal to incite or inhibit the behaviour of others. Whereas the nuclear idea emerges unbidden from interactions among the minds of the individuals comprising the group, the polemic idea emerges from a calculated mind-set of an individual or subgroup, with a particular interest in swaying other minds and group process. This type of leader (or member aspiring to leadership) might depend on bombast, hyperbole, as well as subtler oratory that, by narrowing and focusing feelings and thought, seeks to promote facile and immediate decision making. The polemicist wishes to bend the group to his or her will. Group communication is used to encourage conformity and quell dissension. A mob or crowd group culture might eventuate, guided by the charismatic one, who plays on vulnerabilities. The goal might be to establish one Truth, which the leader believes, or wishes the assemblage to believe.

Chapter Six, "Bipolar thinking leads to polemic ideas", proposes that, although layered over by education, ethical precepts, and the veneer of civilisation, our thinking retains a regressive, bipolar mode, producing polemical ideas: simplistic and personified psychological, moral, and political constructs that drive affects, fantasies, and compelling action scenarios. We gravitate towards bipolarity, particularly when afraid, anxious, or perplexed. Individuals, groups, and larger socio-political entities broadcast—and project and collude to set up others to broadcast—polemic ideas. The therapist's task is to subject these ideas and those who broadcast them (including oneself) to productive thinking, so that they serve the group function of developing nuclear ideas.

Chapter Seven, "Inveiglement", describes a mode of interpersonal influence and control that has particular relevance to group, organisational, and political life. In inveiglement, a person or group is "blinded", that is, diverted from knowing, believing, or thinking about an idea or a perception that exists mentally, or that could be generated. In the former situation, inveiglement may be conceived of as induced dissociation, in the latter, an impingement on the capacity to think and generate thoughts. In both situations, the individual or group becomes mentally bound by polemic ideas, parameters imposed by the other, constricting freedom to think and behave independently. I describe four subtypes: toxic, neurotic, communal, and presentational inveiglement.

Part III: "It's all about 'me'" treats the therapist's psychology—and the group's experience of and response to it—as a nuclear idea that begs for attention. In group, whatever is being talked about—whoever is reacting to whom or to what—the focal conflict, predominating basic assumption, developmental level or stage, its regressions and progressions, dyadic interactions, subgroupings, to some extent, it is all about "me"—the therapist or group leader.

Chapter Eight, "The therapist's psychology as nuclear idea", considers the implicit impact of the therapist's psychology on the group's structure and process. Neither therapist nor member can be aware of many of the important group activities that are unfolding

without verbal awareness, co-determined by the individuals' reciprocally interacting subjective worlds. The participants may learn about
what has been going on when they allow themselves to reflect on their
idea(s) regarding the therapist's psychology and its effects, as they
have come to understand them in the context of the group.

Chapter Nine, "The group beholds its leader", regards the leader
as a looming figure of fantasy, and as an emerging figure of reality.
Psychic patterns that play out in group cohesion, culture, conflicts,
and process are rooted in interaction with this mental object. As the
representative, messenger, even embodiment of truth, the leader
stimulates intense reactions and behavioural tendencies, some that the
group member seeks to hide from himself as well as from others, even
when, at the same time, enacting them in the group setting.

Chapter Ten, "The invited presenter: outrage and outrageousness", contends that the effective therapist must risk being perceived
as outrageous, a challenger of established ways of thinking and being.
Without such leadership, a group—whether in formation or ongoing—is more likely to be marked by polemic ideas: inauthenticity,
conventionality, and stalemate, and occupied by submission to, or
rebellion against, authority. The leader's perceived outrageousness—
and a group or subgroup response of outrage—might signal the possibility of something new: the emergence of a nuclear idea that invites
curiosity and the adventure of learning.

Chapter Eleven, "The group therapist is 'that guy': organising
speech", asserts and demonstrates how, in the development of a new
group, and as an element of any self-reflecting group, the group therapist uses and encourages the use of language to move process from
its underlying basic assumptiveness to the symbolised and articulated
emotional experience from which nuclear ideas develop. Hence, the
leader asserts the Lacanian "third", or oedipal, vertex, expressed
through initiating and inviting verbal intercourse. An essential aspect
of the professional/personal "me" involves, then, the therapist's realisation of, and comfort with, being sexual—that is, in existing in one's
own mind and potentially, in the minds of others, as a complex sexual
being, equipped with a powerful organ of speech.

PART I

THE NUCLEAR IDEA:
CONCEPT AND TECHNIQUE

CHAPTER ONE

Developing nuclear ideas

In the course of leading a group, ideas flow in and out of my consciousness. Some seem to originate from within me, although many emerge from the verbalisations and behaviours of others. Even if the group appears to move on, several ideas linger and begin to impinge. They are now asserting influence on me; unavoidably they affect group process. So, I think about why the ideas or set of ideas has captured my attention: what they have to do with the clinical situation—present and past—and with my psychology, to the extent to which I understand it.

I consider how these ideas relate to what others are saying and doing, linking together, if I am able, unfolding intrapsychic, interpersonal, and whole group themes and processes. It is at this point of connection that a *nuclear idea* begins to coalesce, but it must be examined. I try to see if the idea has relevance to others, and is applicable to smaller or larger milieus, or both. This places the idea in intellectual and symbolic contexts, which also have cultural and historical dimensions.

The idea has to feel vital. I can put it aside but not forget about it. Emotional reverberations energise my thoughts, and realisations sometimes occur that surprise me. If I wish to communicate, I must test whether the idea is comprehensible to other group members. Even if they are not having similar experiences, or are having them but do not see things my way, they need still to understand what I am referring to.

This progression, as I reflect, parallels Bion's (1963) notion of the psychoanalytic object. Bion left the concept unsaturated, to be built upon, although only a few others have written about it, and briefly (Grotstein, 2007, more extensively). I have found the concept helpful in achieving essential therapeutic goals of containment, cohesion, and coherence. As we shall see, developing nuclear ideas provides a way of thinking and working: shifting interest and discussion from "surface" contents to non-conscious or unexplored psychic processes in the individual and whole group, and, thus, to draw attention to multiple meanings—to the metapsychology of our interactions.

Bion's theoretical formulations tend to mystify and obscure their broad clinical utility, and also, tend to exalt the analyst or group therapist as the "seer" or "exceptional individual" (his terms). Bion (1962) conceptualised the psychoanalytic object as emerging from the "discourse and behaviour of the patient" (Britton, 1998, p. 817) and brought to meaning solely by the analyst, who uses observation, theory, his or her own emotional experience, and intuition. The analyst had to maximise the conditions so as to capture the patient's attention, establish a shared focus, invite symbolic thinking, and eventually, integrate the psychoanalytic object within an interpretation. In thinking about his ideas in terms of my own experience as group leader, member, and observer, I have chosen user-friendly words, and those that I believe more closely approximate what takes place in the group situation.

I shall be describing an approach to group that has remained undeveloped in the literature, although it is likely that it is as common in your practice as it is in mine. Evolving from the verbalisations and enactments through which the group symbolises and becomes known, a *nuclear idea* takes shape. The therapist now has an option to test the idea provisionally: to focus attention and redirect group process towards its personal, group, and even societal reverberations.

I conceive of nuclear ideas as emerging from the nucleus of the group process: from intersubjective forces and locations that cannot be fully specified, yet might be possible to observe, name, and utilise clinically. They arise from the indeterminacy of the network of communications and interactions, that is, from within the complexity (Schermer, 2012) of the dynamic matrix (Foulkes, 1964) or "culture" (Whitaker & Lieberman, 1964) of the group, co-created by the therapist's participation and influence, and expressed in the group's "idiom" (Bollas, 1989) and "discourse" (Schlapobersky, 1994), its particular language, symbolisation, and enaction.

While Bion provided a starting point, my application is group relational (Billow, 2003a; 2010a). As concept and technique, the nuclear idea—with its emphasis on meaning and the development of meaning as transformational (Bion, 1970; Bollas, 1987)—integrates the whole group, interpersonal, and intrapsychic foci, and so provides a unified basis for leader interventions.

Key qualities of the nuclear idea

A nuclear idea may evolve from any mental phenomenon that captures attention in the group, and, thus, may be felt, fantasised, and thought about on conscious and non-conscious levels. It might emerge—singularly or in combination—from a member's verbalisations (including the leader's), a group interchange or series of interchanges and enactments, or from the therapist's reverie, which become clarified in language. The idea might articulate an observation, a feeling, belief, or memory that takes place in group, and which might be about the group or any group, or a personality, such as a group member or leader.

A nuclear idea entails a process of thinking and developing thoughts. This process may begin and be abandoned early on, developed somewhat or by some individuals, or elaborated more fully. Still, as Schermer (2012) has emphasised, group participants carry out multiple and complex communications simultaneously, and significant information remains non-conscious and undisclosed. Thinking is never complete, and revealed truths are never absolute, but always subject to the revisions of time, circumstance, and human limitations in tolerating frustration and mental pain.

A nuclear idea possesses experiential, symbolic, affective, and metapsychological resonance. The experiential dimension provides empirical and communicable reference. The leader needs to determine if, and to what extent, its members are hearing, seeing, and talking about a similar or (different) experience. The symbolic dimension refers to levels of embedded meaning, conveyed in speech (metaphor, verbal imagery, etc.), enactions, and the group's sociopolitical culture. The nuclear idea represents and stirs strong feelings: the affective dimension ensures that the idea carries here-and-now emotionally significant weight. Last, metapsychological significance emerges when thoughts extend to general principles of self, group, and societal organisations. People come to think about how they think (and do not think), and, perhaps, when and why.

However, a nuclear idea does not have to become an immediate or even explicit focus of group activity. It can be partially and publically identified, or exist in the shared but unverbalised empathic space of the group. As long as it has resonance in the four dimensions, it operates as a tacit organiser.

Anything that takes place in group has the potential to inspire and develop into a nuclear idea. Something has transpired—an existential and intersubjective moment or sequence of moments becomes partially articulated in words or behaviour. The therapist may take the opportunity to link the idea thematically, to conceptualise further and negotiate meaning with the co-participation of other group members. Let us see how nuclear ideas are introduced and function in the life of four, insight-orientated groups of different types and durations.

Four clinical vignettes

Two groups

A veterans' hospital outpatient psychotherapy group changed leaders, as one psychologist, Lewis, replaced another, Rebecca, who had left the geographical area. The members missed Rebecca, of whom they spoke reverently. Yet, the group took to Lewis immediately, perhaps because Rebecca pushed the group to tolerate the painful termination process, which also included praise for her successor.

Lewis supported the members reviewing Rebecca's person and leadership. This continued long after the group evolved with newcomers. Even after several years, the old-timers would reminisce about "Rebecca's group", and how it differed from "Lewis's group". Recounting the dangerous behaviours they had eliminated or modified, this subgroup of self-described "rough guys" (including several females) declared that Rebecca had "saved our lives". Rebecca had put up with "no crap" and was not afraid of them. "We had to clean up our act, watch what we said and how we said it." "Very strict about rules and following them."

Lewis also queried the group about his leadership, which the senior members described as "more hang-back", "relaxed", "not such a rule stickler". "Rebecca locked the door, while you [Lewis] allow us to come in late." Still, "you can be a ball buster". "If you think someone has an issue that they don't want to talk about, you make us come back to it." "Rebecca did a lot of digging, now we do your fucking work."

One outcome of these discussions surprised the members: they had become and remained "well behaved", even though the style and gender of leadership changed.

Discussion

The core members of Rebecca's group had been through, and shared, a violent period of adjustment—they were old hands at dealing with their own chaos and that of the new members. Perhaps because of Lewis's inviting and non-authoritarian style, it became easier for the members to become his investigative allies. And also, perhaps, they did not need "tough love"—a phrase used repeatedly in describing Rebecca—not because what Rebecca did was unnecessary, but because the old members were more mature, and modelled (and perhaps enforced) maturity for the new ones.

In terms of enaction and symbolic influence, the two leaders—most probably unintentionally—took on parental roles related to earlier and later developmental phases of socialisation. Rebecca was a "toilet training" parent. A clear set of behavioural rules and expectations—a reinforced "yes" and a firm "no"—provided a basis for what the members had called "cleaning up our act", a process that was apparently absent or traumatically damaged in these veterans.

Lewis established or reinforced latency ideals of mutuality and co-operation. In doing "his fucking work", the seniors verbally and enactively transmitted behavioural norms and expectations—now internalised—to the new members. While not abrogating authority, and enforcing it when necessary, Lewis democratically shared investigative leadership, and it was the group members themselves who initiated the nuclear idea of the "two groups". Most probably, he encouraged its clarification and elaboration without forethought or conscious awareness. He was both leader and led, augmenting and creatively surrendering (Ghent, 1990) to the force of the idea of the "two groups".

To emphasise this point, Lewis did not make the old group, the ongoing group, or the comparisons between them an explicit nuclear idea. Here, the leader's role was to recognise and enjoy—allowing the members to think for themselves. The members' pungent language captured key qualities of the groups and its impact on the veterans' thinking and behaviour.

The nuclear idea of the "two groups" functioned as an unnamed "root metaphor" (Srivastva & Barrett, 1988, p. 37), linked experientially to the sensory–affective features of the therapists but stimulated by, and based on, their leadership behaviours, both symbolic and real. It operated as a material entity and as a complex "relational image" (Migliorati, 1989, p. 198), utilised in affectively intense exchanges that referenced the group and also extended to extra-group psychological functioning. "Two groups", thus, possessed the essential features of a well-developed nuclear idea: experiential, symbolic, affective, and metapsychological, bearing on and energising the here-and-now therapeutic process.

The "uncomfortable role" of being in group

I had the unusual opportunity to lead a demonstration group via Skype. The group conference took place in a city outside the USA. In an introductory exchange, the attendees expressed interest in hearing about "truth", "love and hate", "rebellion", and "connection", and I said I would try to address these concepts either in the small group or debriefing.

The room had been set up in preparation for the telecast: I faced a row of participants, with their backs to the large audience of observers. I suggested rearranging the chairs, so that the group of eight was rearranged in a semi-circle. While this improved the observers' sight-lines, my view of several of the members became eclipsed. Further, while I could be clearly seen in close up, the group members, at some distance from the camera lens, were blurry on my computer screen. Since nothing else could be done with the technical arrangements, we began, with fifty minutes allotted.

Not obscured by the electronic compress of our several thousand-mile distance was a familiar jolt of start-up apprehension, which I took as my own magnified by the group's. A woman remarked, "I feel uncomfortable, I can't explain why." Not waiting too long, I asked her if she could try. She repeated herself, and then asked if others could talk. I encouraged her once again to continue. She again appealed to the group, saying indistinctly, "I'm finding it hard to stay in role." Some mumbling among the group members followed, which I could not understand. Then, a man (his back to me) confessed, "We were assigned roles." Another member: "It's difficult not to be yourself."

I responded, "Me too. I was assigned a role and I want to be myself, and I'm uncomfortable too." The room resounded with laughter. "We're all in the same boat," I emphasised. The man tentatively suggested dropping role assignments, which met with exclamations of relief with no dissenters. I referred to the process as a constructive rebellion: modifying the rules of engagement seemed appropriate for the brief time we had together and could make it more likely that we could reach some emotional truths.

A woman addressed the group:

"I don't like the new arrangement."

"But you went along," another woman responded.

"Yes, that's what I do, I go along, then withdraw and sulk until I can't stand it, then protest."

The group seemed to enjoy her honesty and began to enquire further about this aspect of her psychology, about which she claimed to know nothing further.

The protesting woman was in my full view, and I said that she seemed to be angry, and with whom?

"I don't know . . . I guess you."

Although we were talking about anger, our exchange was amiable and she seemed pleased to be addressed directly. Another woman turned to her:

"You could be scary, but I'm glad you spoke up." A third woman said, "Yes, you made it easier for me."

The man who had revealed the role-playing spoke up.

"Maybe I shouldn't have said anything."

I said, "Are you apologising?"

"I started it," he reminded us.

"You seemed to be intimidated."

"No, yes, you're right." He turned enough for me to see the indistinct image of his profile: "I'm the youngest person here."

"And the first man to speak," I emphasised, and then asked him his age:

"Twenty-nine."

I told him that he was old enough to be a full member with equal rights. His thank you seemed emotional, and I felt that our exchange had been intimate, with some special significance for him, possibly related to the theme of being oneself.

And then from the remaining woman, who had been silent, "I'm bored."

I said that might be because she had not taken a chance to "connect" (I was referring to the term introduced by an audience member). Another woman interrupted, "I want to connect, but I am distracted by the audience. Several of them are raising their hands [also indicating boredom]."

I said to her that they were envious and that she could tell them to fuck themselves. My remarks drew another round of laughter from the room, and apparently the hands went down. "That feels better," she said. The woman professing boredom then engaged with several others; she said she no longer felt that way.

I asked if anyone else was bored. An older man said he was not bored, but confused:

"Is this supposed to be psychotherapy? Should I talk about my problems?"

I said that, given our time frame, we would not have time for "problems", and that he should just connect to feelings and to others.

The woman who had first spoken in our group addressed him:

"You were one of the reasons I was uncomfortable. We know each other from other places and haven't always got along. I like that I am in this with you and getting to know you differently."

With encouragement, she elaborated on what she had discovered about him.

Everyone in the group had taken opportunity to talk and address others, and after inviting them to do so once again, I closed the session.

Discussion

I heard the opening remarks as speaking for all: "I feel uncomfortable, I can't explain why." This shared and expectable discomfort gave birth to the germ of a nuclear idea that referred to the current state of our group in formation. When a participant revealed that the group volunteers had been given roles to play, as patients, but wanted to be themselves, I heard an opportunity to include myself, and to refine the nuclear idea by treating the disclosure metaphorically, metapsychologically, and self-referentially: "Me too. I was assigned a role and I want to be myself, and I'm uncomfortable too."

Although making reference to myself, I was really expanding on the nuclear idea: we were discomforted not only by being put into these roles of demonstration leader and members, but also by being in any group and needing to be ourselves, to think for ourselves, and to make meaning.

The use of the nuclear idea put us on task to reach multiple learning goals: it called attention to the painful quandary of any therapeutic or quasi-therapeutic situation addressing the need and discomfort of being and learning about oneself; it invited the members to share in the discovery process; it lessened the asymmetry between leader and members; it provided an example of the therapist's use of self; it opened the door to metacommunication: symbolic language and thinking; finally, it modelled risk taking, constructive rebellion (Billow, 2010a), and the open expression of intense feelings.

When I suggested that the bored audience members could be told to fuck themselves, I was merely extending the nuclear idea in the form of a whole group interpretation. By implication,[2] I was calling attention to a typical and unsurprising dynamic between two types of "uncomfortable roles" in a large group that might impede thinking: envious spectators who cannot actively participate, and the demonstration group members, with specific responsibilities and expectations, assigned or not.

Checkpoints

We were several hours into a two-day institute held in Jerusalem on the topic of "Reconciliation". The members had expressed interest in my writing on "passion", yet I found myself unable to reveal, stimulate, or feel any. In response to increasing conversational lulls, I suggested that people might be anxious. A woman immediately responded that she was "perfectly relaxed", and suggested that it was I who must be feeling anxiety. My acknowledgement sparked no interest or curiosity.

Someone suggested it might be a good idea to return to the theme of the conference. "Everyone here wants peace, yet the process seemed so sad and difficult," another woman lamented. The Gaza residents talked about their difficulty getting past Israeli checkpoints even to attend a meeting on reconciliation; the Israelis countered with justifications for the barriers. Each side related stories of hardship, loss, and terror.

When attendees from other countries attempted to moderate the rising antagonism, the Arabs and Israelis concurred that these suggestions were unfeasible, given the political climate in the Middle East and the influence of the "military–industrial complex". Intellectualisation replaced anger—but no passion.

After a while, I said that despite obvious ethnic and political tensions, the main barrier in the room appeared to be between everyone else and me. I could not locate, much less get through, a checkpoint and become part of this group. After some denials, reassurances, and hesitations, several members came forth with their doubts: I was an American, a visitor, and an outsider; how could I understand their anguish and loss? I acknowledged that I probably understood less than anyone else and would learn and gain more than anyone else during our two days together. I invited the group to deal with me directly when I went "off base".

The nuclear idea, which attended to the group's refusal (Billow, 2010a), located the impasse in an inhibited need to "check out" the leader. With verbal attention focused on the source of the group's impasse (the distrust of the leader as sufficiently empathic and knowledgeable), I achieved a point of entry. Now the group could attend to other barriers—difference and conflict related to ethnicity, citizenry, age, gender, political leanings, and personality. The women came forth to complain that the men—Israeli and Arab—had been doing all the talking. Two young Arab students confessed to being intimidated by their professor, sitting across the room. An Israeli housewife–community organiser confronted what she assumed were bellicose attitudes of the two high-ranking male soldier-psychologists from her country.

Whether reconciliation was possible remained a question throughout the two days, but now we were checking out each other openly and mutually, painfully learning about the glaring and consequential personal as well as socio-political forces and affiliations that are ineliminable aspects of our identities.

Discussion

Supplementing the typical paranoid/depressive dreads and excitements accompanying formation, our group was subject to specific determining influences: fear of, and anger toward, ethnic and religious difference, and a collective, traumatic disillusionment with leaders, local, national, and international. I had been serving as the personification of the distrusted leader, and a "foreigner", too. Calling attention to the "checkpoint" located the predicament a leader must face with an untrusting and angry group.[3]

The nuclear idea provided a point of entry for the messenger and the message.[4] I shifted from being a shared threat and common target to a sufficiently safe physical and mental reference that could be confronted and verbally "checked out". As the common target shifted from me to a nuclear idea of "me" (Part III, this volume), group process shifted from a restrictive solution (Whitaker & Lieberman, 1964), or static, basic assumptive fight/flight (Bion, 1961) stance, to thinking, feeling, and communicating—a self and group reflecting work group. The salutary effect was to destabilise the pre-existing ethnic subgroups and prejudices so that members could relate to me, and then to each other, as individuals. Resistances behind the refusal unfolded, bringing to the fore intersubjective factors related to age, gender, status, and member-to-member (horizontal) transferences.

Not being missed

A recent incident occurred in one of my analytic groups, this one of thirty-five years' duration.

"I'm just letting everyone know that I'm going to miss the next couple of weeks," said one of our members of four years.

He was surprised when people enquired as to his plans. I was surprised by his surprise and asked him, "Why are you surprised?" A woman of many, many more years piped up,

"I can understand that, I don't expect people to be interested in me when I'm not here. But I'm interested in you."

"I'm not surprised, I feel the same way, I will miss you, but I know I'm not missed," echoed several others.

I found this curious, given that people regularly began with "Where's so and so?" "How's so and so?" Absences were noted and talked about. In individual sessions, group mates often referred to and enquired and worried about other members.

"Everyone seems to miss everyone else, but nobody feels they're missed," I summarised. Several members initially dissented, but they re-examined their feelings in the interlude that followed, which revealed personal narratives:

"My father practised 'children should be seen and not heard'."

"I don't know why my parents had children, we seemed to be ignored."

"My sister was the pretty one; I was supposed to be smart, and if I wasn't, forget about it, I mean, forget me."

"It was about my mother, never about us."

"With my father, talk about sports or he disappeared behind a book. I have to concentrate on not being the same."

When I asked one of the speakers how her feelings affected her group participation, others joined in, so that our discussion extended to our group's culture and process. Members had registered, but had not previously talked about, the group's greeting and departing rituals: how and if they were addressed in the waiting room and who said goodbye and to whom. Only some of the members anticipated a friendly reception at the start of the session. Group etiquette included monitoring frequency and duration of "talking about oneself", "taking turns", and "attempting to interest others, but never being sure". Post session introspective preoccupations more than occasionally involved review of possible injury of others and fear of guilt-inducing retribution.

No matter the mutual reassurances and offers of disconfirming evidence, members echoed lingering doubts concerning their clarity, perceptiveness, and value to others. One individual's ironic evaluation of our discourse brought appreciative laughter: "What an 'up'. No wonder I love this group!"

Discussion

"Why are you surprised?" I asked the member who was the subject of enquiry, not expecting resonance from so many. I had stumbled upon a group mythos—a belief shared by the majority of members, which was captured by the nuclear idea, "Everyone seems to miss everyone else, but nobody feels they're missed." My intention was not to interpret, direct group process, teach, or confront the members with reality, but to provide an opportunity to assess and publicise the depth of the commitment to an emotional belief that had surprised me. My words were spontaneous and ironic, perhaps obvious, yet they captured an important and unexamined emotional truth located in the member-to-member relationships, and with deep personal resonance. Here was a group where each member testified to the value of the others. Iterating the sense of not feeling missed in the face of contrary data made vivid the power of trauma and the difficulty of modifying or eradicating its roots and effects on how we think and what we think about.

As therapists, we often do not know where an enquiry will take us. With little therapeutic effort, the nuclear idea segued to throw light on group cultural interactions, which, unbeknown, had most likely reinforced pre-existing inhibitory self-stereotypes and strategies of group participation. Thus, a nuclear idea has the potential to serve as a selected fact (Bion, 1963, p. 11), to the extent that it clarifies, re-organises, and brings illuminating depth to prior and ongoing events in the group. From here, as in this vignette, further examination and generation of intersubjective meaning may continue.

Not mentioned in our discussion, and perhaps universal, is the harsh reality of not being missed. Not only Oedipus and those traumatically neglected or used, but the child in all of us deals with the ungraspable fact of not being wanted for oneself, or missed. As parents once claimed their sexual relationship, our loved ones claim their privacy. And, too, a future looms wherein we—like our long-departed group members—will not be remembered.

Our group left the nuclear idea before such existential elaborations were consciously thought about and explored. A nuclear idea might stimulate an infinite network of associations; we had articulated and interpreted some but not all of its emotional elements. While an exploration of a nuclear idea may be carried out adequately, it cannot be done all at once, and never completely.

Nuclear ideas as container–contained

A productive mind and a productive group are always in the process of growth and transformation, affected by the perspectives supplied by other individuals, ongoing experience, and one's own thinking processes. I contend that every group—to the extent that it is organised as a group—organises itself by developing relatively stable ideas of itself and of its leader (this volume, Part III).

Developing the nuclear idea provides a framework for how the therapist—and the group itself—goes about the task of containing.[5] The therapist and group exist as material entities and as representations. Primarily, it is the latter—the individual and group's conceptions (and preconceptions) of its leader and the group—that contain and are contained by the group. Each member is capable of generating particular and even unique nuclear ideas, and the group as a whole develops nuclear ideas. They exist and await discovery and development.

Let us review the four case vignettes.

Two groups

The nuclear idea, while arising anecdotally and remaining unnamed, assumed essential holding and transformational containing functions. As the contained, it focused the pungent discussions of "Rebecca's group" and "Lewis's group", serving as an ongoing and fertile source of formulating and clarifying individual and collective meaning. As the container, it "held" the members individually and collectively, stabilising the transition and the relatively smooth initiation of new cohorts. In its dual function as the container–contained, the nuclear idea spurred cohesion and coherence (Ezquerro, 2010), organising, expanding, and making known a range of "well behaved" experiences, interpersonal, emotional, and mental—actual and potential.

Uncomfortable roles

As the container of dynamic meaning, the nuclear idea of "uncomfortable roles" revealed and made manageable a locus of anxiety that to some extent defined a core dimension of the group in formation. We were "in the same boat", I had declared, a containing reference to our shared discomfort, which we then addressed realistically as well as psychologically (and metapsychologically). Acknowledging my own discomfort as the leader reduced our emotional distance and fostered empathic bonding (*symbiotic* container–contained interactions, see endnote 7).

The justifiable rebellion against the sponsoring organisation's role-playing instruction, the benevolent intragroup confrontations, and the leader's playful "tell them [unruly audience members] to fuck themselves" were enactions directed to reduce discomfort. They made sense because of the clarity and safety provided by the nuclear idea.

Checkpoints

Until the introduction of a nuclear idea, group process was marked by the parasitic variation of the container–contained. The unproductive intellectualisations, denials of anxiety, and emotional flatness suggested a nuclear idea of the formative stage of our workshop: it was untrustworthy, antagonistic, and unsafe. Thinking and thinkers were avoided or attacked, as in the silent hostility directed towards me, and the group's unwillingness to challenge a participant's bald assertion of "no anxiety". The "checkpoint" idea encapsulated important socio-political aspects of the attendees' experience that were both metaphoric and real, perhaps too real and too dangerous to contain in language without the group leader's active interventions and benevolent presence. I tolerated the participants' projections without retaliating by withdrawing my subjectivity, such as by falling silent, claiming not to be affected by anxiety, or offering lofty interpretations. As a metaphoric extension of a political reality, the nuclear idea invited the attendees to carry out a "checkpoint" in words, rather than surreptitiously halt the process and sabotage the group. Revealed, too, was the suppressed idea of the leader, an outsider of questionable status as a sufficiently containing figure.

Not being missed

Each member's characteristic defence patterns and anticipatory fantasies relating to not being important, cared about, or missed contributed to the inhibited participation that characterised a dimension of our group. The nuclear idea brought to light but did not resolve a "common tension" (Ezriel, 1950). Neither could it, for "not being missed" and related ideas remain everlasting sources of existential anxiety, common to us all.

Still, in being broadcasted, a core nuclear idea of our group sufficiently contained the members as they went on to explore unresolved historical relationships, revisit trauma, express anger, and mourn.

Connection to established group theory

In his encyclopaedic review, Ettin (1999, p. 133) found a unifying thread in the writings of major theorists who understood group formation and function in terms of "inductive, bottom-up empirical-additive processes". Using different vocabularies and theoretical formulations, these authors described similar communicative patterns of "associative discourses" clustering into recurrent topics and prevalent themes that expressed central and shared psychodynamics. The group occupied itself with dealing with basic struggles, explicit or obscured, configured as "basic assumptions" (Bion, 1961), "common tensions" (Ezriel, 1950), "focal conflicts" and "group themes" (Whitaker, 1989), "barometric events" (Bennis & Shepard, 1956), and/or disruptive subgroups (Agazarian, 1997). The group as a whole, with the therapist's assistance, comes to attend to these events and negotiates normative decisions and solutions. Each member "reverberates" (Foulkes & Anthony, 1965, p. 152) with the group, identifying and participating in his or her own way. The cohesive pressure of the group's accumulated affects, ideas, and developments fosters a curative culture (a "work group" (Bion, 1961)), in which the members reduce neurotic tendencies (Bion, 1961; Foulkes, 1964) and restructure their personalities and relationships (Whitaker & Lieberman, 1964).

According to these theorists and others (e.g., Rutan & Stone, 2001; Yalom, 1995), group process is "bottom up", that is, member-inspired and inductive. However, the therapist utilises techniques that are "deductive, top-down theory-based" (Ettin, 1999, p. 150). Possessing a transcendent vantage point encompassing an overall conception of what will take place, the therapist discerns prototypical patterns in which conflicts are expressed and resolved by the group. The therapist's role is to understand and to help the members understand and deal with conflicts, which the therapist knows about, and "allows" to develop, so that the group resolves these on its own.[6]

These modern theoretical formulations present valuable models of disarray, personal and group dysfunctionality, and conflict resolution. Certainly, the therapist possesses special knowledge and technical skills, and maintains a separate and unique role in the group. Nevertheless, relational theory—a "postmodern" theory eschewing reliance on theory and redolence of pre-established ideas—assumes that the defining characteristics of group life are co-created by the members' (including the therapist's) conscious and non-conscious participation, maintained and worked through intersubjectively (Grossmark, 2007; Kieffer, 2007; Wright, 2004).

A group advances via a "hermeneutic spiral" (Gayle, 2009), a process of regression and progression, from experience through expression to co-created understanding. The therapist is being challenged continuously by his or her own affectively based mentality, as well as by pressures emanating from other members. Feelings of persecution and depression are unavoidable. Along with other group members, then, the therapist simultaneously participates from the "top" and from the "bottom", sharing and contributing to tensions and conflicts and participating in efforts to define and resolve them. In effect, the therapist is pulled up from the "bottom" and pulls others along by developing nuclear ideas and responding to those suggested by others.

I briefly compare the nuclear idea to "focal conflict", a linear, two-vector, tension reduction model of group process. Whitaker and Lieberman (1964, p. 19) conceptualised the events of a therapy session

> in terms of a slowly emerging shared covert conflict consisting of two elements—a disturbing motive (a wish) and a reactive motive (a fear) . . . [that] pervade the group as a whole , and are core issues engaging the energies of the patients . . . A group solution represents a compromise between the opposing forces.

When the members find a solution for a focal conflict, the group moves on to the next, and so on, such that the successful solutions contribute to the "group culture", expanding the repertoire of possibilities for coping with "group themes" (Berk, 2011).

When observed psychoanalytically, *every* thought, affect, or action, is a compromise formation, made up of conflicts among wishes (or drive derivatives), defences, self-punitive trends, and painful affects (Brenner, 2002). Thinking involves restraint of motor discharge, and, consequently, an increase of mental tension (Freud, 1911b). Creative mental activity is not characterised solely by the incremental build-up of manageable experience, but also involves intense episodes of emotional turbulence: breaking down existing meaning, confronting what is unknown or confusing, and tolerating upsurges and releases of the irrational. For these reasons (among others), productive group work *always* involves anxiety, and *always* involves compromise between opposing forces: pleasure and unpleasure (Freud, 1911b), aggression and reparative love (Segal, 1957), and truth and falsity (Bion, 1965).

To the extent that he or she is able to identify them, the group therapist focuses on these compromises as they emerge and play out on intrapsychic, interpersonal, and whole group levels. "Basic assumptions", "focal conflicts", "common tensions", and other theoretical formulations are themselves potential nuclear ideas. Each represents a particular focus: the therapist's opinion of what is going on. How and if the therapist intervenes varies according to personal style and theoretical and technical orientation.

No theory, formulation, or perspective best fits all group situations. For an opinion to be actualised effectively, rather than imposed autocratically on the group, the therapist needs to engage the thinking of other members: to determine if, how, and why they find a specific idea contextually and personally relevant. Group members might have competing ideas that more directly address truth needs— ideas that are more accurate and salient, or simply, a user-friendlier lens to observe how and what the group is thinking about (and not thinking about, and why). Also, a group might not be ready to develop a particular nuclear idea, or just not interested in doing so, no matter how luminous, and the idea might have to wait, along with its initiator.

If a nuclear idea is of "genuine psychological use" (Ogden, 2004), its four-dimensional reference points will make themselves known, sooner or later. The "common tension" or "focal conflict", such as is involved with the feeling of being a member of "two groups:, creating "checkpoints", "being uncomfortable", or "not being missed" will enter experience sensorially, and/or be inferred from the group's verbal and non-verbal expressions. Affects will be felt and expressed. Symbolic dimensions of the "common tension" or "focal conflict" will be linked or generalised to other personal, social, and metapsychological contexts.

The nuclear idea extends discourse to the metapsychological

A nuclear idea may involve a premise, a working hypothesis, a strategy, non-conscious working through, or an exploration and interpretation of group, subgroup, or individual traits, fantasies, and dynamics. But it is more than a conflict, tension, theme, or an interesting process that is addressed by naming and connecting to individuals, subgroups, and the whole group. The therapist listens for, and seeks to develop, a metapsychological mind-set and focus of discourse, which at the same time does not get bogged down in intellectualisation. Developing a nuclear idea—if it truly represents the four dimensions of experiential, affective, symbolic, and metapsychological import—becomes a living event of self–other awareness that changes the psychology in the room.

The nuclear idea vitalises thinking and being, particularising the vague or theoretical, and making abstract and universal the concrete. A "common tension"—such as being a part of "two groups", "uncomfortable in role", in need of "checkpoint", or feeling "not missed"—clarifies group process. But presented and treated as a nuclear idea, the formulation extends the scope of thinking. The nuclear idea of "two groups" is far-reaching, condensing the past and providing a forward-directed model of "good behaviour". "I feel uncomfortable in taking a role" broadens to the metapsychological (and sociological) question: "What is the nature of being in a group?" Derivatives of "checkpoint" reflect intense internal, interpersonal, and socio-political realities, fantasies, and cultural myths that are both ancient and as current as today's newspaper. "I feel I'm not missed" relates not only to group realisations and negotiations, but also to spiritual dimensions that are timeless and irresolvable.

A relational stance, which makes the therapist's subjectivity available for inspection, provides a model of an emotionally reflective self.[7] When incorporated in a nuclear idea, the therapist's subjective experience offers metapsychological reference. For instance, my report of feeling unable to get through a group "checkpoint" also implied that I would not stop thinking for myself, even if my thoughts were unwelcome. Treating the "checkpoint" references metaphorically and metapyschologically involved accessing and publicising some of my fantasies, anxieties, affects, and thoughts in relationship to the group participants' barriers to me and to their own thinking. Perhaps, in revealing a metapsychological dimension of my subjectivity, including allusions to my own helplessness and the group's power, the nuclear idea put the participants in a less dependent (and frightened) position. The members became willing, and able, to observe and understand the rationales behind their own (non) thinking and, in so doing, to think for themselves.

The "uncomfortable role" vignette provides another clinical example of the nuclear idea's extension into the metapsychological. My self-report of how I felt also conveyed a sense of how I thought, and that I would share rather than withhold my thoughts about my thinking. My therapeutic action encouraged other members, who came to report on their thoughts about thinking. One woman spoke of her "going along" with the thinking and action of others; another woman spoke of her anxiety about broadcasting thoughts in the presence of the first ("you can be scary"). A man spoke of his uneasiness of being the youngest and presenting his ideas. Others acknowledged impaired thinking processes: boredom, distraction, and confusion ("Is this psychotherapy?").

A nuclear idea provokes the curiosity drive and extends its reach from the personal, interpersonal, and social to the metapsychological. Without assuming formal leader status, all group members may participate as drivers of this function. They are not leaders of the group, but they may initiate and even lead this discourse (as in the "two groups" and "not being missed" vignettes). The assumption here is that each group member is capable of being a thinking, interpreting subject, capable of doing conscious as well as non-conscious psychological work (Grotstein, 2000).

The nuclear idea is the type of intervention that expands the category of what is thinkable (see Levine, 2012; Ogden, 2011). When effective, it serves as "a point of departure for new meanings and places not yet known" (Levine, 2012, p. 27), for generating new thoughts (Ferro & Besile, 2009, p. 92) and new ways of thinking. Furthermore, since its goals are transformational and not merely informational, the nuclear idea often stimulates, rather than resolves, tensions and conflict.

Summing up

The lexical representation of the nuclear idea is often simple in grammatical structure, and straightforward in experiential group reference, but generalisable and complex in symbolic and affective resonance. Something has transpired—an existential and intersubjective moment or sequence of moments that subsequently becomes named and (partially) articulated. It is built on and refined by the group interaction, linked to a shared database of here-and-now verbalisations, non-verbal behaviour, and enactments. As a thought or a series of emotional thoughts that are thought about, nuclear ideas are self and group reflective. They offer opportunities for the leader or therapist to focus, refocus, or challenge the group, orientating the members towards the search for meaning on personal, interactional, group, and metapsychological levels. As we have seen, the nuclear idea can be the organising principle directing the enquiry, the focus of the enquiry, or the result of the discovery process.

The therapist may choose to develop a nuclear idea thematically, conceptualise further, and negotiate meaning with the co-participation of other group members. However, a nuclear idea has to catch on, that is, to function in dynamic relationship with thinking, so as to involve the group or some members in an emotional experience associated with learning. It cannot be rushed or imposed on the individual or group; it emerges from the intensity of the clinical experience. Thus, a nuclear idea is provisional, tested in terms of its affective saliency and capacity to generate interest and thought. It can go flat, or be ignored, or applauded. It is not an oracular pronounce-ment, and should not preclude the potential for competing, and perhaps better, ideas.

The value of a nuclear idea might seem brief, as the idea becomes absorbed in the individual and group's development. Alternatively, its influence might be long-lasting, an idea revisited on different levels of awareness and group process and which continues to propel thought, function as a symbolic, affective, and metapsychological narrative, and have an impact on behaviour. Relatively stable, core nuclear ideas of the leader and of the group serve containing functions.

The frequency with which nuclear ideas are explicitly made the focus of group investigation varies according to the type, stage, and process of a group, and the membership composition. They might remain as tacit organisers, or be developed explicitly. That which may potentially be treated and developed as a nuclear idea might not seem to interest particular members, or involve all members equally, or be the optimal in significance to the group and its process. Nuclear ideas differ, then, in depth, breadth, creativity, and relevance to group and the particular needs and wants of the individual members.

The nuclear idea (a) gives opportunity for new meaning and depth to any experience that has occurred before or is ongoing in intrapsychic and group relations; (b) focuses participants' attention and provides a mode of entry; (c) establishes a shared activity and common goal of understanding; (d) privileges group members as potential sources of transformation; (e) conveys a sense of order to, and mutual appreciation of, the group; (f) creates interest in and valorises attending to other nuclear ideas, such that metapsychologis-ing becomes part of group culture and process.

It has been my intention to introduce and make accessible a previously undescribed essence of relationally orientated group psychotherapy. As a concept, technique, and description of group process, the nuclear idea does not put the wine of previous theorists in new bottles. Rather, it builds on their excellence, removing the "impurities" of "top down" leadership ideals and remnants of "hegemonic" (Wallerstein, 1988), autocratic psychoanalytic assump-tions. In introducing, distilling, and putting into practice key concepts of relational thinking, varietals of nuclear ideas offer a qualitatively different experience for the therapist and the group. Indeed, develop-ing nuclear ideas circumvents (and might even anticipate) the type of meaning deprivation that leads to a profusion of exaggerated basic assumptions, common tensions, and focal conflicts, and which encourages unproductive rebellions and refusals, and static resistances.

All group members of a psychodynamically orientated group share in the invitation to attend to, develop, and harvest nuclear ideas, and to their quality. I emphasise once again that the therapist's influence remains primary. In offering him or herself as a meta-psychologising subject and relating likewise to other members, the therapist sets up a culture and process in which the group comes to listen for and develop nuclear ideas.

CHAPTER TWO

The four dimensions of a nuclear idea (experiential, affective, symbolic, and metapsychological): on scrutiny

"Man will only become better when you make him see what he is like"

(Chekhov, 2006, p. 113)

S crutiny's passionate gaze is directed inward and outward, towards self, other, and the others—the whole group, society at large, and the universe itself. It has been a focus in myth, theology, ethnology, political philosophy, social and aesthetic criticism, and empirical developmental research. In this chapter, we investigate scrutiny through the lens of the container–contained. I will illustrate how scrutiny may, as a nuclear idea, come to serve as both the container and the contained, and, also, how the very experience of scrutiny may drive or inhibit the development of nuclear ideas. For scrutiny has been, and remains, ever-present and consequential— potentially harmful, or life affirming and, especially, therapeutic. Punishment, exile, death; praise, status, creative achievements, and personal growth are possible outcomes.

Scrutiny is an instance of curiosity, which may be bounded or unbounded. For curiosity is associational: it follows consciousness and the derivates of non-consciousness, producing links, the precursor to new meanings. Scrutiny, in contrast, centres on a particular object or theme. It evolves towards organisation, rationality, bounded by an expanding set of connections. Productive thinking involves both: curiosity, more wide open, and scrutiny, more concentrated, allowing meaning to be established as well as suspended.

Curiosity may be active or passive, aggressive or timid, interactional or voyeuristic, without the will or means for thoughtful pursuit. While curiosity is not necessarily directional, scrutiny is focused. Scrutiny is effortful; it investigates, may test hypotheses and reflect on itself. Its consequences feel more imminent, with no return to innocence. In addition, as we shall discover, there are mental and social situations where scrutiny is unwelcome.

Still, we seem destined to endure scrutiny: "You cannot even die, / But Nature and Mankind must pause / To pay you scrutiny", lamented the nineteenth-century poet, Emily Dickinson (1960) in "The hound" (Part Five). ". . . Judgment comes in many forms / But never scarce or shy / A lifetime of scrutiny", intones the contemporary punk-rock band, Bad Religion (Gurewitz, 2007)

Such sentiments—in keeping with my clinical experience—must be acknowledged and dealt with, since scrutiny is a prominent dimension of psychoanalytically orientated group work. Tubert-Oklander (2006, p. 203) writes that

> the psychoanalytic process is not just something that happens but something that evolves under the scrutiny of those who participate in, are challenged and drawn by, and reflect upon and conceptualize it in their dialogue.

Indeed, one of the tantalising pleasures of doing or being in psychotherapy is the arousal of one's curiosity, and the anticipation and excitement that there will be new knowledge and experience. However, I have found that as we are eager to exercise our curiosity, and be the object of others' curiosity, we are less comfortable and shy away from scrutiny. Curiosity begins with no responsibility—until curiosity narrows to scrutiny.

I abbreviate a series of group psychotherapy sessions to describe how each member's mental relationship to the prospect or experience of scrutinising or being scrutinised played out experientially, symbolically, affectively, and metapsychologically, providing the essential qualities of a nuclear idea. To establish a basis for empathy and personal relevance for the reader, I first convey the experience of a particular interval in the life of our group. My representations of the participants and verbatim reports of dialogues are geared for you to share in the process of developing a nuclear idea.

Group process: co-creating the nuclear idea

I begin with Session 4.

"You're on," a group member said to Donna, "we've been waiting for the update."

Donna had been dating a new man for a few months—"very nice", divorced, an out-of-towner with several children. "How do you feel?" "Would you think of relocating?" "Did you let him know you want to have a child?" The questions came fast, and Donna hesitantly answered each one, until she began to cry: "I know everyone is interested and caring, but I feel like I'm under scrutiny."

Wishing to relieve her sense of being an exclusive focus, I interjected and addressed the entire group.

"What's wrong with 'scrutiny'; isn't that something you want from group, from each other?"

A chorus of "no way" surprised me. "What about you [therapist]," Marvin asked sincerely, "do you like to be scrutinised?"

I answered without much thought, "Go ahead, I like scrutiny."

Ignoring the interchange with Marvin, Danny reacted to my earlier question: "Who wants to be in the spotlight!"

"You do," Joan teased, "like now," setting off some jovial go-rounds and sparring, until Jonathon's clarification. "Spotlight, but not the hot seat, Danny likes to control the lights."

"What about it? Danny, tell us about your new girlfriend," Donna dared him.

"OK, I don't mind, I'll show you." The recently divorced Danny regaled us with a description of his dating adventures, until members told him to slow down and specify: "Does she know how religious you are?" "What about her children, does she want more?" "How do you know she's telling you the whole story?"

Danny turned to me with some embarrassment: "Am I making sense? You can explain. He already knows about the situation, we discussed it in individual [psychotherapy sessions]."

Joan (irritated), "You know Rich isn't going to do your work. If you can't tell us what's going on, you're setting yourself up with her."

Danny reddened. "All of a sudden I feel very uncomfortable. When I try to explain, I think you [the group] are thinking that I am being naïve, that I don't know what I am talking about and that you are going to say 'I told you so'."

Donna, in resonance, "Sometimes I feel bombarded by reality. Like earlier, when everyone was asking me questions about my boyfriend. Last week-end he said 'I love you', and I felt depressed on the way home. I wondered if he was the 'right one'. My mother made me question every boy I ever dated. Reality was her negativity."

Joan: "I evaded my mother's questions as much as I could, even lying. That's why I don't talk about myself here—even though I talk a lot."

Danny: "My father made me bring home receipts—even from the deli. To 'teach me' to account for everything. So embarrassing, in front of my friends."

It did not seem necessary for me to make the link to Danny's embarrassment in this group session. My attention had shifted to certain interactions from previous sessions, and at first I merely followed my reverie, without knowing why.

Session 1 (three weeks earlier)

Jon arrived, half-an-hour late. This was not unusual, and we assumed rush hour traffic from the city to my suburban office, or, when he missed a session, we assumed an emergency (he was a physician). But where was Ben, why did he miss so many sessions? Marvin angrily questioned whether Ben should be allowed to continue. Joan said Ben was "vacant" whether he was there or not, and she tuned out. But Jon was very important.

"I guess I could make more of an effort to be on time; I feel bad for Ben, maybe he's getting some of my anger."

"What do you mean, 'more of an effort'?" someone asked.

"You're not seeing patients?" another member continued.

"No, this is my afternoon, I'm off, free. I don't rush to be on time, that's obvious."

"You mean all these years, you could be on time?"

"Yeah, I guess I never thought I was that important," Jon reflected.

Several members seemed flabbergasted: "You contribute so much, you're so open and helpful to other members too. You must know that."

"I'm not as open as you think, obviously, I monitor my vulnerability. I can feel great here, but also leave feeling like crap." Jon reflected, "I can't say I really feel like a regular member. I know I'm helpful and maybe 'special' to some of you. I can feel special but not a down-to-earth person. In my family, no one was taken seriously—the sense that family mattered and that we cared for each other with common goals. Mom was the star, and I was her bright light. Anything I did well was exaggerated, but she could put me down anytime. I ended up protecting myself from her—didn't trust her attention, too unreal—treacherous, she could use me to shame my father—as if to say 'why can't you be as wonderful!' I don't know which was worse, her praise or punishment."

Session 2 (two weeks earlier)

Ben walked in as several members were expressing gratitude to Jon for coming on time.

Liza exclaimed, "Both Ben and Jonathan are here at the start of a session."

Tom (to Jon): "I'm glad you took us seriously."

Marvin (to Ben): "We were talking about you too, and why you stay in group since you miss so much."

"And come so late when you do," Joan added.

Ben: "I'm glad to be here, when I am."

Marvin: "Yeah, but it isn't fair to the rest of us."

Liza: "You never tell us when you're going to miss. I always call Rich if I have to. Do you? I don't think so."

Rather than apologise, promise to do better, and withdraw, which had been his pattern, Ben became uncharacteristically emotional.

"Look, I appreciate your wanting me to be here, but I'm not going to do it. I'm not going to do what you want because you want it. I had to suck it up with my father, stay out of sight. He'd be drunk, smoking up the house, and ready to beat the shit out of me. I come when I come, and when I want to—I want to when it isn't an incredible hassle. You don't know my day. I drove 400 miles seeing clients. No matter what you may think, my way, not yours. Don't try to control me. It pisses me off."

Tom said, "It's like 'fuck you'. Like you're still a member of a street gang."

Ben, once a truant and runaway, now a highly successful financial adviser, took some pride in correcting Tom's version of his teenage years:

"I was my own independent agent, stealing and torching cars, I didn't need a gang."

Not everyone was happy with Ben's assertion of independence, but we agreed that a new voice had spoken.

I now return to Session 4. I had been in reverie while listening to the group, and now Tom was speaking, in resonance with Danny.

"You want to hear about an embarrassing dad, you should have sat at our dinner table growing up. All five kids getting grilled by my father, in turn. Here's a question for you [to the group]: 'How many four cents stamps in a dozen?'"

"Three," several members responded.

"No, it's 12! That's the kind of thing he did. Not to teach us, but to make us look stupid and show how clever he was."

"So you keep a low profile in group," Liza observed.

"That's right," said Tom resolutely.

I felt some inner press to speak, perhaps to spare members unnecessary pain in retelling and reliving traumatic histories. I had decided that it would be therapeutically advantageous to concentrate on an emotional idea: a type of anxiety situation, now being represented in and by the group experience.

I said, "I now understand why Donna thinks it's a bad thing to be under scrutiny, and everyone agrees 'no way'." I reviewed the comments of the members who had spoken, elaborating on their reports of what "scrutiny" seems to represent, formerly, elsewhere, and in our group: versions of embarrassment, shame, humiliation, degradation, and so forth.

I connected my reveries to our topic. For I had realised that Jon and Ben's longstanding enactments were propelled, in part, by fear of scrutiny.

Jon had habitually come late to "control the spotlight", a phrase he applied to Danny. A steady focus felt "treacherous". The group stood for his mother's gaze (see Scheidlinger, 1974), making him feel too good or too bad, but not safe and accepted. Ben feared group scrutiny as a violent, controlling father. His hunger for affection emerged in his appeasements and wishful promises. For the first time, he seemed to take command of his rebellious provocations. He would continue to "torch" us with unaccounted absences, but now with some awareness of his anger and its alienating consequences.

I bridged to Jonathan and Ben and normalised their actions with a group interpretation: "It seems that everyone has a way of saying: 'fuck you scrutiny'!"

The collaborative process expanded, refining the nuclear idea and also adding further complexity. Rachel, who recently joined the group, volunteered,

> "I don't like revealing myself. I love group, don't get me wrong, but the circle. It is like all the dinners with my family, at a big round table and we were supposed to talk and tell about our day, but a big act. Couldn't talk about anything real. Not to say that you [other members] don't, I'm not ready."

Liza said she looked to me for direction, but was afraid if I seemed not to approve.

> "There's always a moment of panic, waiting for you. And if you don't say anything, I think 'uh oh'."

Another member concurred:

> "Every time you speak you flash a scared look at Rich to see if he approves."

Joan turned to Rachel, as if Liza had not spoken and been responded to,

"I don't want to do group Rich's way either."

Danny said, "We know that, Joan, you don't listen to anyone. We were talking with Liza."

"Shut up," Joan smiled, "you're right, I'm sorry Liza, but how did you get to be judge, Danny?"

Donna retrieved the nuclear idea, now focused on scrutinising and being scrutinised by the leader. "I like to sit across from Rich so I can see his expressions. He's my compass, I check in to see if I got it right."

"You make it obvious; I try to check him out without being so obvious," Jon acknowledged, and when I enquired, other members came forth.

"When Rich looks at me, it's my cue . . . I'm supposed to talk."

"When he looks at me it means whatever someone is saying applies to me."

"I just look away, or look down. Avoid his eyes."

"I don't like to sit next to you [Rich]; when you turn to me, it's too intense."

"When you ask me a question, you already know the answer, and I'm afraid I won't get it right."

"Or he won't approve if it doesn't agree with him."

"I check out how he greets us in the waiting room, what kind of a mood he's in, whether he seems glad to see us."

"I wait to see if he notices that I got a new hairstyle, or anything. Or remembers from last session."

"I'm amazed he can remember something I said from ten years ago. It makes me wonder whether he spends his free time re-reading notes."

"Or has a hidden camera."

Towards the end of the session, Marvin turned to me: "The group was great tonight; you were very active. Rich, was something going on?"

I had been thinking and writing about the concept of the nuclear idea. Scrutiny—in its appearance in our group as clinical example—unexpectedly and delightedly caught my attention. But I now felt myself becoming an uncomfortable object of scrutiny, and recalled my glib invitation at the group's onset: "Go ahead, I like scrutiny." Marvin caught me red-handed, and I felt shabby, for I knew I was not going to respond candidly.

I maintained my demeanour with a quizzical look, feeling guilty for playing the psychoanalytic trump card: answering a question with a question. I had lied to myself that I "liked" scrutiny—when directed to my person—and now I knew better. In refusing Danny's sincere enquiry into my psychology, I, too, was saying "f-you scrutiny."

Session 5 (week following—midsession)

Marvin: "So where's Ben, a lot of good we did."

Danny: "Forget about him, why are you so obsessed? Are you back seeing Rich?"

"I'm not obsessed, screw you. This is my family," Marvin persisted.

Liza and Joan chimed in: "Cop out, answer Danny's question."

Marvin complied: "Nah, not for a while, you know, my hang-ups Rich and I discovered in 'individual'."

Marvin had not returned, now eight months after his self-imposed "summer break" from the combined dyadic–group format. He reminded the group,

"You know, I had the dreams that Rich and I were lying on the floor, touching each other all over. And what I was feeling about my parents."

And then, perhaps to preempt the group: "It's not about worrying about being gay . . . I'm not. You don't believe me. It's about my parents, what I've discovered about my relationships. They fondled me, not Rich, monitored everything I did, and didn't let me grow up. Now I don't want to."

Danny: "When Rich and I talk about my parents, I go home and bring out my talit [prayer shawl], pray for forgiveness. Sometimes I pop a Xanax."

For a while, the theme focused on guilt about behaviour towards parents, or speaking about parents, living or deceased, and then the group moved on to seemingly unrelated subjects. I did not reintroduce the idea of scrutiny, its pleasures and dreads, as when "touching each other all over", but I believed we still were exploring as well as enacting its relational reverberations.

The four dimensions of the nuclear idea

I organise the material around the four dimensions of a nuclear idea. These dimensions are overlapping and non-exclusive. They are interactive and fluid, harmonising in various permutations as thoughts develop into expressible ideas.

The experiential dimension

The experiential dimension refers to something discernible: denotative, rationally explainable, and socially available, so that individuals can be reasonably certain that they are hearing, seeing, and talking about a similar experience, or can come to awareness and understanding of difference. Additionally, there is the experience of sensation involved in mental activity, which seems to "ground" our thoughts: the thinker often experiences thoughts first as a perception (see Chapter Three).

While we scrutinise in our mind, the "eye" and "seeing" are its common metaphors.[8] Scrutiny may originate in any sense, however, as when two animals sniff each other, or in all the senses, as when the therapist utilises "clinical feel".

In human development, the prolonged, mutual "eye love" (Beebe & Stern, 1977) between mother and infant involves the visual sense, but also touch, sound, and movement (exteroception–interoception). In this "dance", each partner scrutinises and makes moment-by-moment adjustments in response to the other's shifts in behaviours. Scrutiny, thus, may propel bonding, mutual recognition, and the formation of the child's (and mother's) identity, but it must be judicious and co-regulated. The mother maintains interest, empowering the infant to seek and avoid engagement, without anxiously "chasing" after it (Beebe & Lachmann, 2002; Beebe & Stern, 1977; Stern, 1971; Tronick, 1989).

Scrutiny arouses the senses, then, and the anticipation of consequence that may be pleasurable, or dreadful. Very early, the infant makes efforts to titrate the intensity and duration of scrutinising or being scrutinised. Ethnologists note that most animals do not sustain long periods of such looking unless they are about to fight or make love (Eibl-Eibesfeldt, 2007).

In *Three Essays on Sexuality*, Freud (1905d) associated scopophilia with the sense of pleasure involved in looking at other people's bodies—and, by extension, their psychology—as objects. However, for Lacan, here lies the origin of our human predicament—the essence of our "lack". Human recognition is overlaid with misrecognition, and the visual object is a lure for the subject's unquenchable desire for self-completion through the other. "The eye and the gaze—this is for us the split in which the drive is manifested at the level of the scopic field" (Lacan, 1978, p. 73).

The experience of scrutiny in the group sessions

The sequences of sessions shared some pleasure in scrutinising, but unanimous dread of being scrutinised. The palpable sense of scrutiny was marked linguistically by intense imagery and metaphor, extra linguistically by laughter, tears, blushing, interruptions, and emotional outbursts, and behaviourally by physical positioning, lateness, and absence.

In Session 4, the members determined that Donna was "on"; but scrutiny brought her to tears. The group "spotlight" turned on Danny, who reddened with embarrassment. We discovered that being an attracting "bright light" stimulated the late-coming Jonathan's sense of being "great" or "crap", and neither felt safe. Tom felt "stupid", Liza, "panic", and Ben vacated or became "pissed off" when scrutinised. Some members kept a "low profile", avoided my eyes, or, like Joan, evasively rebelled against "Rich's way" and refused to reveal. Everyone experienced a sense of scrutiny's "negativity".

Except for me, or so I had thought. Imprudently, I had not truly considered how being scrutinised impacted on me personally—until it gathered with sudden emotional power in response to Marvin's enquiry. I felt anxiety, fear, and embarrassment, redoubled by shame and guilt for hiding these reactions and avoiding the group's gaze. With my own emotional experience of the nuclear idea brought to life, I could become a fuller participant.

The symbolic dimension

The symbolic dimension refers to levels of embedded meaning conveyed in speech (metaphor, verbal imagery, etc.), patternings of resistance, transference–countertransference enactments, and group, personal, family, religious, and socio-political narratives. Scrutiny has, as we shall see, deep and broad symbolic resonance—cultural, religious, historical, and contemporary reference.

Scrutiny places us in two minds: forbidden and feared–essential and desired. For the scrutinising subject lives uneasily with the awareness of also being the object of scrutiny. The discourse, which dates from antiquity, manifests in such mythic symbols as the evil eye, prevalent in ancient Greece and Rome, in the foundational religions, Judaic, Christian, and Islamic, and in modern cultures worldwide (Dundes, 1992).[9]

The All-knowing One scrutinises our deeds and even our thoughts. He tests the pious and wreaks havoc on those who look where they are not supposed to: for example, Eve and Lot's wife. On "judgement day", His angels scrutinise the soul of the departed and assign the person to heaven, purgatory, or hell.

Sartre referred to "le regard" (the look), asserting that the state of being watched threatens one's very being. Like the gorgon, Medusa, whose gaze could turn its object to stone, "the eye engrosses and corrupts its object" (Davies, 1991, p. 134).[10]

Foucault (1975, 1995) called attention to how the asymmetry of the "inspecting gaze"—seeing-without-being-seen, such as in the panopticon (high surveillance prison) or in classical psychoanalysis—represents the essence of power. Similarly, the physician (or psychotherapist) gathers influence via the "clinical gaze", which allows access to "truth" unavailable to the diagnosed other.

Classic and contemporary literature offer cautionary tales involving zealous scrutinisers: Narcissus, Psyche (with her illuminating lamp), Oedipus, the "curious impertinent" husband (a story within Don Quixote), King Lear, Hamlet, Javert, Miss Havisham, Poe's Usher, Kesey's Nurse Ratched, among many others. Cupid, Cordelia, Ophelia, Hester Prynne, Jean Valjean, Pip, Madame Butterfly, McMurphy and Toni Morrison's Pecola have suffered from being the scrutinised.

However, scrutinisers also are symbolically endowed as leaders, idealised for representing the best in human relations. Those categorised as truly devout (the rabbis, priests, imams of the establishment religions), these wise elders achieve credibility, social status, and power by analysing and deconstructing surface readings of doctrine, to arrive at deeper meaning.[11] Socrates praised the virtues of an examined life, and self-scrutiny benefits practitioners of any discipline—

lawyers, doctors, ballet dancers, and, certainly, clinicians such as ourselves.

In literature and popular culture, scrutinising talents define heroes such as Sherlock Holmes, American private detectives, and such characters as Superman, blessed with X-ray vision, or with mind-reading capabilities. The personal and scientific or artistic journeys of scrutinisers such as Galileo, Louis and Marie Pasteur, Darwin, Edison, Freud, Michelangelo, and Seurat have entered the popular culture, mythologised on stage and cinema.

Scrutiny plays out in symbolic imagery, transference configurations, and enactments

I had not considered myself a scrutiniser. Like the mother who does not insistently "chase", I attempt a light clinical touch, being careful not to overstress my presence or interventions. Moreover, I strive to protect patients from excessive scrutiny, monitoring timing, intensity, and duration of my or a group's exploratory excursions into the minds of others.[12]

After all, other group members, and not I, tenaciously pursued Donna, egged on Danny, monitored Jonathan and Ben's attendance, and attempted to oversee Marvin's return to combined therapy. Still, I became the repository of the members' disowned and projected scopophilic drives and wishes for completion.

To be expected: in my opinion, it is an aspect of the psychoanalytic process to position the therapist as the Scrutinising One, a position also extended to the group as a whole (via personification). By virtue of status of power and authority, the therapist's sentences (and silences) are multivalent and formidable: pronouncing a sentence, sententious, legalising, legislating (see Derrida, 2002; also, Cunningham, 1994).

My symbolic powers were fearsome—my close presence "too intense", "look away, or low down". Like the Sphinx, I "already know the answer", possessing private knowledge from a "hidden camera" and re-read notes, and making group members "afraid [they] won't get it right". Tom and Rachel kept "low profiles" to avoid my power to draw them in.

I served also as the Scrutinized One, the group "compass", "checked out" as to "expressions" and "mood", and monitored in terms of noticing and remembering others. In looking at me for direction and "cues", Liza spoke for apparently many of the members, who lived with "moment[s] of panic . . . scared if you do not seem to approve".

Added to these perhaps universal member dynamics directed at leaders were intensely personal narratives, which revealed idealised as well as traumatogenic versions of parental figures and the families they created. "A lifetime of scrutiny", mutually initiated in the infant–parent relationship, traumatically violated in upbringing, and now, desired and feared, contained and played out within the confines of our group.

Donna experienced the group's scrutiny as emanating from her "bombarding", negativistic mother. Liza feared maternally tinged criticism and judgement. Any or all of us could stand in for Joan's intrusive mother, and she refused to contemplate our insights. To withstand anticipated maternal treachery and enhance his safety, Jonathan metered his entry into sessions.

For some members, the group—me particularly—also personified a claustrophobic, degrading, even violent father, and members did not submit easily. Expecting the paternal one-upmanship of "I told you so", the flustered Danny darted in and out of the "spotlight". Tom lay "low", anticipating replays of fatherly humiliation; Rachel stayed on the periphery, suspecting a manipulative insincerity in my role as the group's progenitor. Marvin distrusted the therapeutic "touch", in both its regressive and progressive aspects, which brought him too close to the male figure. Finally, we discovered the ferociousness behind Ben's withdrawals and absences—the defensive and retaliatory father–son dynamics behind keeping "out of sight".

The affective dimension

As I have emphasised in Chapter One, a nuclear idea must be of more than intellectual interest, but also represent and stir strong feelings. The affective dimension ensures that a nuclear idea carries emotionally significant weight. *Passion*[13]-the loves, hates, and curiosities that accompany scrutiny—has consequences that cannot be foreseen or necessarily desired. While offering a pathway to discovery, scrutiny might entail a painful separation from, and alteration of, established links, and in often unexpected ways. Paranoid and depressive feelings are unavoidable and must be tolerated (preferably, without Danny's felt need of Xanax). "Truth is stark and leaves its mark as limited constraints / And the most difficult part is accepting what the future may bring" ("Scrutiny", Gurewitz, 2007).

Looking too deeply and extensively might violate current religious, cultural, or scientific norms, or be evaluated as invasive and provocative, prejudicial, sexually inappropriate, immoral, or illegal. Indeed, in challenging the myths of the prevailing cultures, scrutinisers and their ideas have provoked scrutiny and intensely negative affective reactions in others. ". . . Judgment comes in many forms / But never scarce or shy" ("Scrutiny", Gurewitz, 2007). Socrates had the choice of banishment or death for promulgating this type of scrutiny among the young. The retaliation for Galileo's investigations in astronomy was forced recantation and silence in the threat of execution. Spinoza was excommunicated for his philosophical enquiries.

Other scrutinisers were more fearful and circumspect, such as Newton, who kept private his mathematic discoveries until he was informed that Leibnitz had independently published the same discoveries. In similar circumstance of a competitor with the same ideas, Darwin delayed publishing his idea of natural selection because he was afraid of the disapprobation from religious circles. Freud, anticipating an anti-Semitic backlash to his controversial investigations, sought to keep the Swiss Catholic, Jung, in his inner circle (Grosskurth, 1991).

Scrutiny may be misguided, misapplied, too little, or too late.[14] In our time, scrutiny seems too often directed towards the type of "passion" pertaining to sensationalism rather than emotional substance and meaning. A question exists regarding the extent new media technologies—the Internet, cell phones, global positioning satellites—will facilitate unprecedented monitoring and observation, so that we bring Orwell's Big Brother on to ourselves.

Our group process: suffused with strong affects

In our group, scrutinising scrutiny, its agent or subject, we all could and did feel "not nice": "embarrassed", "crap", "stupid", "panicked", "vacant", "pissed off", "caught red-handed", "shabby", "guilty", "pray[ing] for forgiveness". Everyone shared a sense of scrutiny's "negativity" and we both ruptured the group gaze and sought relief and comfort in it. Some members gained insight from confrontation and feedback, others were mainly self-reflective, even private, while still others expressed themselves publicly through affective outburst, denial, and enactment. Still, I am confident from these very reactions that the shared group experience had deep emotional relevance—we each used the group in our own way to develop and integrate the containing nuclear idea.

The metapsychological dimension

The psychoanalytic process "evolves under the scrutiny" of its participants (Tubert-Oklander, 2006) and the scrutinising process itself is subject to scrutiny. The container becomes the contained: an organising nuclear idea comes to be "held" by the thinking of the group and further developed, ideally, so that it comes to represent a generalisable, human "truth". In effect, the intersubjective metapsychology of the group comes about through the very process of self–other scrutiny. Ongoing, recent, and past events undergo reflection and review, as their emotional relevance to the here-and-now relational frame is clarified. Here, also, lies opportunity to expose and re-scrutinise the symbolic dimension—the personal, cultural, and socio-political myths that underlie, and might even define, experience. By tracking inner responses and (semi) spontaneous interactions, and the attendant affects, fantasies and thoughts, the group and its members achieve metapsychological attunement: an "emotional state of awareness of an emotional state" (Bion, 1965, p. 34).

Scrutiny reaches metapsychological significance in our group

We struggled, as individuals and a group, to allow into our private and public consciousness the palpable experience of scrutiny, deeply held myths about its force, and its passion. To some extent, we evaded scrutiny, but, to different degrees, each came to scrutinise scrutiny and benefited from the process.

Whereas "scrutiny" retained its particular individual and group references, it also came to stand for a generalisable psychological principle, an existential "truth" that freed the concept from its immediate contexts. I have come to a greater understanding of what scrutinising means in human relationships—being the scrutiniser or the scrutinised—and I am more sensitive to its influence. I refer to "scrutiny" in introspection and reverie, and in formulating and presenting my ideas, clinical and otherwise. Evidence suggests that other group members have been similarly affected.

Developing the nuclear idea of "scrutiny"

Nuclear ideas develop from existential and intersubjective moments—or sequences of moments—that subsequently become referenced and further conceptualised, often by the therapist's specific interventions. In the case example, Donna's plaint, "I feel like I'm under scrutiny", stimulated a rhetorical question, "What's wrong with 'scrutiny'; isn't that something you want from group, from each other?" The chorus of "no ways" surprised me and stimulated my curiosity.

The nuclear idea evolved as the result of a sequence of events, becoming an emotional experience associated with learning by the matrix of mutual participation, in which we addressed "scrutiny" from a number of different perspectives. As is typical in clinical situations, a nuclear idea emerged as a complex co-construction: here, directed by the therapist in interaction with the participants' (including the therapist's) thought, language, and behaviour. As we have seen (Chapter One), the direction of influence also works in reverse, as the therapist discerns the members' developing nuclear ideas.

Of course, the therapeutic achievement is making a nuclear idea a mental reference for all participants. Taking from Bion's book title, *Taming Wild Thoughts* (1997), gathering disparate experience into a containing nuclear idea represents the taming of the "wild thought". "Taming" refers, then, to revisiting, developing, and presenting in a form suitable for sharing an idea that stimulates and integrates on different levels of awareness, specifically the experiential, symbolic, affective, and metapsychological.

Functioning as a nuclear idea, "scrutiny" focused the participants on a single narrative line, stimulating associations to the here-and-now process, the group culture, and the impact of the leader. "Scrutiny" also referenced intersubjective experience: historical and contemporary, transferential and fantasy-based, cultural, and, perhaps, biologically built in. Scrutiny reached metapsychological significance as we came to consider and reconsider scrutiny itself—how and why we approached and avoided scrutinising and being scrutinised, in our group and elsewhere.

Summary: the four dimensions of a nuclear idea

Four integrated qualities describe a nuclear idea.

- The experiential: it sufficiently relates to experience to provide an empirical reference point, comprehensible to self and potentially communicable to others.
- The symbolic: it carries symbolic weight, and exists in a particular context: personal, cultural, and historical.
- The affective: it carries here-and-now affective charge, arousing basic or so-called primitive levels of feeling regarding love, hate, and curiosity and the related fantasies and anxieties accompanying the paranoid–schizoid and depressive positions.
- The metapsychological: it stimulates self- and group reflections that might extend to examination of basic values, ideologies, and modes of thinking and being.

In our group, the prospect, reality, and discussion of scrutiny stirred intense negative and positive valences, along with curiosity towards each other and then towards our collaborative focus: the nuclear idea. When we could approach scrutiny itself, coming to understand its associated paranoid–schizoid and depressive affects, fears and fantasies, we could reconsider certain long-standing patterns of enactments that had evaded being addressed comprehensively.

I conclude on a paradoxical note: no need exists to scrutinise the group session to locate a nuclear idea. In the clinical situation where individuals are thinking emotionally, a nuclear idea will emerge, and with a feeling of conviction.[15] Scrutiny—the experience of being scrutinised and of scrutinising—came to reveal itself in the course of our group process. As the group leader, I allowed my attention to follow my reveries, which led me to a nuclear idea, and I waited until I felt and understood some inner press to speak.

CHAPTER THREE

Grounding the nuclear idea:
sense and clinical sensibility

"During the past long and difficult years he had trained all of
his senses. It was as if he had sharpened the blades of his hearing, sight and smell"

(Mankell, 2005, p. 313)

T
he "blades" of hearing, sight, and smell, a metaphor from the
Swedish crime writer, Henning Mankell, provides an introduction to the metapsychology of sense, and the role sense plays—
phenomenologically and symbolically—in the development and
utilisation of a nuclear idea and, hence, in the life of the clinician and
the group.

As Chapter Two elaborated, the nuclear idea has four dimensions.
Sense maps on to the experiential, with links to the affective, symbolic,
and metapsychological, that, arguably, rest on a sensory foundation.
For sense experiences are powerful motivators, as in seeking contact,
satisfying psychosomatic need, pursuing physical activities, and
taking aesthetic pleasure. Sensory stimulation vitalises experience
and the language with which we describe experience. The taste of
Proust's famous madeleine unlocked the psychological and the

metapsychological: a lifelong and complicated network of emotions, thoughts, memories, and associations.

The clinician's leadership skills are enhanced by heightened awareness to sensory cues, and from utilising sense data to reach group members and focus attention. Perhaps more than we realise, we reach for sense, and without sense reference, we cannot grasp or even talk about psychic reality.

Sensation, symbol, and sensibility

Advances in relational, developmental, and neuro-psychoanalytic research have renewed our interest in sensorial experience.[16] Ferenczi (1956) had emphasised the "intimate connections, which remain throughout life, between the human body and the objective world that we call symbolic" (p. 194). For example, imagery of ingestion describes our own thinking processes, as in *food for thought, chewing* over a proposition, and *digesting* an *upsetting* idea. Lexically, "sense" refers to the sensorial. It also has metaphoric reach into the sphere of ideas, as in such usages as *common sense, sensible, nonsense,* and *sensibility.*

Freud (1923b) stated, "The ego is first and foremost a body-ego, ultimately derived from bodily sensations" (p. 26). We connect first via the body—eyes, skin, mouth—and in maturity, the relational ego remains an embodied ego, imprinted and continually affected by what we see, hear, touch, taste, and smell.

Out of the flesh of bodily experience, the world becomes known and symbolised via processes of association, condensation, and displacement of one experience on to another. Sensations are linked into perceptions and develop through successive levels of non-verbal representation (Benveniste, 1998). In infancy, images cohere and quite early, pre-articulate groupings, naming, and more sophisticated levels of categorisation are applied. Hence, pre-established signifiers, which are social categories and culturally mediated, modify sensory experiences (Vygotsky, 1962).

A continuous exchange of meaning flows among the bodily, mental, and social spheres, constructing and reinforcing each other (Douglas, 1982, p. 65). Sensory experiences continue to influence our thoughts and words. In the process of reaching a nuclear idea, we borrow from the physical world, transforming our feelings and thoughts into ideographs (images), bodily sensations and pressures, sounds, gestures, and, via further transformations, into words.[17]

Bion's "common sense" applied to a group relational perspective

Bion (1963) called attention to sensory dimensions of our thinking, in his description of the *psychoanalytic object*, with its extensions in "sense, myth, and passion." As did Freud,[18] Bion assumed that we can never fully grasp perceptual or psychic reality; both remain unknown and unknowable. As psychological beings, we link emotionally from "mind to mind", and this process begins at birth (perhaps pre-natally).[19] Accordingly, clinical thinking requires both intuition and sophisticated models, either of which may become distracted by physical presence of objects. The language used to describe and develop our focus is characterised by analogy and metaphor; its sensorial nature might mislead, derail, or obstruct attending to psychic reality and the possibilities of developing and communicating ideas.

However, at the same time, the domain of sense supplies a crucial reference point: to enable the patient "to see that what he [the analyst] is talking about is something that is either audible, visible, palpable or odoriferous at the time" (Bion, 1970, pp. 11–12). The patient and analyst each has his or her take on what captures attention in the clinical situation, influenced by their own psychodynamically constructed narratives ("myths") and emotional reactions ("passions"). Sense functions as a shared reference, so that "common sense" (Bion's pun is intended) serves as a crucial vehicle for "transformations".[20]

If the participants cannot find sense in common, "the grounds for the failure in correspondence must be regarded as significant in itself" (Bion, 1963, p. 11). For Bion, inclusive sensory disparity served as a marker of psychopathology, as, for example, in hallucination or surreptitious alteration of perspective, both of which promote misunderstanding and obstruct therapeutic effect.[21]

Our contemporary emphasis on perspectivism and relativism has made me cautious about assuming an easily established common sense. In fact, I take for granted sensorial asymmetry in my interpersonal relationships, and accept a "failure in correspondence" as unavoidable—a constraint and an opportunity—in intersubjective reality. As a progenitor of relational theory, perhaps Bion might have come to agree that establishing common sense is more a goal of productive work than a precondition.

Sense rarely presents itself as a singular, shared aspect of physical reality, and significance might reside in that which is not held in common. Sense exists as each individual's amalgamation of several or many senses at different levels of intensity, fixity, clarity, and communicability. Some people are visually orientated, others to sound, bodily movement, even smell. Some are synaesthetic. As a group member commented humorously, "Don't look at me in that tone of voice!" To different degrees, we privilege internal sources of stimulation (interoception) to inform our view of outer reality.

Sensation and perception are active and interactive processes. Both are further transformed mentally, but mental activity feeds back to sense and perception as well. Hence, ongoing encounters in group alter and widen and make more complex these experiences. The very way others look and sound can change, as we know them better and "see" them differently.

Sense, thus, has a potent relational or interactional component, also developmentally significant (Schore, 2003). Bonding, empathy, containing–contained, introjection–projection, mutual attraction–repulsion, these psychological processes—subject to mutual influence—share a concordant but also, a necessary discordant sensory basis, experiential and metaphorical. Without disparity, perception of difference and the acknowledgment of individuality are not possible.

Bion (1970, p. 44) went so far as to recommend that the analyst suppress or suspend one sense modality to enhance the effects of another, "in a manner analogous to the use of alternate eyes". Indeed, it is useful to turn away from visualising a speaker, for example, better to hear undertones and other nuances of verbal expression. However, the group therapist does not have to artificially blind himself, as Freud suggested the analyst do, but merely acknowledge limited vision, and trust that the members supply many sets of eyes, to see what we may not, and ears to hear what we may not. Other group members are capable of using their perceptions to fuel their own intuitive leaps into the realm of psychic reality.

Notions of the therapist's exalted status as "seer", "mystic" (Bion, 1970), "analyzing instrument" (Lipin, 1992) or "telephone receiver" (Freud, 1912e), are vestiges; we no longer assume that the analyst or therapist may maintain a mind free of personal influence. During the clinical hour, sensations arise from the therapist's own internal experience, not only "projected into" him or her from member and group, and not entirely co-created. The clinician's sensations are continuous, often subtle and out of awareness, acted upon, and communicated.

The therapist does not merely utilise the domain of sense to reference commonality, as per Bion, but he or she is sensed by the group, and senses being sensed. In listening, the therapist's body speaks, as in smiling, nodding, looking towards and away. The movement of eyebrows or the tone of voice conveys sympathy and understanding, curiosity, perplexity, or challenge. Like other members, the therapist tenses in enduring mental pain and relaxes in prolonging mental pleasure.

I assume that all of us struggle with the concrete nature of human experience. We need sense, and we cannot maintain contact with our own minds—or the minds of others—without collaborative senses. "Seeing is believing"—but with the contact and support from others, we learn to disbelieve, to widen perception, decentre, to discount but not neglect the obvious. Entertaining multiple perspectives—our own and that of others—allows one to see further, deeper, and differently. When a nuclear idea reaches my consciousness, it is often because group members, arousing and modifying my sensorially influenced cognitions, have led me to something less obvious, and no less salient.

Are the sense impressions co-incident, epiphenomenal, primary, or secondary to our abstractions? I leave this as a philosophical question, subject to further psychological investigation. In any case, our words cannot stray too far from their links to sense, or else our communications (including interpretations in particular) risk becoming vague and experience-distant. In transforming experience, creating and recreating narratives, we bring in fresh sensations, and these have an impact on our ways of being—the sense of self, others, and the groups within which we live.

No way of perceiving is definitive or "true", and while this does not bestow equal validity to all sensory perspectives, each may be interesting and informative. We may note, attend to, and believe we are thinking about a similar experience, but the individual's sensorial representation might determine its personal significance. As in the following clinical situation, ascertaining the particular sensory qualities of a nuclear idea might be a prognostic imperative.

The sense of the group

An important but usually overlooked task is for therapist to be aware of each member's sensory experience *of* the group. In the following example, the therapist left unexplored sensory qualities of a troubled member's relationship to the group, with worrying consequence.

Clinical example: saliency

Paul had a history that included two suicide attempts, the last four years ago. For two years, he has been a member of a group with several members who had been or were significantly depressed (hospitalised, although not suicidal). When the group therapist asked how Paul was feeling, he said "real good". He added that he was due for an evaluation at his place of employment, expressing confidence that his job was not in jeopardy.

His response satisfied the therapist, and the group moved to other topics. But after about ten minutes, Ivan interrupted and addressed Paul: "I'm sure your evaluation will be good, but what if it's not, would you consider hurting yourself?"

"I haven't done anything like that in four years."

The therapist, in a protective gesture to Paul, commented to Ivan that he wondered if the ongoing conversation was making him anxious, and did he want Paul to "hold" his anxiety for him. Ivan replied, "Maybe, but Paul hasn't said he would not consider hurting himself, and didn't really answer." Paul said he had answered, but felt cared about by Ivan.

Jeannie addressed Paul: sometimes she thought about hurting herself, being a single mother with physically ill daughter, but could never do that to her. "I could think that way when feeling very bummed, but never would do it," said another member. "It's natural, given what people in this group have been through," said a third.

The therapist commented that the group was letting Paul know how important he is to them, but could the members consider that they were putting their own self-doubts on Paul? The therapist succeeded in moving the group focus off Paul. Then, when the session was past its midpoint, Ivan interrupted again. "I'm sorry, and maybe it's something about me I don't understand, but I don't feel good about how we left things with Paul. It's a crummy economy, all sorts of crap is happening to good people, and Paul didn't say what he would do."

"Would you tell us if you felt suicidal?" someone asked. Paul volunteered that "these things come on suddenly, but I haven't been thinking that way." Rona said she didn't blame him for no one wants to dwell on the past and all the bad things that have happened, but she had been speaking on another subject, and felt ignored. "Would you promise to come back to group, no matter how you thought?" Jeannie asked.

Several members turned to the therapist, and as if to gently remind him about his patient: "Paul likes to live on the surface." "He's Mr Supportive." "Mr Positive." Another member: "I'm really angry at you Paul. We all care about you and I don't know if you care about us. I know we've been helpful to you here, but I don't know if you think about us when you aren't here."

Maintaining his whole-group stance, the therapist closed the session by iterating the interpretation that group members were "ridding themselves" of their own anxiety and self-destructive feelings and placing them in Paul to "hold".

Discussion

The therapist believed that Paul served as the "group patient", localising the members' fears of annihilation and fragmentation. But the question remained: what was Paul experiencing in his "guts" about the group that could keep him from plummeting into despair should he receive sudden bad news? The therapist seemed to have no thought about the sense of the group for a potentially suicidal member: its visceral power as a containing, protecting, and limit-setting core nuclear idea (Chapter One).

The therapist might have considered the vector toward Paul as representing (a) Ivan and other members' intuiting and responding to Paul's unacknowledged need for help, and that this centred upon (b) investigating his unelaborated nuclear idea of "the group" and, in particular, its sensorial representation.

The group's rebellion—in which the members defied the therapist's interventions and twice circled back to Paul—emerged from a legitimate difference in assessment of, and approach to, emotional truth (Billow, 2010a). The therapist concluded that the group did not wish to "hold" their own visceral reactions. However, it is more likely that the members formed a visceral sense of Paul's precariousness, and concluded that he did not sufficiently share in, or retain, their idea of the group, which included a sensorially experienced dimension of life-supporting caring and concern. The optimistic Paul was impassive.

Working from a different mind-set, the therapist constructed his version of the group's psychic reality. He articulated a hypothesis of the group's *projecting* their repressed fears and anxieties into Paul, while the members were working from an unstated hypothesis that Paul was inadequately *introjecting* the group and, therefore, insufficiently holding on to it as a containing nuclear idea. Their anxieties signalled concern for Paul, and were not primarily about themselves.

In supplying self–object caring functions, group members attempted to foster a "transmuting internalisation" to solidify and, thereby, protect Paul's self-structure (Kohut, 1984). To make the nuclear idea of the group memorable and retrievable in an emotional crisis, "We're here for you" had to be impressed with forceful sensory–enactive impact upon Paul's subjective experience. That was the truth that Paul needed to believe in and "hold" on to.

Further discussion: the four domains of the nuclear idea

To review once again: in the group setting, *sense* exists in dynamic relationship to structure, interactional process, and content (the experiential dimension), which themselves are linked to the personal, social, and cultural narratives (the symbolic dimension), and to the emotions (the affective dimension) that each participant brings to, and becomes evoked by, the experiential immediacy of the here-and-now situation, and extended to wider personal, social, and existential situations (the metapsychological dimension) (Chapter Two).

In the case example, the therapist constructed the narrative of the group process based on explicit group analytic theory. The welfare of the whole group remained the primary object of his communications. However, the nuclear idea that he was attempting to develop—group fears and defences related to projected anxieties of annihilation and fragmentation—failed to capture the group's attention. That is, the therapist's idea did not become a nuclear idea for the group. The idea lacked salient sense, because the therapist repeatedly deflected from an experientially close reference point, that is, Paul, or, rather, an empathic experience of Paul.

The members' emotions concentrated on a single member (and their empathic identifications with him), enhanced by thoughts and fantasies of rescue (related to anticipatory fears of suicide), histories, and narratives of familial bonding (as with the mother and her ill daughter), symbolic and affective links to the group culture of caring, and their evaluation of Paul's metapsychology—how and if he would self and group reflect, before acting precipitously. Paul's sense of the group—its presence, absence, or insufficiency—became a common reference point for the members but not for the therapist.

The members, rather than the therapist, gathered latent and manifest themes into a coherent nuclear idea of "the group", which they tried to impress upon Paul, and perhaps upon the therapist, too. The nuclear idea should not, and did not, become a point of fixation, which seemed to be the therapist's uneasiness as the group circled back to Paul. Rather, in fostering the re-visionary progression (and regression) typifying productive container–contained exchanges, a salient nuclear idea keeps "truth"—and group process—fluid, moving between concrete and abstract levels of conceptualisation.

The collective activity in which members attested to their concern and questioned Paul brought agency to those who came forth. In eliciting and contrasting Paul's sensory–affective reality with that of the other members, a prevailing nuclear idea of "the group" became further delineated and more complex, and, yet, more emotionally and intellectually accessible, too.

Sense-words symbolise concepts of group formation, identity, and process

Noting the extent to which physical and bodily referents are used as models and descriptors of social–psychological relationships emphasises the impact of sense on group theory, as in matrix, boundaries, structure, holding, valence, symmetrical, parallel process, container–contained, homeostasis, role suction, and introjection/projection. Physical terms give conceptual shape to group formation and process, as in group-as-a-whole, subgroups, systematic transactions, pathways, and small/median/large. These terms are merely symbolic, not descriptive of fixed entities. A single "viewpoint" might foreclose clinical responsiveness (a containing function) and creative approaches to our work (see Part II, on polemic ideas).

For instance, in the above example, the therapist fixed on a model of group-as-a-whole that narrowed his interpretative options. The group needed to think clearly about the potential predicament of one of its members, and anticipate otherwise unforeseen consequences of a sudden change in Paul's job status. The therapist's predetermined and rigid group-as-a-whole perspective[22] closed off sensory–affective channels that could have provided important sources of information regarding specific group members, Paul particularly.

To some degree, both therapist and group members conceptualise group and group process in terms of discrete sensory properties, distinct from the physical properties of individual therapy, and these contribute to the symbolic and affective dimensions of their experience. For example, from group members:

"When people don't show up, I feel that something is missing, almost like I've lost a limb and need to recover."

"I have more space, I'm freer when the group is small."

"I don't like to talk when someone is absent. I like to feel everyone's presence, not just some people."

There are obvious differences between the two modalities of combined individual–group psychotherapy that exist in material reality, but what is significant, if not completely determinable, is how the two modalities remain both unified and split apart in psychic reality. Here are opposing comments from two individuals discussing individual *vs.* group treatment; the physical referents are influential:

"I can talk one-on-one, maybe one-to-two, but not when I see so many people in a whole group."

"I can hide behind others in group, not like in 'individual' [therapy], so I can talk when I want to."

Bion (1961) held that group is only an illusion. Nevertheless, I confess that in leading or joining a new group, in no time at all my own sense of "groupishness" turns an amorphous aggregate of "just some people" into something with particular sensory qualities: "a group". Each group and each session develops its particular colour, shading, rhythm, and pace. Illusory or real? Perhaps no more or less than the notion of our individuality and separate subjectivities. As a musician uses notes, or a painter uses his palette, I use words to bind together sensory aspects of my group experience, listening for, developing, and presenting nuclear ideas. But something ineffable remains.

Senselessness

Senses alert and direct us to psychic qualities that are not sensuous, although accompanied by senses: that is, experienced sensorially, and described in the language of sense. Even if they are sometimes misleading or plain wrong, we depend upon physical cues to make inferences about who people are and how bodies and minds are functioning.[23] We gaze into eyes to see how people are hearing each other, and nuances of sound may convey insight regarding psychosomatic need (as in soothing). In studying bodily movement, we intuit the impact of insertion or expression of an idea. We cannot function without a sense of sense.

Clinical anecdote: deprived of sense

I had been conducting a day's workshop in a Scandinavian country. Only about a third of the eighty participants had an adequate grasp of English, and I had no familiarity with their language. Still, with a talented translator at my side, the lecture–discussions and small-group demonstrations worked well.

Now, in the midst of a conducting an experiential large-group session, I began to experience a vague dizziness that I could not attribute to jetlag or fatigue. Without a raised platform, I could not see many of the speakers. And, although I could hear the voices, my inexperience with the flat inflection of my hosts' language made it impossible for me to decode vocal nuance of emphasis and feeling.

With sight and sound cues missing, I lacked adequate sensory information, and began to experience symptoms of sensory deprivation. I used my predicament to link to the assemblage: "I can hear what you are saying, but I cannot comprehend if you are saying anything personally meaningful. Are your words affecting you as you speak? How are they affecting each other?"

These remarks created some confusion, even with the translator's help, and the members attempted to clarify for each other what I had been asking. I iterated, "I can't tell whether you are being 'real' or being gracious to your guest."

There was a buzz among the participants, and then someone called out in English, "We're not shitting you." And from another, "Billow wants to know if we are shitting ourselves." And from a third participant, "My mother is full of shit. Some of our teachers here, too." That worked! When the laughter settled down, we continued, and I was no longer symptomatic.

Discussion

I had been deprived of necessary sense to gather my feelings and thoughts. Questioning the group about the psychic reality of my experience focused the members on the reality of theirs. When the participants began to reference "shit", my pronounced sensorial experience was auditory. The humorous inflection of the participants predominated over other potential sensory associations, such as visual or odiferous, and it was sufficient to restore my psychic orientation towards the group and its process. I got the message, which I trusted as authentic. We had discovered a reassuring, mutually containing nuclear idea: we were not shitting each other. In thinking about their ambivalent relationships to family members and faculty, the members took the nuclear idea further.

Somatisation

Sensation is not just a passive process of environmental impingement. Sensations come to carry symbolic value, that is, ideational and affective significance. This is particularly clear with somatisation, where ideas and associated affects are expressed or avoided via experienced bodily sensations. While somatisation reflects an individual's defensive style, its occurrence in group provides the opportunity to look at the person's psychology and links to other members and the group itself. The following are examples of somatic complaints, reported or witnessed by the group, ripe for participation in developing a nuclear idea.

Gastrointestinal. Harris functioned as a well-behaved, professional, family man and group member. Others wondered why he remained in group. Only gradually did he allow his psychology to become a focus of attention. He revealed an inner world filled with "gagging" sensations, which he linked to feelings of panic, self-doubt, and guilt. "It's like my acid reflux; I can feel something rising in my throat, like I can't breathe. I feel it whenever I ask for the group's attention, or tell them about myself. As a child, I was supposed to be perfect, not complain or be in any trouble. My older brothers took care of that." Harris's gastrointestinal symptoms, now publicised, represented a sensory (and also metaphorical) aspect of a complex nuclear idea, generalisable to all of us: he had upsetting feelings that needed the group family to attend to.

Excretory. When Marla, a new member in her first session, talked about her husband's affair, Judith—herself a betrayed wife—excused herself to relieve diarrhoea in the bathroom. Judith's distress reinforced Marla's predominant fantasy of group as public humiliation—something Marla already had been enduring as a consequence of her husband's behaviour. Judith pleaded with Marla to stay in group; for the first time Judith connected her pervasive stomach cramps to previously unformulated or vague ideas, evacuated via her bowels. These related to untrustworthy men and silent female witnesses, originating in her family of origin but relevant also to unexplored aspects of her relationships to both the men and women in our group. While it seemed difficult for the overwhelmed Marla to immediately comprehend Judith's thoughts, she was sufficiently impressed by the reflective group process to maintain membership.

Muscular. I observed a member tapping his foot and asked him to translate the "Morse Code". He smiled: "I have to relieve body tension." Understanding this aspect of his metapsychology, members now could focus on the affective and symbolic basis of his sensory experience, linking his displeasure to ongoing here-and-now process. In effect, the nuclear idea (and process of reaching it) became the mode of containing "tension" and, also, dissipating its physical intensity.

From Tamara: "It doesn't happen right way, but after a bad group, my pubic floor tightens, and I get this burning in my vagina. That's why I came to therapy; to make it go away, not make it worse." "What happened last week to make it a 'bad group'?" several members enquired, non-defensively. Treating "a bad group" as a potential nuclear idea invited Tamara to bring to conscious awareness the suppressed roots of anger that the tightening and burning signified.

Auditory. A group member clapped her hands on her ears, as if to dampen sound: "Lots of group voices—yelling at me." Other members did not share her sense, but, following their curiosity, encouraged the woman to attend to her experience, which she linked to her family of origin.

One member to another: "Your voice is like a siren, I'm really getting a headache." While the receiver hated the sensory form of the message, eventually she grabbed on to the idea and utilised it to attend to her behaviour.

Circulatory. From different members: "I have to talk or I'll burst. I'm palpitating." "When you come into group and glower, my heart speeds up and I hear it." From a group therapist in supervision: "When I think about running this group in particular, I get all pumped up, no matter how tired, an adrenalin rush." In these instances, sensory events stimulated a dynamic network of associations that we could think about and integrate.

Body weakness and sleepiness. Whenever group strayed too far from Allen, or conversely, when group process involved emotionally difficult material, Allen reported sensations of being "weak and tired". He could drift into a semi-stuporous state through intervals of group sessions. While Allen sought the group's attention, this did not necessarily extend to anxiety-producing nuclear ideas, which he both approached and avoided.

Selma, a longstanding member of another group, habitually missed attending after "breakthrough" sessions, or even after those when she had been complimented for being helpful or self-revealing. "I just felt too tired to come. I guess I can't take positives." She would not contain and develop a "positive" idea of herself.

Hallucination

Hallucinations occur on a continuum from small accompaniments in normal interactions to gross distortions, as in psychosis. Hallucinations reflect not only central nervous system modifications, but peripheral sensory activity may itself be altered. They are motivated, and, like all mental activity, they have symbolic and affective import and may be utilised to develop—or avoid—nuclear ideas.

In negative hallucination, an individual (including the leader) fails to hear, observe, or think about that which is obvious to most others. Freud (1920g, p. 11) asserted that "most of the unpleasure we experience is perceptual unpleasure". In efforts to avoid anxiety and pain, we might fail to perceive, voluntarily or not, and, thereby, fend off unpleasant impingements of psychic reality.

In positive hallucination, the individual distorts perceptual reality, or substitutes one image for another, in an effort to blur, modify, or reverse the valence of unpleasure. Perhaps every successful group leader is the beneficiary of positive hallucination, as he or she most probably is seen and heard as more beautiful or handsome, mellifluous, quick-witted, younger, and thinner. Probably, too, positive hallucinations are involved in the idealised transference–countertransferences that spur bonding and group cohesion, and which relate to core positive nuclear ideas of the leader, and defences against negative ones (Part III).

Hallucinatory transformations are common and frequent, particularly in moments of stress, and subtle and difficult for the clinician to appraise. Since they might be transitory, simultaneous with normal perceptual processes, they could evade recognition. For example, I fortuitously pursued a group member's assertion that she did not like me right now. She responded with a relieved smile: "Oh, I thought you said that *you* didn't like *me*. It's OK if I don't like you. Now I like you." The woman realised that her not liking people often flowed from the distorted perception of their not liking her. She resolved, in her words, "to take a second look". The exchange became a salutary model, witnessed by other group members and applied to what they referred to as their own "paranoid tendencies".

Clinical sensibility: dancing to one's own tune

In an earlier section of this chapter, I suggested that sensory correspondence between or among individuals is limited and partial, and that what remains discordant might be most valuable for the therapist to discover and pursue. I present now three clinical examples. In the first, I judged it imperative to advance group process by privileging my integration of sense experience and my formulation of a nuclear idea over those of several influential members. In the second, I came to realise that I had misjudged the correspondence between my sensory experience and the group's, which became an opportunity for me to learn about a different subculture. In the third, sensory correspondence did not reduce what I judged as a productive tension between ideas and wishes of a group member and me as the therapist.

The perceiver and the perceived

For the second demonstration group of a day's workshop, fresh volunteers rushed to take chairs. Almost immediately, we fell into a sombre mood, most probably in response to Erwin's arrival, the last to join our circle. He was an older man who sat unsmiling and inert, until he broke the silence: his wife had died several months previously and he needed to speak. Erwin's mourning drew in many of the participants, who revealed their own bereavements. Two individuals, while acknowledging the difference in the type of relationship, reported grieving their analysts, both recently passed away.

I remained relatively quiet, saying finally that while we all could relate to life's pain, it took confidence and trust to reveal deep loss. My comments seemed to free the group to turn tentatively to other subjects, and soon, to my role as leader. Some members commented that I was being very different from the morning's presentations. In both the lectures and demonstration group, I had contributed to moments of boisterous laughter and controversy (see also, Chapter Ten, on outrage and outrageousness). One man in the morning's meeting—and now in this group—had said he was so angry that he wanted to blow himself up, a reference to being a suicide bomber.

I said that this group was different, and my disposition too. Members explored the implications. I seemed to be demonstrating relational options to respond "naturally" without pre-determining how and when, according to certain to role expectations. I reaffirmed a basic principle: authenticity is contagious, and spreads from leader to member and in the opposite direction, too.[24]

Then, Marty, an African-American woman sitting next to me broke in, saying that she felt "invisible" and that the other black people were the only ones who made eye contact with her. She acknowledged that she tended to focus on race and was the one to bring it to attention at meetings. She always checks out who is black or might be black. Several Caucasian members protested that they were not racist; they felt connected to Marty and looked at her as much as at anyone else. But she continued, extending her contention to our sponsoring organisation and clinical settings in general.

Indignation mounted. The self-described "suicide bomber" now revealed himself as Palestinian. In an effort to counter Marty's assertion of prejudice, he drew attention to his physical proximity to a "friend", an Israeli—apparently they had introduced themselves to each other during the morning.

Marty drew only modest interest and support from the other black members. The youngest in our group qualified: "It is important for me to be identified as a *woman* of colour." From the mix of domestic and foreign accents, it was not clear who identified themselves as Afro-Americans. No one seemed to want to be conscripted into Marty's subgroup of the disaffected, except for Howard—a white man.

I knew Howard from other national and regional group meetings. He was what Gans, Rutan, and Lape (2002) have described as a "demonstration group recidivist", a frequent volunteer and active and senior member of several group organisations. We had affectionately tangled during previous lecture–discussions and several demonstration groups. I read from Howard's physical movements that he was gearing up for a fresh opportunity to air his own grievances. "Calm down," I said, my smile returned by Howard, and I continued for the benefit of the ongoing demonstration and the larger group of conference attendees: "Don't even think of raising the gay flag. This is about Marty and her relationship to the group and me." Howard shared in the round of laughter.

I turned to Marty in an empathic *tete à tete*, complimented her for bringing forth issues of race, but suggested we let other people get a chance to express themselves and see where the group goes. I said that, as the leader, I wanted to keep our new group from breaking down into "black and white". If we had time, racial issues would assert themselves, but in a more personal, group-related context.

Marty and Howard were not satisfied completely, but they went along. Each in turn had enjoyed our visual embrace, re-engaged with the group, and carried on comfortably enough.

Discussion

In a new group, particularly, all members are faced with Marty's problem of "invisibility"—an often suppressed but pervasive nuclear idea—and, to some degree, physically enact desire for recognition. Erwin asserted that he "needed to speak". But even before he had uttered a word, his mournful visage asserted early influence on group process.

Marty turned attention to herself by referencing race, which is sensorial, cultural, but also context dependent. Group members had attested to their efforts to connect to Marty visually—why was she asserting "narcissism of small differences" (Freud) and refusing the group's embrace? I judged that she needed more from "me" (Part III), the leader, whose dissimilar behaviour in the two demonstration groups had been the ostensible subject of interest. Marty took the opportunity to define and test her ideas of relationships, to both the leader and the group at large, by mounting her protests and invoking a race polemic (Part II). In my enactive *tete à tete*, I supported and demonstrated what I took as her legitimate self–object need for member–leader connectivity without submitting to her agenda, which I considered an inveiglement (Chapter Seven).

I judged Howard's behaviours similarly: "flagging" attention to an aspect of his difference was simultaneously an effort to maintain individuality, connect to the leader, and become a part of our group. Because I had a history with Howard, subtle visual cues had a distinct meaning to me and influenced my consideration of what was going on and the polemic that was about to occur. My idea of him was more articulated than the other group participants. Knowing something about his metapsychology, I believed I could intuit and provide some of the attention that he desired, and save the group time that we did not have to come to learn what his surface behaviours signified.

From infancy onwards, we experience the other through sensorial observation of bodily and verbal features, but we differentiate ideas of who is "like me" and belongs to "our group" based in part on an intuitive process of bonding. The gaze between infant and others particularly is important in promoting the idea of secure attachment (the symbiotic level of the container–contained (Chapter One)). For Marty and Howard, I made a concentrated effort to initiate a powerful sensory–affective experience they had not allowed themselves: a mutual gaze with the leader.

I do not believe you see black or white or straight or gay when you look into another's eyes and feel human connection. Sense triggers symbolic–cultural references (myth), and *vice versa*, but when we feel bonded, the attendant affects release us from pre-established attitudes. Exterior features that mark human difference retreat into the background; in the phenomenological foreground are the interoceptive sensations associated with bodily warmth and muscular relaxation. In group process terms, bonding exchanges modify divisive fight/flight dynamics and support constructive pairing and dependency—the rudiments of mutual recognition.

The leader must remain alert to how each member uses varying self-presentations, and their effects on the group's orientation towards thinking (see Chapter Seven). Each group member asserts influence in taking a role as the perceived and the perceiver, the sensed and the one who senses. Sometimes, the leader harmonises by supporting the members' efforts at being experienced in their own perceptual terms. Erwin's physical presentation defined him as mourner, and alerted us to the ever-present reality of mental pain.

In utilising clinical sensibility, the leader must also be willing to de-centre members from their customary and often stereotypic self-presentations and perceptions of others (see Agazarian (2012) on stereotypical *vs.* functional subgroups). If a group focuses on black and white, for example, the members might not be open to sensing other salient features of the visual and auditory field. I did not think it useful to "see" Marty or Howard primarily in the mode they proclaimed wanting to be seen, or for the group to see me as bounded by my behaviours exhibited in the morning's session.

To generate creative thinking, our group—brief as it was—had to tolerate prompt removal of such social masks as "mourner", "black person", "woman", "Palestinian", "charismatic leader of the morning's session", and so forth. Social signs and signifiers limit the visual and sensory field and might encourage or prolong stereotyping, narrowing the range of potential emotional experience and the likelihood of useful nuclear ideas.

Culture influences the experience of sensations

About sixty conference attendees were taking seats for debriefing—it was the last half-hour of my two-day workshop, taking place in the

Southern region of the USA. One of the participants complained that there was no seat for him within our large, two-ringed circle. Someone had taken his seat, or his seat was removed along with the seats of those who had left. He found no satisfaction in the group's response and began to interrupt the proceedings with provocative comments: "How come no one owns [taking my seat away]?" "Does no one notice or care—why not a provision for me?"

At first, I was dumbfounded, then curious as to what might be emerging symbolically in lieu of an orderly debriefing. Was he a mouthpiece of the dissatisfied and insufficiently nurtured? Was he inveigling us into continuing a large-group experience? But after a few minutes, one of the seasoned professionals at the conference said, "You know, I can't say this to patients, although I wish I could. But I can to you: 'Get over it!'"

I heard the remark as sardonically amusing, and assumed that there would be sufficient good cheer between the speaker and spoken to end the issue. However, the remark offended the listener, and, more surprisingly yet, turned the whole group against the speaker, who was morally condemned. I began to formulate some hypotheses—an emergent nuclear idea related to defences against termination—but not adequately confident, I put this line of thinking aside to register my confusion. One of the women explained: "Richard, this is not how we talk to people in the Deep South. We don't insult people to their face . . . we smile at you, and you don't realise until later that you've been stabbed in the back."

Relieved at having enquired before acting on my clinical inferences, and benefiting from cultural translation, I suggested an incipient nuclear idea. I closed the conference with reference to the "insult" of termination, given that we are "unseated" from fantasies of and desires for uninterrupted connectedness. I thanked the group for how much I learnt from the workshop, to its very last minutes.

Discussion

I was in my own country, hearing my own language, but I needed a translator before I could develop a nuclear idea with sufficient accuracy. Members of a different subculture had heard the same words differently. We each brought a mythos to this moment, which drove different clinical sensibilities. To my Northern ears, "get over it" was music; to my Southern colleagues, the phrase was noxious and discordant.

Case example: the therapist serves as sensory-based nuclear idea

It was not the first time that I allowed a degree of anger to be present in addressing a member of one of my psychotherapy groups. While Andrea, the receiver, accepted my intervention, and understood my frustration, Mark protested.

> "You sound angry, Rich, I don't like it. I hate it when you address me that way. Are you angry?"

We had been here before, Mark acknowledged, anticipating the group's impatience.

> "I know, I know, Rich's delivery doesn't bother anyone else the way it bothers me. I agree that Andrea was very provocative, but there was a better way to speak to her."

When Mark insisted that I address him, I said I was sure that there were many better ways, and invited Mark to offer his. Andrea was often ignored in response to the very behaviours that had provoked me, and I took this interaction with Mark as another chance for her to get sorely needed feedback. Mark conveyed the message to Andrea articulately and compassionately.

Andrea took some pleasure in reporting preference for Mark's delivery over mine. Mark, however, demanded something more than I had offered, which was appreciation and admiration of his way of communicating, but I made no promise to try to do better.

> "You're not troubled by how you speak sometimes. I wish you were."

I agreed that I was not troubled, but added that, as always, I do not dismiss, but think about what he says. Mark continued,

> "It happens just once in a while, but it really gets to me. OK, I registered my comments, I'll let it go."

"For now," another member teased. For we all knew about Mark's sensitivity to how people speak and how we should "do" group his way. His experience of me stimulated transference to his harsh and unsympathetic mother. Mark desired my being measured and more neutral in tone and cadence—even oracular, but less personal—and I refused to comply. I would rather incur his displeasure than abort an opportunity for us to revisit an ongoing nuclear idea involving Mark's psychology: his wish to control others (and himself) to avoid sensations and associations linked to traumatic maternal experience.

Discussion

Although traumatic personal history contributed to Mark's discomfort with my speech, controversy remains in theoretical and clinical writings regarding the display of the therapist's sensory–affective sensibility. Eradicating the therapist's subjectivity is neither possible nor desirable (Renik, 1995)—but countertransference should not serve as a rationale or justification for narcissistic gratifications and injudicious behaviours. I am also aware of not promulgating what Racker (1968) identified as the "myth of the analyst without anxiety or anger", which itself may become iatrogenic, presenting an unrealistic and unachievable model of mental health.

More than other participants, the therapist serves as a sensory object and source of stimulation. In my sessions, the relationship of the group and its members to "me", the leader, regularly becomes a focus of attention (i.e., a potential nuclear idea; see Part III). My sensorial impingements—plus and minus—represent the domain of sense.

Members make their own separate and collaborative judgements about the myriad bodily movements, facial expressions, and vocalisations that reveal my impatience, disapproval, embarrassment, caring, warmth, unexpressed amusement, and so forth. In bringing forth their perceptions and opinions about my behaviours in the realm of sense, members such as Mark have an opportunity to discover personal symbolic relevance and explore their affective responses.

In my opinion, the therapist who is open and relatively relaxed regarding confrontations with his or her own clinical sensibility makes less likely the development of stubborn and clandestine individual and group resistances, rebellions, and refusals. The therapist's willingness to embrace his or her own psychology as a nuclear idea, that is, to share in the process of self-revelation (which is unavoidable, anyway), encourages and supports a group culture centred on meaning-making (Part III).

Sensibility matures

The world of sense is not purely native. Sensorial experience can be educated, and develops and matures, influenced by the group context. For example, difficult music might take many hearings, sometimes decades, to be heard and considered beautiful (as in Stravinsky's *Rite of Spring*).

Likewise, the therapist's sensibility—the very sharpness of one's clinical "blades"—might disturb, frighten, or alienate, but can also excite, invite, and inform the uninitiated, or those operating from different cultures and belief systems. Interventions and interpretations operate on many levels, including the sensorial–phenomenological and metaphorical. They have under- and overtones, may cut deeply, and leave a lasting impression.

In a well-working group, members (including the therapist) learn to widen and deepen their sensory channels, to become more aware of, and comfortable with, their own responses and ambivalences, and more accepting of difference, dissonance, and lack of correspondence. Previously avoided, censored, or censured sensory materials—while not always transformed into sources of pleasure—become an invaluable basis for the development of complex thoughts and feelings.

Summary

Sense experience serves as sign and symbol, as metaphor, analogy, illustration, and model. Sense fixes experience, yet may fixate experience and so interfere with developing abstract thoughts. Thus, sense is both necessary for, and a potential distracter from, group process.

Even while being appreciated for itself, the domain of sense—to provide the basis for a nuclear idea—needs to be linked to psychic qualities: to the personalities of the members (including the therapist), the group culture and process, and the live clinical interaction. Group therapists need to keep this question in mind: how are the senses being used to convey and/or obstruct thoughts about psychic experience?

Reference to sense in group brings experience near and grounds group discussion. Members have concordant and discordant sense experience; often, it is from lack of harmony and correspondence that nuclear ideas arise and meaning accrues. Attention to, and exposure of, the field of senses enlarges those held in common, and also highlights those that are not, or can never be, held commonly. Sensations are appreciated for the associations and realisations they stimulate, for what they teach about oneself and others.

Sense exists in relationship to personality and character, to the symbolic meanings brought to experience and to the affects that are aroused. As a dimension of a nuclear idea, it is worthwhile to consider sense independently, as this can point to new paths of knowing, and provide creative links to ongoing individual and group processes. To emphasise this point, sense experience sets off a cascade of potential meanings, and it is these meanings that sense triggers that is important.

Calling attention to multiple sensory perspectives and their connections to symbolic and affective elements might serve to develop a particular nuclear idea. The sensory domain—what members see and hear and experience internally—becomes elaborated and better articulated. In the process of widening and deepening awareness of sensory experience, and linking it to feeling and meaning, the group member expands metapsychological awareness for that which can be tolerated psychically without a retreat into somatisation, intellectualisation, or hallucination.

CHAPTER FOUR

Processing nuclear ideas via four communicative modes: on hostage taking

Hostage taking is a pervasive phenomenon in human relations, in groups, and societies. It exists literally, figuratively, and psychologically, and is both a phenomenon in the mind and in the outside world. Historical texts, including religious writings such as the Old Testament and the Koran, and literary writers make numerous references to threats, blackmail, ransom, and kidnappings, reflecting that hostage-taking has been a relational pattern of interaction for thousands of years (Allen, 2006). Judaism, Christianity, and Islam share the Old Testament as a religious source and also share an image of God as a terrorising, hostage-taking, father figure. A "jealous God" (self-description) exacts obedience with litanies of threats and punishments—death of the firstborn (Exodus, 4:23; also 11:5), boils, tumours, incurable itches (Deuteronomy, 28:27), and retribution wrought on great-great-grandchildren (Exodus, 20:5).

Shakespeare presented illustrious emotional hostage takers: the temptress, Cleopatra (who first kidnapped herself to Caesar), the petulant Hamlet, a master guilt-inducer, and the envious Iago, captivating Othello with jealousy. Somerset Maugham's *Of Human Bondage* (1915) dramatised the human vulnerability—perhaps a universal wish—to being taken emotional hostage by those we love. Bellicose threats, weapons of mass destruction, banks "too big to fail", seizures of land and people—hostage taking remains in front page headlines.

While I am referring in this chapter to psychological and not actual hostage taking, the motives and some of the methods are similar: control and extortion by producing anxiety, often in the form of threats or outright terror. I present a dramatic incident that occurred in one of my groups, and which served as the experiential basis for developing a nuclear idea. As I cycled through the four modes—not always with complete success—we discovered how group members (including me, the leader) hold, or may seem to hold, others as hostage by their words and actions. By conceptualising and revisiting a series of affectively intense, but seemingly disparate, interactions as a type of symbolic relationship, we were able to rebalance ourselves and contain the experience as a nuclear idea.

A member angrily departs the group

Overview

The group and its leader remained in various degrees of disarray following the dramatic exit of a member, Miranda, several weeks earlier. Her angry departure, in mid-session, while in keeping with unresolved, action-orientated aspects of her psychology, also related to the particular culture and its informal conventions that our group had established.

Over a three-year period, casual post-session conversations in my office driveway evolved into lengthy pow-wows. Two members began to call each other and text between sessions, and then a network emerged that included email addresses of all members. In time, the group established a custom of meeting for dinner after sessions, with a subgroup of core attendees, some irregular regulars, and several who seldom attended.

In the group, I described some pitfalls of the new arrangements as they were developing: the formation of cliques, secrets, sacrificial loyalties and betrayals, substitution of real for therapeutic relationships, limitation of self expression and mutual feedback, and so forth. I was assured that all members were invited, outsiders excluded, and that important topics, interactions, and insights would be brought into our group sessions.

I regularly expressed curiosity as to who attended these meetings, who did not, and what went on, and how the attendees and absentees felt about it all. I am not naïve and I shared my belief that I was receiving heavily edited versions, so I came to, and expressed, my own conclusions. This created controversy, and the group credited me with amazing insight; suspected me of having "inside information", or challenged me as "nosy", off-centred, or wrong, and lambasted me for feeling jealous and left out. All of which I acknowledged as possibilities and discussed, without deterring my focus on the interplay between the group and aftergroup.

I had my reasons for not otherwise intervening, such as by forbidding the dinner meetings. I am averse to functioning as rigid rule-maker and avoid, as much as possible, serving as a superego figure, which I believe limits creativity and has iatrogenic effects: too much goes or remains underground and the group becomes fearful and covertly paranoid. Further, the concept of "acting out" is undergoing re-evaluation (Ivey, 2008); "enactments" are inevitable, provide sources of data not otherwise available for analysis, and form a background for the emergence of new forms of engagement and experience (Aron, 1996; Davies, 1999; Hoffman, 1992; McLaughlin, 1991). Finally, my own early group therapy experiences in the heyday of the 1960s included weekly aftergroups, mandated by my analyst and meaningfully integrated within the psychotherapeutic process.

Sessions 1 and 2

Now, we return to Miranda, a vivacious and attractive young woman and popular in group. She was generous and supportive, but could exhibit a big temper and a nasty streak that threatened to wreck her marriage; controlling the latter personality qualities became an ostensible *raison d'être* for her initially joining us. In no time she found her disparaged husband in group: Donna. Like him, Donna was "negative and mopey", and easily offended.

I worked with Miranda to put her observations in helpful words and benevolent tone, encouraging her to use her inherent sensitivity and compassion. Still, she continued to send conspiratorial "vibes" to other members, which created some group tension. As for Donna, she had to learn to roll with the punches, not withdraw or spitefully strike back in the face of criticism, to work on some of the personal qualities that had threatened her marriage to a man not unlike the mercurial Miranda.

Donna was among the occasional attendees of the dinner aftergroup, while Miranda was a central player, consigning her husband to babysitting duties. Towards the end of a group session, Miranda announced unexpectedly that she was leaving group and began to thank us. No one had forewarning, and we were all surprised. She had threatened to leave on several other occasions, and I believed that— between the group and aftergroup—we would resolve the situation. After some negotiation, she agreed to return to discuss her plan and her reasoning.

The next meeting began with other subjects taking our attention, and I assumed the aftergroup and/or the network of extra-group emailing and texting had dissuaded Miranda and the issue was resolved. Towards the middle of the session, Marvin asked what she was thinking. "I came back because Rich asked me to. But this is my last session. I have had enough of group. It's time to take responsibility and not blame my parents." She had learned what she needed, and wanted to say goodbye. She could take tennis lessons with the money. I was a brilliant therapist and she would always be grateful. What of a termination process? I reminded her, joined by other contesting members. Miranda reassured us: she had no intention of leaving the aftergroup.

This sat well with several people, who seemed relieved. Others suggested she still should remain in group anyway, with everyone present, including its leader. "I need time in group to process your leaving," one member protested. "I need to think about this too. At least come back next week."

Perhaps it was a testament to Miranda's affecting persuasiveness that I seemed to be the only person in our sophisticated group who was flabbergasted with her very idea, and, with less grace than I would have liked, I said that attending the aftergroup was an impossibility. An aftergroup could consist only of our ongoing group.

"What would happen if we met with Miranda?" Liza asked.

"You would have to leave group," I responded, with an alacrity I continue to regret.

Several members reported being shocked or surprised that I came on so strong. Marvin defended Miranda's proposal and said I was being dictatorial. Tom questioned whether I had the right to make decisions for what takes place out of group. Concurring, Marvin asked rhetorically, "Is Rich God?" Liza said it was unlike me to take this kind of control, and it unnerved her; she loved Miranda and wanted to see her, but did not want to lie to me or go behind my back. Danny said that it was my group and I could do what I wanted, and that he did not want to get kicked out.

I had regained my composure sufficiently and clarified that people were free to get together socially with whomever, at any other time, but gathering right after our group was different. The confidentiality of our meetings had to be protected. A former member would be privy to the emotional drift from group to aftergroup—a need for talk and decompression was unavoidable.

Susan, perhaps the closest of Miranda's aftergroup cohorts, interrupted, "I'm not sure it's fair that we pay for the group and you don't, Miranda, and it's not about the money." Marvin disagreed, "They're different experiences, why should she pay?"

Irritated with what I took as an absurd direction of the discussion, and recognising our time constraints, I broke in. "If Miranda does decide to leave, the group moves on. How could new group members be integrated in an aftergroup with former members?"

A tearful Miranda interrupted my logic, and, cursing me, bolted from the room. From the office window Marvin observed Miranda's crying, her car boxed in by Tom's in the driveway. Marvin left the room to encourage Miranda to return. "She's very upset and wants to leave," he reported back to us. Susan angrily declared that she disrupted the group enough, and she should just wait, but Tom passed his keys to Marvin. "You could let her out if you want."

"This is a shock to her and she doesn't understand," Marvin recounted upon returning, alarmed. In the remaining half hour, the group attempted to make sense of Marvin's rescue operations, their own feelings towards Miranda, and their reactions to my uncharacteristic limit-setting.

I said it was unfortunate when we had to end, and reminded the members that I would be away and that we would be missing the next two weeks.

Session 3

Our next meeting began with only a few members present—I wondered whether the empty seats represented a reaction to last session and/or to my vacation.

Liza began by detailing her elderly mother's ongoing visit.

"If I interrupt her she gets mad; if I disagree with her she gets hurt. She claims she has no money and then buys a big condo—three bedrooms that no one uses. She complains of abdominal pain, thinks she has cancer, and then eats a pastrami sandwich. I had to take her to the emergency room—just wind. I hadn't realised it was always like this—all about her."

A few supportive comments broke Liza's monologue: "She's only staying a couple of weeks, thank god!" "Keep her busy." As latecomers drifted in, Liza briefed them, partially repeating herself each time: "My mother is still driving me crazy; maybe I need to go back on heavier meds." Finally, we reached full membership and Liza said, "That's all, thanks for listening, we can move on."

The subject turned to the seceding member. Who had spoken to Miranda during the past two weeks? How did she feel, was she all right? Only Marvin had spoken to her. Others had texted and received no reply.

"Did you tell her what we discussed after she left?" a member asked with some irritation. "No," Marvin replied, "she just wanted to curse and she said she hated everybody for going along with Rich."

Susan reported, "She texted me back a 'fuck you' and I'm letting her sit with it."

"You were her best friend," an aftergroup regular reminded her.

"I'm going to call her in a few weeks when she calms down, although I am shocked by her reaction," Susan replied.

Liza regretted not doing more: she could have reasoned with Miranda, let her know that she loved her.

Donna had been quiet during Miranda's outburst, and now she addressed the other members:

"This is how she treated me, her husband, Rich, and now you. I resent that you are so caring and don't seem to care about how she hurt my feelings. And you, Rich, let this happen by not putting down firmer limits until you said she couldn't attend the aftergroup. You weren't protecting me."

I acknowledged her assertion, ignoring its accusatory tone. "Yes, I felt I had to protect the group's boundaries."

"What about my boundaries? I know Miranda talked about me in the aftergroup," Donna continued relentlessly.

"I don't see what would be so bad, Rich, we could take our feelings back to group," said Marvin, interrupting Donna's accusations, and tearfully pitched for a Miranda-inclusive aftergroup.

In the previous session, some members felt I could have said what I said without being so harsh, and I had agreed. Now members challenged Marvin and I received almost unanimous support for my interventions and explanations. "You were in a difficult place." "You had to say what you said."

Donna reminded me, "None of this would have happened if you hadn't forbidden the aftergroup."

"Could he have done that?" Liza asked, and Tom replied, with a trace of resentment, "Rich could do whatever he wants, it's his group."

"Oh?" I enquired, to invite discussion.

Liza interceded with some anxiety: "I don't want to spend the whole session talking about Miranda."

I said we were not talking about Miranda, but responding to a group event, and that we could learn from it.

"How?" someone asked.

Not wanting to predetermine the direction of discussion, I said, "We'll see," which seemed to be satisfactory, for the moment.

Conversation returned again to Miranda: how did we think she was feeling, was anybody planning on calling again, and so forth. Several people had expected Miranda to return, or fantasised that she would. "She brought a lot of good feeling into the group, always so positive and giving," Marvin reminded us, and then iterated his concern. When members attempted to zone in to his psychology, he protested and became tearful again: "I really miss her, that's all. I know she is suffering and that makes me feel bad. Don't you guys have feelings?"

Danny interrupted, good-naturedly, "Guilt trip. Fuck you!"

Marvin: "No, I mean it, Danny," and he remained close to tears.

Danny continued, "I learnt a lot from what Miranda did. I'm not calling or texting her again. I learnt to say 'fuck you' and not buy into her bullshit." And, switching targets, he added, "That's why I can say 'fuck you' to you, Donna."

"Well, 'fuck you' too, Danny!" Donna retorted, with an uncharacteristic grin.

Liza, to Donna: "I really like that you're not crawling up in a ball and getting sad."

"And making me feel guilty," Danny added.

"I feel much freer to speak my mind without Miranda, even though I know it would have been good for me if she stayed," Donna replied.

I, too, found myself with the adequate communicative tools—mental, emotional, and linguistic—to pull different themes together, connect individual psychologies to each other and to the group process, and the "here and now" to "then and there". Marvin's delayed rejoinder to Danny provided a propitious moment.

"Don't control me, Danny, by laying the 'guilt tripper' label on me. That's a guilt trip too. [To the group, challengingly.] I know, you all are thinking Miranda's my mother."

I said simply: "I'm thinking that Miranda is everybody's mother—father too—when you feel held hostage." With the group's attention, I added data: "Some of you were late and missed Liza's predicament with her mother."

Liza interjected: "Thank god for Prozac, she could drive me insane."

I elaborated, focusing on the process as representing an idea, a type of mental relationship: "being held hostage," and, hyperbolically referring to the recent series of interactions and echoing Liza, I continued, ". . . we could go 'insane'."

The conversation continued as if I had not spoken.

Susan, to Donna: "I didn't like it when you blamed the aftergroup for talking with Miranda."

Donna: "But I feel betrayed . . . you're not supposed to talk about members not present, and I know Miranda didn't like me."

Danny: "So why didn't you talk about it."

"I was afraid. Look how she exploded here. I felt we all had to walk on eggshells, you too, Rich."

I did not dispute. "So Miranda held me hostage, and the group, too." The group now picked up the metaphor, and the concept behind it.

Liza: "I don't like it when you hold us hostage, Donna, it is like my mother. I'm afraid to hurt you and make you cry."

Susan: "Or else you get mad and withdraw. But Liza, when you go on about your mother, I feel I have to soothe you so you don't fall apart."

"So you are Liza's captive and have to pay ransom," I elaborated, but Susan disagreed. "That's putting it too harshly."

I continued, "You don't want me to upset Liza and make you anxious?"

Susan (sheepishly): "Maybe you're right, but shut up."

Some good-natured laughter followed, and then a pause.

Peter, another member, turned with some trepidation to Tom: "You know, you can be scary, too, and when you are in a 'mood', I'm afraid to confront you. I just shut up, like I did with my father."

Marvin: "Yeah, Tom, you can hold us hostage, just like Rich thinks Miranda did."

The personality of group attention shifted to Tom, and new players such as Peter emerged, along with monologues, dialogues, and subgroup exchanges that often seemed only tangentially related to our subject or to each other. Some communications were concrete or circumstantial, or left incomplete. Furtive glances were passed, suggesting that not everything that people felt and thought about was being broadcast. This was to be expected, of course. Still, we were developing a nuclear idea: thinking, feeling, and putting into words experiences of taking and being held hostage, past, present, and ongoing.

Case discussion

Most, if not all, of us have been distressed by individuals who shout, threaten, walk out, slam doors—fierce in their displeasure. We have been lulled by uninterruptible monologues and have trodden carefully about the easily wounded, like Liza, the semi-despondent, like Marvin, or the incipiently angry, like Tom. We have shared Susan's righteous anger, felt Danny's retaliatory "fuck you too", and Donna's ambivalent disappointment and relief when a valuable but volatile individual departs from our lives. And, as group members, we have had to cope with fear-inducing injunctions of the leader, such as my forbidding a certain type of aftergroup.

Miranda's fervid displays of affects encroached on mental space. All members had difficulty remaining in contact with their own minds, and, for moments, our mentality was held hostage, as evidenced by the group's unthinking reception to Miranda's absurd plan, my stupefaction about its approval, and my impulsive *diktat*. We cycled through paranoid–schizoid and depressive feelings and fantasies, spinning out a series of polemic ideas (Part II), many expressed through dramatic outbursts and provocative enactments. Marvin was teary and protective of Miranda; he could think of little else, and attempted to have the group similarly preoccupied. Susan stirred indignation, and her rhetorical question was not designed to pursue further discussion: who was Miranda to benefit from group without paying? Danny brandished his "fuck you's" as if they could free himself, and us, from feeling controlled. Liza spoke for, and at times embodied, the guilt-ridden, Peter, the frightened, Tom, the angry, rejected, and confused, and Donna for the persecuted and the triumphant.

Hostage-taking played out at every level of group interaction: intrapsychic–intersubjective, as in vertical and horizontal patterns of transference (e.g., "Miranda is everybody's mother"), and in subgroupings and whole-group processes reflecting the three types of basic assumptions (Bion, 1961).[25] Miranda both *fought* and *took flight*, stirring us to take one or both positions. In restraining the group and threatening enforced flight (*exile*) for disobedience, I, too, morphed into a fearsome hostage taker. Miranda had become a Magus, conjuring rites and rituals that threatened my leadership and the group itself. Perhaps too abruptly, in Session 2, I broke her spell over the group and her pairings with various members. This had included me, ineluctably drawn to her sadomasochistic embrace. In Session 3, the vocal naysayers, except for Marvin, stayed silent, so that the group voiced near unanimity that I had done the right thing and had done it well. To disturb a dependency basic assumption, and the attendant reliance on a too-comfortable idea regarding "me" (see Part III) as the Infallible One, I had to bring to light the members' and my own re-evaluations of my leadership qualities.

Probably, all of us felt shifting combinations of fear, anger, concern, anxiety, regret, spite, sadness, relief, in different degrees and proportions, which contribute to the emotional experience of being held hostage. These powerful reactions: feelings, fantasies, wishes, and fears, perhaps at different moments for different members, coalesced and came to be mentally and interpersonally organised. We had co-constructed a nuclear idea: investigating how group members link to themselves and others—and to, respectively, the group and aftergroup—via hostage taking.

Hostage taking became not just something we were, and perhaps remained, immersed in, but it also became a thought about how people interact. Reaching metapsychological status, the nuclear idea contributed to our working though process. In abstracting that which had been intensely felt as real, to some extent removed us from transference–countertransference impasses and the group from its reliance on basic assumptions. Energised and also rebalanced by the containing nuclear idea, we could think, feel, mourn, and move on.

The therapist's modes of interaction co-create nuclear ideas

To a significant extent, the therapist serves as host and, thereby, defines the rules of engagement and the group experience. While we take some responsibility for comfort and welfare, our benevolent invitation makes unstated demands and provides unsuspected risks to the strangers who "group". Perhaps not surprisingly, the word, "host" has antithetical tension, related to its etymological roots in "hostile" and "hostage" (in Latin: *hostis*, "stranger" ,"enemy", or *hostia*, "victim") (see Visser, 2009). I had made an explicit ultimatum regarding the structure of the aftergroup: allegiance or exile. The sense (Chapter Three) of my being a hostage-taker was no longer subtle or underground, yet its impact on the group—and on me personally— remained to be clarified.

In *Resistance, Rebellion, and Refusal: the 3 Rs* I asserted that, to the extent to which the therapist is expert, it is in pursuing a search for emotionally meaningful ideas, which I referred to as "truth with a small 't'". The "Bionion shift" (see Ogden, 2011) in contemporary psychoanalytic theory—placing the drive to know ("K") in a position of pre-eminence, even over drives of love and hate ("L" and "H")— influenced and continues to influence both my formulations and how I address them. I assume that interest in truth remains basic, and, to be effective, the therapist must monitor, evaluate, and respond to the truth needs of the various individuals and the group itself, as well as detect and minimise the impact of falsity. Our therapeutic task is twofold: to pursue that which is painfully immediate and most meaningful, while, at the same time, shielding others from that which is immediate, but too painful to become meaningful.

In dealing with the group's dynamic forces and actions, the group leader operates in four communicative modes, captured under one or more of the following rubrics. Diplomacy, integrity, sincerity, and authenticity are tactics of discourse (Austin, 1962), or relational modes of speaking and listening, adopted by the therapist with and without awareness. They are intimately interrelated, reflecting communicative skills that the therapist utilises in interfacing with the group as its cycles through inevitable strategies of resistance, rebellion, and refusal.

The four modes supply conceptual references for the leadership stance one has adopted, allowing the therapist to be more aware of what he or she is doing, and why. Exploring them may serve to disentangle and address some of the technical issues that concern the contemporary relational psychotherapist regarding topics of truth, intersubjectivity, presentation of self, and self-disclosure. The four modes of diplomacy, integrity, sincerity, and authenticity allow us to reflect on the therapist's actions and make inferences about its effects on the members and the group as a whole—how my own thinking and behaviour impacted upon the development of a nuclear idea (see also, Kieffer, 2010).

Diplomacy

The mode of diplomacy includes the therapist's monitoring and, if necessary, regulating or mediating power arrangements among members and subgroups to foster ideals of mutual respect and freedom of expression. The therapist must be able and available to protect vulnerable members and minority subgroups, to establish and maintain a climate of safety. Without such leadership, the group is more likely to become anarchic (Billow, 2010a,b) and in danger of fragmenting (see Hopper (2003b) on incohesion). Or, the members and leader might collude to form a truth-evading establishment, marked with inauthenticity, submission to authority, and conformity.

In being diplomatic, the therapist is both political and strategic, trying to influence the group to use its power in co-operative, truth-seeking interrelationships, rather than to express power in forms of retaliatory rebellions or refusals. Patience—timing and tact—would seem to characterise diplomacy; however, spontaneity, emotional openness, transparency (self-disclosure), and confrontation could be effective in establishing and maintaining thought-provoking relationships.

Unavoidably, and continually, group members witness the therapist's diplomatic manoeuvres: leadership theories and techniques as they are put into practice, and which bring power, control, and directionality to group structure, process, and culture, in part by privileging and prohibiting types of interpersonal interactions (see Hoffman, 1996). Tom's observation/plaint seemed unarguable and begged for further group investigation: "Rich could do whatever he wants, it's his group."

In all groups—family, therapeutic, and societal—tensions of friend–foe, love–hate, dependence–independence, security–freedom, exist between leaders and followers. Each constituency risks feeling, or even being, held captive by its own roles and felt needs and to the other's. I, perhaps, liberated the group from Miranda's captivity, but unavoidably reinforced custodial bonds to me.

Integrity

The mode of integrity emerges from the therapist's moral and ethical principles, and how they are applied. Integrity involves strength and consistency, and also flexibility, for no one set of rules or principles can do justice to all group circumstances. Samuel Johnson (1759/1985) clarified that "integrity without knowledge is weak and useless, and knowledge without integrity is dangerous and dreadful". As clinicians, we emphasise *self*-knowledge, of course.

The therapist's sentences are multi-valent and unavoidably formidable: pronouncing a sentence, sententious, legalising, legislating (see Derrida, 2002; also, Cunningham, 1994). Every gesture and utterance—what the therapist says, and does not say—carries moral weight. Apropos is Donna's grievance: "Rich, you let this happen by not putting down firmer limits [Miranda] couldn't attend the after-group."

Practitioners must "fight off the bewitchment by the dream of an ethical algorithm—a universal and invariable code of procedures" (Jonsen & Toulmin, 1988, p. 7). Indeed, as Nietzsche (1980, p. 63) asserted, "The will to a system is a lack of integrity". Boundaries, if they are vigilantly defined and securely fortified, offer some protection from capture and being held hostage. But untraversible boundaries limit cultural exchange, the productive conflict that ensues from the import and export of different personalities, ideas, and practices. I did not believe the group would want to be, or should be, deprived of the unknown and unpredictable: creative opportunities provided by the interactions between two subcultures—group and aftergroup.

In not outlawing the aftergroup, I carry responsibility for the disarray and my strident proclamation that followed. However, I would carry a greater weight of guilt by applying pre-ordained conventions to a group of lively and sophisticated adults who understood—and now experienced with emotional complexity—the risks as well as rewards of their decision-making. Painful and confusing, and still not completely resolved, the ramifications of our enactions have been intense and informative. The process has produced the nuclear idea.

Sincerity

Sincerity conveys felt feeling and conscious intention. Sincerity derives from the developmental stage of idealisation: an intermediary and unstable intersubjective platform preceding the "depressive position" (Klein) and secure bonding. Splitting, rather than mature thinking that tolerates ambivalence, is prominent as a mode of organising experience (either/or; good/bad; in/out, in thought and feeling). Sincerity is categorical: either you love/are loved or not, and, hence, in its direct transportation of a feeling, sincerity is always simple, and sometimes simplistic. Consciousnesses of sentiment and its public expression do not necessarily advance relationships. One can be sincere yet self-deceptive, ineffective, inappropriately seductive, wilful, or misleading.

The disarray surrounding the departing member threw our group into impassioned sincerity. Miranda's tears of dismay, the pining for the missed member, the feelings of guilt, the volley of angry "fuck you's", the therapist's fearsome polemical decree, each expressed an unembellished emotional impulse with moving sincerity.

In hostage syndrome (also called Stockholm syndrome after a well-publicised case in that city), the hostage reduces anxiety by identifying with the attitude and cause of the hostage-taker (identification with the aggressor). In the sessions under discussion, Miranda first claimed the role of hostage taker, with Marvin as prominent hostage-spokesperson for those loyal to her. But others were revealed to be hostage-takers, too, including me. Loyalties shifted, and, despite my own ambivalent reaction, others came to appreciate the sincerity of my proclamation.

The group re-established relative harmony as the members came to identify with their leader and his laws. While there was immediate gain in the relief of anxiety, there was also loss of emotional complexity. In reducing conflict, the overt struggle with hostage taking and takers, I feared I had deprived the group of opportunity to think and, therefore, to develop nuclear ideas.

Authenticity

In contrast to the felt assurance of sincerity is authenticity, in which struggle exists among competing motivations. Authenticity remains an uncertain, incomplete process: mentally integrating conflicting feelings, thoughts, and motives, directed to those we love and also to those we find troublesome and wish to reject (at various moments, the same individuals). Authenticity represents, then, the achievement of the depressive position, its hallmark being the toleration of ambivalence while maintaining a balanced and humane outlook. Translated into Bion's (1961) group terminology, sincerity remains wedded to basic assumption mentality while authenticity encompasses work group thinking as well.

Whereas sincerity is categorical and simple, authenticity is dynamic and complex: tension exists between self-awareness and expression. In functioning with authenticity, the therapist communicates with conviction, while acknowledging that his or her interventions are based on ideas, which are also opinions, and that they have limitations. Most obvious are those arising from character, professional training and orientation, the emotional intensity of the group situation, and non-conscious influences.

Some of what I learnt and report on here came from "doing" and from "being"—committing to words in the immediacy of group interaction. Alford (1994, p. 203) writes,

> With the speaker's voice I may show myself to others and so come to
> know who I am. Not just because self-revelation allows me to know
> myself as I am mirrored in the eyes of other . . . but also because in
> speaking for myself I must make a public commitment as to who I am.

Some realisations have emerged and been clarified retrospectively. In
thinking and putting words to publication, "my spoken words
surprise me and teach me my thoughts" (Merleau-Ponty, 1964, p. 88).

This much I know about myself now: I am made anxious by anticipation of being held hostage and also of taking hostages. I assume
that my anxiety is universal and enduring, and based on conflictual
identifications with one's first hosts/captors, parents, and the culture
they represent. These figures, along with others, such as the group
theorists and practitioners who influence me, provide models of how
to host and how not to host.

Miranda's plans to attend the aftergroup impinged on the group's
boundaries and the role of the individuals as group members. As
conservator of our ongoing group, my response was also personal
(Chapter Eight). Too personal to me, yet my impatience, annoyance,
and disapproval came to seem reassuringly "human" to the members,
reaffirming their bonding to me and respect for my leadership. I had
attempted to communicate a democratic, experimental attitude, and
share decision-making, such as in the formation and functioning of
the aftergroup, but I still had to provide limit-setting leadership, even
if delivered with less than ideal pitch.

Authenticity requires "strenuous" mental activity, an "exigent"
(i.e., demanding) standard of being true and of representing truth
(Trilling, 1971). It is also humbling, perhaps depressingly so, for
authenticity recognises the reality that neither therapist nor group
member can simply love and remain sincerely accepting. Uncongenial
circumstances of social life inevitably are stimulated by group process
and must become part of an authentic group experience.

Building the nuclear idea

In our group, there were multiple symbolic communications and
enactments related to hostage taking, and it took time for me to
discover, formulate, and elucidate what I took as a unifying theme for

investigation. "Hostage taking" became an emotional experience associated with learning by the matrix of mutual participation, in which we addressed the idea from a number of different perspectives. In the case example, the nuclear idea, "hostage taking", clarified our situation and reduced its intensity, so that the experience could be contained, thought about, and interpretations could be offered.

Hostage-taking myths commonly, even pervasively, are entwined in group structure and process. Hostage taking also represents a metapsychological "truth": a universal dimension of human experience: internal, interpersonal, sociopolitical, and religious. While members look forward to group, and often report it to be the emotional centre of their week, they also lament being "tethered", "trapped", "guilty when playing hookey", fearful of retaliation for making the therapist and the whole group angry, and so forth. As leader, I can feel and fantasise similarly towards my constituents and our groups.

In later sessions, we developed other nuclear ideas that had been stimulated by Miranda's eruption, such as "boundaries", "inveiglement", "limit setting", "Rich's role as therapist", and "what kind of person is Rich?" The relationship between group and aftergroup begged for further exploration, and, thus, the idea of "our group" remains a superordinate and core nuclear idea to which we return.

CHAPTER FIVE

When the group refuses a nuclear idea: on Facebook

A prime constituent energising and informing process joined my group without invitation and remains without my choice. An infiltrator revolutionised our culture and structure, affecting the content and direction of our discourse. Facebook had entered as "social fact" (Durkheim, 1982). No one had asked for my opinion or consent.

Durkheim held that our identities and behaviour as individuals, groups, and societies are best studied and explained by reference to forces outside of, and beyond, the individual. Exterior and more powerful than any person, the social fact exercises a degree of coercive social force. It informs and organises broad and diverse institutions and practice: legal, economic, religious, aesthetic (Edgar, 2002; Mauss, 1990), and, as I discovered, therapeutic. A social fact might alter or even revolutionise what is considered "true" and, also, how truth is pursued.

In *Resistance, Rebellion, and Refusal: The 3 Rs*, I described how many forms of interpersonal behaviours involved in group organisation and process might be conceptualised as a series of moves and counter-moves to express, redirect, modify, or block the search for emotional truth. In revolution, assumptions regarding how such truth should be pursued are challenged, and so bring a group to a new phase. Revolution is, thus, both a mental attitude and a strategy of social action, modifying certain principles and modes of operation. The cultural change may be positive and negative, progressive but problematic, and with its own set of unforeseen consequences that need to be understood and attended to.

A revolutionary change can occur without an obvious revolt, or result from a single or dramatic event. Revolution might arise organically, as part of a social organisation's development and evolution, or be imported, in response to economic, political, or, as in this group, technological contingencies.[26] Only in retrospect might the speed and significance of revolution become apparent.

The members had begun to connect via Facebook. Within a few months, a new idiom (Bollas, 1989) had been introduced and established, altering sources of information and communication, boundaries of time and location, reducing confidentiality, and abrogating anonymity. Facebook asserted and reasserted itself as an ongoing theme of group interaction.

To be sure, I would have preferred to make explicit and explore some of the functions Facebook served in the intersubjective context of our group and elsewhere. However, the other members were content to keep Facebook as a communicative medium without further overt thought. For them, the "revolution" was over and was not a source of intrapsychic interest or public debate. Facebook seemed merely an enjoyable convenience, common and of no more symbolic significance than a mobile phone.

It is always interesting to consider what grabs a group's interest and why some ideas seem to float along without being—or seeming to be—responded to. Facebook served as a material entity, as a structure-modifying "social fact", and as complex symbol, utilised in affectively intense group exchanges. Operating on many levels, Facebook achieved the criteria for a nuclear idea (Chapter Two). It had experiential, affective, and symbolic reference, and was ripe to be developed metapyschologically.

A focus of attention had become a nuclear idea for the leader, but the members disavowed interest. Still, I could clarify my own experience, being witness to its influence on our feelings, thinking, and behaviour. In this chapter, I record my efforts to monitor, evaluate, and respond to Facebook's revolutionary effects, to uncover and explore Facebook's symbolic value, the truth needs that it addressed, and the purposes it served.

Clinical vignette

This long-term psychotherapy group consists of ten men and women between the ages of forty-five and sixty-two. This is how we might begin.

Robin (smiling, to Donny): "You're an idiot! You take up so much space."

Donny: "You're so aggressive! No one tells you to look."

Robin: "I have to scroll through to see my other posts."

Donny: "Your 'other posts'. Your wall is five times larger than mine. How do you have time for anything else?"

Robin: "I'm interested in other people. Novel concept?"

Donny: "Interest or gossip? You showed your boyfriend my page."

Robin: "But you friended him."

Paul: "Donny is an egomaniac, that's all. He needs a lot of attention, from anybody, he doesn't care who."

Donny: "I have a following. They expect a witty saying, a thought of the day. It's my job to entertain and keep them happy."

Eleanor: "Some of the ideas are very good. It must take a lot of work."

Donny: "It does. And some of them are my own, from group."

Robin: "You show pictures of yourself wearing a tuxedo [sarcastic]. That keeps people happy?"

Donny: "The women check me out. They tell me they like a man to look sharp. It helps my social life."

Eleanor: "You don't need help, a lot of women like you, especially when you are being yourself. I do."

Robin (to Donny): "Listen to her. I feel the same way."

Mark: "He doesn't believe it yet, he doesn't trust women, he's two wives down [divorced twice], and lots of cash."

Donny: "Maybe never trusted, except the women here."

Paul: "He's doing it again, getting a lot of attention, dominating the group."

Donny: "Are you jealous?"

Paul: "No, well maybe I am. [To Donny] Where did you go all dressed up?" Robin answers for him, naming a well-known and expensive restaurant.

Mark (to Paul): "Do you want to be his date? You're so *into* Donny and what he does and where he goes."

Eleanor (protectively): "Paul looks to Donny as a role model."

Paul: "I guess I do, he's a chick magnet."

Mark (pursuing his implication): "Could you handle the chicks?"

Paul: "Probably not. I'm not sure how 'into' them I am."

Some members—the speakers, others, maybe me—might stay with the repartee and reflect and deepen meaning. Or, someone might indignantly implore intervention: "Here we go again", or exclaim, "I need to talk about something." The disapproval or expression of need usually moves us to other subjects. I am comfortable either way, and remain relaxed. Symbolic meanings do not immediately or easily reveal themselves, and problematic character traits and behaviour might benefit from repeated confrontation. Group repartees "radiate" associatively, asserting retroactive influence (see Green, 2000). What members were saying to, and observing about, each other and themselves represented difficult emotional truths, which would reverberate played with and interpreted from multiple perspectives, contextualised, and recontextualised in the course of group life.

During a session that followed this not untypical start, it was likely that we would return to topics directly or indirectly referenced in the Facebook inspired byplay, such as Robin's "aggressiveness", Donny's insecurity and distrust of women, Paul's transference and/or possible sexual feelings towards Donny, Eleanor's earnest protectiveness towards Paul and others, and so forth. Even the byplay itself—referenced by the exasperated "Here we go again"—has segued into interpersonal exploration: why would certain members spend so much time "gossiping" and others spectating?[27]

Discussion

Responding to the revolution

The Facebook revolution rose "bottom up" from the members out of the nucleus of the group experience, itself nestled within the larger context of a changing culture. I had never issued the traditional injunctions against extra-group contact, but group members were psychologically savvy and knew the usual proscriptions; this did not seem a propitious time to insist on adherence to the therapeutic "frame" (Langs, 1978) and strictures of anonymity and confidentiality. And, given the reality of the social fact, a strategy of prohibition would have represented an effort to deny a cultural force greater than myself. In attempting to quash the revolution via the assertion of autocratic control, could I have succeeded in depriving these mature adults of Internet freedom to see and be seen?

Besides, I respected the decision-making skills of the members and their capacity to address and correct undesirable choices. I attempted to offer neither sanctions nor prohibitions; both are enactments, impacting and impacted by leader–member relations, the group's development, and the here-and-now process.

As social fact, Facebook emerged in the entire world because it serves social, cultural, and personal purposes. I had confidence that whatever emerged enactively involving Facebook could be utilised to discover something particular about its metapsychology, as it applied to our group microcosm.

Still, leadership was required to guide the group through its crosscurrents of multiple needs, so that Facebook, and how the group used it, received suitable psychological attention, without demanding too little or too much of our focus. *The New York Times* columnist, Thomas Friedman (2011, p. A35) opined,

> in the hyper connected world, in the age of Facebook and Twitter, the people are more empowered and a lot more innovation and ideas will come from the bottom up, not just the top down. That's a good thing— in theory. But at the end of the day . . . someone needs to meld these ideas into a vision of how to move forward, sculpt them into policies that can make a difference in peoples' lives and then build a majority to deliver on them. Those are called leaders.

Rather than passively submit to, or rebel against, Facebook's social impact, I surrendered creatively (Ghent, 1990), retaining faith in the drive for emotional truth and mental growth that exists in all of us. I could wait to see where Facebook would take my thinking, what I would observe and come to understand about the group, its members, myself, and what, if anything, I needed to do as leader.

The members had wished to establish certain modifications, all of which involved extra-group contact among the members. They had their own beliefs about how the group should best be run, and this involved challenging certain prevailing rules and practices of our profession. The revolution involved no direct confrontation with me; rather, the members unilaterally altered group socialising norms. Not, then, primarily directed to testing or overthrowing my authority by violating and weakening boundaries, the goals of the Facebook-inspired revolution have been to inform the membership, strengthen bonding, and create a new social context.

Indeed, while the boundaries and modes of communications have expanded to include the computer, mobile phone, and tablet, not so the group's purpose or preferred mode of interaction. I have retained my position in the hierarchy of status, power, and influence. My therapeutic values—psychoanalytic, group relational, and otherwise—predominate.

Facebook fosters cohesion and coherence

Facebook functions as what the French sociologist Mauss (1990) referred to as a "gift", a "spiritual mechanism" for reciprocal exchanges benefiting both givers and receivers. Facebook serves as a welcoming offering to new members, an effective tool in maturational rites of passage, a joyful, electronically conveyed proclamation of life, a buttress in illness, and a memorial in death. Facebook, thus, fosters bonding, cohesion, and coherence, the last referring to organising principles that enable higher levels of functioning (Ezquerro, 2010).

I marvel at the ease and speed with which members come to conform to the group's Facebook norms. For example, after an extended period of individual treatment and my persuasive efforts, Eleanor entered the group unconfident and in her word, "paranoid": "I didn't want even to let you [other members] know my last name, but now [after seven months] I don't care. I mean I like to be able to see what's going on, to contact you if I want to. Like now that I am worried about Seth [absent, recently diagnosed with a skin disease]."

Avid users metaphorically walked the Internet-shy Phyllis to dating sites, teaching her to electronically groom her Facebook self-presentation, and negotiate with potential suitors. Facebook provided a scrapbook of Phyllis's and the group's collective accomplishments. Over time, her postings and discourse relating to her postings reflected the victories of late marriage and pregnancy. Like proud grandparents, members express delight in her wall of baby pictures.

When Mark's sister unexpectedly died, group members who could not attend in actuality, or chose not to, electronically participated in *Shiva*, the Jewish post-funeral ceremony. Mark's Facebook postings connected the members not only to the deceased relative, but to Mark himself, so that mourning became a sustaining group event.

Facebook invites graphic entry into the user's life, introducing the group to a self-selected collection of historic and contemporary characters, not the least being the member him or herself, in the pose of mate, parent, pal, child, vacationer, athlete, host, victor, and so forth. Assuredly, the group does not take Facebook at face value.

In the vignette presented above, Donny's Facebook images were subject to truth-inspection, loving and helpful, although not administered in the most polite language or tone. "Idiot . . . egomaniac . . . needs a lot of attention from anybody . . . wearing a tuxedo keeps people happy? . . . you don't need help . . . when you are being yourself". Paul attempted to convince himself (with Eleanor's collusive suggestion) that Donny's images served as Paul's heterosexual role model, but Paul accepted Mark's more likely and sexually ambiguous truth of his being "into" Donny, the man.

On other occasions, the group examined Robin's "aggressive" usage of Facebook (and of other people), such as in breaking the expanded group boundaries by inviting her boyfriend to view Donny's page. That led to a reconsideration of the unstated rules of Facebook use and related topics that bordered on the metapsychological: post-session socialisation, trust, confidentiality, the relationship between Facebook posters and observers, and to the group leader, a non-user.

Thus, while the group members would not treat Facebook itself as an explicit nuclear idea, it served as the vehicle for the expression and development of other nuclear ideas. The free-flowing discussions inspired by Facebook encouraged retrospection, introspection, and mutual confrontation. In revealing individual histories and current concerns, Facebook motivated truth seeking, and also, truth-inspection: how and why members present themselves in various social situations (see Chapter Seven, on presentation of self). Hence, Facebook returned the group to itself, and to our here-and-now. I consider it a meaning generating "gift" to Facebook users and onlookers alike.

Facebook considered metapsychologically

Members band together and enact "equivalences", so that the group—its organisation, process, and symbolic content—becomes a microcosm of the social facts and the larger existential contexts that embed the group. Equivalences serve multiple goals, including the desire to achieve control and mastery over feelings of personal and social helplessness and powerlessness (Hopper, 2003a,b).

In my opinion, all groups and all individuals attempt to deal with these existential issues, and the ensuing pain of separateness, isolation, and loneliness. The Internet serves as a medium to fulfil the myth (and basic assumption) of achieving union and, with union, deep knowledge of self and other. Considered in the light of its metapsychology, then, Facebook usage—and the ongoing group dialogues involving Facebook—may be appreciated as regressive–progressive efforts to communicate desire and fulfil need. Whereas the ongoing group enactments are not an antidote to feelings of fragmentation and annihilation, they allow members to be part of something they create and make meaningful.

I should add that only one of my groups makes use of Facebook as an enactment. I believe this attests to the strength of an appealing and magnetic subgroup that consists of extensive Facebook users. Hence, whereas Facebook represents a social fact, its impact on a psychotherapy group is partially dependent on receptivity of the local environment.

Facebook invites members to cross a threshold into a wider social context in which the users and visitors, the givers and receivers, are empathically embraced: likewise, a well-functioning group. Facebook exchanges enactively represent an aspect of a nuclear idea of our group as a friendly place. That is, the group treats itself as its own Facebook page. Thus, in facing Facebook together, the group views its equivalence, views and re-views itself.

The group faces its leader

While not everyone in the group had a Facebook page (and the group did not create its own Facebook page), all were familiar with its use and, also, they frequently communicated with each other via emailing and texting. Except for me. I confine professional Internet exchanges to the occasional making or changing of an appointment and have limited familiarity with Facebook terminology or operation.

I remain Face(book)less, the outlier, taken care of and also derogated. Members patiently explain some of the electronic options regarding seeing and being seen, at the same time gently deriding me for my ignorance. As the mythic parent who does not "get it", I am tolerated, perhaps even cherished, for my perceived limitations. Whereas I do not believe I would be excluded from Facebook contact (blocked or defriended), I think the members enjoy and benefit from my absence. My disadvantaged status serves as an intimacy equaliser, reducing therapist–patient asymmetry, since among themselves the members have sources of information and private relationships in which I do not participate. Facebook participation serves as an equaliser between those individuals who also see me individually and those who are solely in group; they bond over my limitations in cyberspace.

However, relative *naïveté* put me at some emotional remove, and provided impetus to study the ongoing enactments. As a nuclear idea, Facebook gave me a productive way to self-reflect: to think about group, organise my mixed emotional responses, and measure my interventions. The nuclear idea allowed me to settle down, to be patient and enjoy its use in the members' narratives. I was free to follow my thoughts about Facebook, whether other members wanted to or not. Over time, I could assess and evaluate its impact.

In some ways, the members' Facebook usage represents an electronic form of the traditional aftergroup, but I believe it also represents an enactive breaking of a parental taboo. For little debate exists that I tolerate but have limited interest and patience for some of Facebook's group and extra-group proceedings, and there is some consensus that I disapprove of them. While this is true—traditional training and indoctrination are difficult to eradicate—it is also not true. In my surrendering to Facebook's social force, the members faced a leader in a productive struggle less with a rebellious group than with my own way of thinking and therapeutic mode of doing. I came to appreciate the "gift" of Facebook's electronic imprint, which informs us all.

Nuclear ideas function preconsciously

As a revolutionary infiltrator, social fact, and a multi-faceted enactment involving all members of our group (myself included), Facebook stimulated new meanings and depth to experiences, past and ongoing. While the group members did not treat Facebook itself as an explicit nuclear idea, it served as the vehicle for the expression and development of other nuclear ideas, focusing attention on the behaviour and personalities of certain members, subgroupings, and the predilections and limitations of the group leader.

In all groups, who the leader is and what interests the leader registers. My curiosity regarding Facebook's usage in our group (and elsewhere in the members' lives) remains unconcealed, as is the members' pleasure in only partially satisfying it. I assume, then, that our members are thinking about "me" (Part III, this volume), and, therefore, about Facebook usage, with more preconscious dimensionality than they are aware of, or willing to admit.

Postscript

Early in a group session, approximately ten months later.

> Donny: "I'm trying to get a thousand people, that number seems important" [to subscribe to his page].

> Another member: "Why is that so important?"

> Paul: "He likes attention."

> Donny: "I do, I love it."

> Robin: "I like attention too, but I wouldn't want to be so exposed on Facebook. You share everything, as soon as you meet someone."

> I took an opportunity to broaden psychological meaning: "We've never really considered why Facebook is so important to so many of you, not just for Donny. [Addressing him.] What about feeling powerful in getting so many people involved?"

Donny: "Definitely. It has given me a lot of confidence."

Elliot, who had not joined previous discussions and was not part of the group's Facebook exchanges (as far as I knew), now launched a vignette. He had "Facebooked" a college friend from thirty years ago, and entered a series of spirited discussions, and then the friend suddenly stopped responding. "I felt dropped, kind of lonely." Robin said that sometimes that happens. She becomes excited at connecting to an old friend, and then loses interest. Still, she checks in every day. From other members: "I start the day seeing who has posted." "I do it before going to sleep."

I tested in my mind and rejected "So Facebook is a good mummy, waking us up and tucking us in." Instead: "Facebook gives people a sense of comfort, not only attention . . . being attended to."

Donny: "I was so lonely as a child. I can spend hours preparing my page, knowing that people read it."

The group was sufficiently sober and reflective. At last, we could begin to use Facebook as an explicit nuclear idea. "It connects me to the world—I get updates on what's happening with people I care about." "My source of news, I don't have time to read the papers. I get the news from my friends, what they think is important." "So Facebook empowers people to take care of themselves, to get what they need from others, not only attention," I confirmed. Only later did I realise that the remark referred also to the members' relationship to me.

From a "group family" perspective, Facebook represents a vehicle for mutual growth among caring siblings, and, as such, an affirmation of independence from the parental figure, without intimations of exclusion.

A nuclear idea can lie dormant, undeveloped for a lengthy period of time, and then surface. My patience had been rewarded. The discussion led me to consider what Shapiro and Ginzberg (2001) referred to as the "persistently neglected sibling relationship", and why it was overlooked in our group and with this leader (see also Ashuach, 2012).

PART II
THE INFLUENCE OF POLEMIC IDEAS

CHAPTER SIX

Bipolar thinking leads to polemic ideas

I now introduce the concept of the polemic idea, which functions in tension to creative thinking. To review briefly: the nuclear idea harnesses potentially explosive emotional material, but which is used for peaceful purposes that are rational and productive. Developing the nuclear idea necessarily stimulates thinking, an emotional experience associated with learning (Bion, 1962); its primary effect is not to propel or quell action. The nuclear idea eschews manipulative rhetoric. If consensus is established, dissension and abstention are encouraged and respected as representing possible and alternative versions of, or paths towards, emotional truth.

The polemic idea, in contrast, focuses on controlling emotional responses and has its goal to incite or inhibit the individual's and group's action. Whereas the nuclear idea emerges unbidden from interactions among the minds of the individuals comprising the group, the polemic idea emerges from a calculated mind-set of an individual or subgroup, with a particular purpose to sway other minds and group process. This type of leader (or member aspiring to leadership) might depend on bombast, hyperbole, as well as subtler oratory that, by narrowing and focusing feelings and thought, seeks to promote facile and immediate decision making. The polemicist wishes to bend the group to his or her will. Group communication is used to encourage conformity and quell dissension. A mob or crowd group culture may eventuate, guided by the charismatic one, who plays on vulnerabilities. The goal may be to establish one Truth, which the leader might sincerely believe, and wishes the assemblage to believe.

Shakespeare's *Julius Caesar* (1961) provides a dramatic example of the power and effectiveness of the polemic idea. Mark Anthony uses irony, repeating "Brutus is an honorable man" to persuade the Roman senators and masses of the opposition, to switch allegiances and incite war.

Groups and sociopolitical organisations, to the extent that they function as thought-inhibiting establishments (Bion, 1970), are disposed towards adopting and promoting polemic ideas. As emanations of establishment beliefs, texts, doctrines, and written and unwritten laws and customs, polemic ideas present readily absorbed verities and slogans that ease individuals and groups out of the anxiety and conflict that often accompany free thinking and decision making.

Polemic ideas may excite or smooth emotions, for they convey clarity and conviction. The effect—intentional or not—is to unify and direct individuals and groups to follow predetermined modes of thought and behaviour. Haidt (2012) proposed that, given our "tribal" nature, individuals gather around and cohere into groups by adopting certain symbols, ideas, ancestors, books or gods, and treat them as sacred. In effect, groups construct "gangs"—internal and external—and fight and even die for competing value narratives, blinded by the "rightness" of their own ideas.

Polemic ideas are endemic in sociopolitical life, limiting freedom of thought in national and international affairs, affecting relations between genders, races, religions, sexual orientations, and so forth. However, polemic ideas are not necessarily bad or immoral, for example, "Cigarettes Kill". They may be inspirational and support what is believed to be the good and just. For many in the USA, the simple word "Hope", referring to Barrack Obama's presidential campaign of 2008, propelled thinking and behaviour.

As Smith (2008, p. 202) asserts,

> as soon as we observe and name anything, it quickly becomes reified and idealized; our psychoanalytic culture, as much as any other, is

built on such moral high ground. . . . [E]very analytic approach can be shown to have its own idealizations, from the currently much debated idealization of neutrality to the sacrosanct notion of empathy.

We convey polemic ideas—explicitly or implicitly—in encouraging an individual to join or stay in our groups, negotiating frame and boundaries, registering approval, interest, impatience, and so forth.

Nuclear ideas exist with unclarity. They often emerge from surrendering (Ghent, 1990) to a level of identity diffusion and fluidity, stimulated by being in group. Polemic ideas, in contrast, anchor one's sense of identity, but they might come to serve as intersubjective bulwarks, carrying certainty and conviction.

I now consider overweening the mode of mental organisation and thinking leading to polemic ideas.

Polemic ideas emerge from bipolar thinking

Polemic ideas are located in surface and deep strata of intersubjective life, reflecting the influence of the earliest phases of cognitive–emotional development. By way of "paranoid–schizoid" mechanisms of splitting and projection (Klein, 1952), the infant comes to organise its experience via pre-verbal, bipolar[28] ideas.

Klein theorised a life-preserving motive driving the primitive cognitive organisation: to protect the self from the danger of annihilation by the destructive impulses deriving from inborn envy and the death instinct. Without adhering to orthodox Kleinian theory, we may appreciate Klein's phenomenological description of the functioning of the early ego: how the infant negotiates need, frustration, and aggression through defences of splitting and projective identification. Bipolar perceiving and thinking represent developmental milestones, cognitive–emotional achievements for the infant.

But, however layered over and developed by education, ethical precepts, and the veneer of civilisation, our thinking retains its earlier, paranoid–schizoid mode, producing simplistic and personified psychological, moral, and political constructs that drive affects, fantasies, and compelling action scenarios. Bipolar thinking remains, then, a "fall-back position" in individuals, groups, and societies, and is activated in situations of anxiety, felt powerlessness, and threats to identity. Thus, Benjamin (1988) describes how the achievement of empathic mutuality ("recognition") goes awry in situations of conflict. The individual loses the capacity to trust the self and yet be open to the feelings and ideas of others. "Opposites can no longer be integrated; one side is devalued, the other idealized (splitting)" (p. 50). The stage is set for domination: by one's own polemic ideas or those of others.

The greater the sense of experienced discomfort, fear, or uncertainty, the more likely our mental response will be influenced by a level of thinking that is both primitive and violent: we perceive an enemy or group of enemies that must be vanquished, along with any challenging or modifying ideas.

Gangs in the mind

I return again to the infant, and its hypothetical inner experience. Since its thinking remains fluid and fragmented, the developing infant finds itself in a fantasmic world of "bits" of me and not me. During this normal maturation process, the infant gradually takes mental ownership of its fragmentary concepts of people and anthropomorphised objects, and amalgamates them into simple categories: good and bad, friend and foe, strong and weak, and, on the social level, us and them.

Even as more mature forms operate, the individual continues to organise and personify experience via the simplified structure of the paranoid–schizoid mode. Each of us lives with us and them, "gangs in the mind", and we feel both protected and persecuted, and use them to persecute others. I appropriate Rosenfeld's (1988) phrase because it conveys the notion that a particular type of group exists in the mind: "a powerful gang dominated by a leader, who controls all the members of the gang to see that they support one another . . . it has a defensive purpose to keep itself in power and so maintain the status quo" (p. 249). The leader is, of course, an aspect of the thinker oneself, "disguised as omnipotently benevolent or life-saving", who recruits other aspects of the self, which promises "to provide . . . quick, ideal solutions" (p. 250).

Rosenfeld used "gang" metaphorically, in reference to aggressive narcissism in certain patients, rather than as an aspect of self-organisation or as a dimension of group thinking and behaviour. That is,

Rosenfeld did not direct his remarks to the group, but to the internal world of disturbed persons. Still, they supply a useful conceptual bridge between individual and group psychology.[29] I conceive of polemic ideas as providing the vehicle—for the individual, the group, and the social network—to promote the idealised, simplified solutions that Rosenfeld referred to.

Clinical anecdote: shifting bipolarities

Sometimes, it is difficult to know who is dominating whom with polemic ideas, and who initiated regression to bipolar thinking. For instance, Lauren reported to our group about the state of her marriage. She was, in her words, "diligent and hard working", and her husband, Jim, was not. She had many ideas about how their relationship could improve, and she offered them often and forcefully to her husband and to us. Like her husband, group members could only agree. Group cohorts supported Lauren with suggestions, including divorce.

At one point, I spoke to Lauren directly: "Your ideas might be valid, but you're ramming your reality into Jim's mind, and he is going to feel bullied and he'll react." I realised that I, too, had felt bullied, and, with other group members, I had become a torpid witness and unwitting accomplice to Lauren's distress.

Lauren's thoughts about her marriage operated like a "gang in her mind", which she set loose on her husband and the group. Lauren's "gang" bullied husband, group, and Lauren herself, controlling mental space and our psychic freedom to think for ourselves and to link up ideas collaboratively. In outwardly submitting to her by offering or agreeing with her "quick, ideal solutions" (Rosenfeld), we formed our own collusive gang, providing us—and, most probably, her husband—a tempting combination of passive revenge and swift exit from enslavement, both mental and enactive.

Like her husband, I would be avoiding "hard work" by not challenging her to think about her contribution to relational difficulties. I had to formulate and present in a sympathetic and inviting manner a nuclear idea regarding Lauren's bipolar mode of thinking and persuasive style of communicating and how it provoked compliance, but also, retaliation and abandonment, even by our supportive group. Polemic ideas and their enaction, brought to self and group awareness, were contained by the process of negotiating a nuclear idea.

In bipolar scenarios of power–powerless, the politics of master–slave (Hegel), good–bad, victim–victimiser, shift suddenly and subtly. As with Lauren, the polemic instigator wants something that can be withheld: mindless recognition, submission, completion. Tables turn, roles reverse, tempering the triumph and mollifying defeat.

Thinking thoughts and badness

Bion described a basic human tension between the essential need for knowledge of the "truth" of one's emotional experience and the desire to evade frustration and pain—the often unavoidable accompaniments to developing a nuclear idea. "Truth seems to be essential for psychic health" (1962, p. 63). But to reach truth, one must not be bullied by the fantasy of truth's "badness".

> All objects that are needed are bad objects because they tantalize. They are needed because they are not possessed in fact; if they were possessed there would be no lack ... [Thoughts] are bad, needed objects to be got rid of because they are bad. (Bion, 1962, p. 84)

The sense of being threatened and overwhelmed must be tolerated without succumbing to splitting, excessive projective identification, or evacuation.

Case example: the group becomes the "gang"

Myra entered combined individual–group treatment after being suddenly widowed at age thirty-eight. She had been a submissive, repressed wife, became an overly possessive mother, and remained, in her words, "sheltered" by her parents and a "worry wart". After a few years, she arrived at certain emotional truths that had profound effects on her thinking and subsequent behaviour: she realised she had been extremely lonely in her marriage, as she had been in her childhood. Now she felt explosive anger toward her parents and her deceased husband, yet, also, "happy and free for the first time in my life".

Myra maintained a warm, if emotionally limited, stance in group, yet she began to attend sessions wearing heavy makeup, revealing outfits, and strong perfume. She had become an "evening person", discovering a late-night world of nightclubs and bars, and men who were available "to play". Internet dating sites preoccupied her day life, and she could do without her twice-weekly individual sessions.

In group, we advised her to slow down, to think about what she was doing and why—which she acknowledged liking, for it was the first time in her life people seemed interested in who she was and what she wanted. The group had become her first real "friend", she told us tearfully. We heard her poignant realisation first as a metaphor, representing emotional growth. However, we discovered that "friend" was a simplistic notion of non-judgemental approval, revealing the fixated bipolarity typical of the paranoid–schizoid mind-set susceptible to the polemic idea. She acknowledged difficulty in thinking about us as separate individuals, bringing to each of us a range of different feelings and unique thoughts. "Intimacy," she reflected, when the word was brought to her attention, "I have to learn what that means. I've never had it."

"Not even with yourself," a group member volunteered, encouragingly.

"This is going to be a lot of work," Myra soberly replied.

However, gradually, she came to hear the group's communications as a polemic: moralistic and conventional. "You're sounding just like them [her parents]," she teased. No matter how variable the membership and individual opinions, she heard one voice spouting establishment verities. We had become part of the gang of id suppressing, enslaving objects of her past.

She soon said her goodbyes.

Discussion

Inviting and stimulating the learning process, psychoanalytic group therapy necessarily disturbs fixed beliefs, values, and relationships, and even one's sense of self. The clinical situation threatens to become a bad idea, a source of danger. I have suggested (Billow, 2001) that on some level, group members—therapist and members alike—hate each other, fear and dread the work, and seek to blame others for being subjected to the very experience one seeks, participates in, and benefits from. "Myra is us," to paraphrase the comic strip character, Pogo, who said, "I have met the enemy and the enemy is us."

With the anxiety Myra experienced ("this is going to be a lot of work"), Myra retreated to an internal polemic idea. The "work" became the bad object, controlling her wishes to act out her impulses. Like Myra, all group participants are liable to think in terms of "them" and "me", clustering unwanted thinkers and unwanted thoughts as "them". In effect, productive work involves tolerating the presence of powerful bad objects—thoughts and thinkers—and learning to get along without splitting, evacuating, or otherwise countering mental links, as in Myra's fleeing from the group.

Establishments enforce polemic ideas

Groups often operate by de-differentiation and exclusion. Freud (1921c, p. 118) wrote, "opposition to the herd is as good as separation from it, and is therefore anxiously avoided. But the herd turns away from anything that is new or unusual". To escape from the provocations of the mature mind and mature relationships, individuals tend to collude and revert to bipolarity. Groups are aroused to action when their system of polemic ideas is disturbed

Finding the scapegoat, an outsider or singleton—whether someone different in the group, or external to it—might help to create cohesion. Throughout life, individuals mass and seek and assert power over "suitable targets of externalization" (Volkan, 1985). Other persons, subgroups, countries, religions, animate and even inanimate objects (e.g., religious symbols) become vehicles for polemic ideas, in which to put unintegrated experiences of good and bad, security and love, fear and hatred.

Democratic as well as fascistic governments, well intentioned as well as malevolent families, leader as well as member—all groups and all individuals are vulnerable to bipolar thinking. Social structures: families, schools, religions, government, professional associations, might endanger those who wish to individuate and diverge from the establishment's order.

De Tocqueville's (2003) observations, although hyperbolic, have contemporary resonance:

> I know of no country in which there is so little independence of mind and real freedom of discussion as in America. . . . The master no longer says 'You should think as I do, or you shall die; but he says, 'You are free to think differently from me and to retain your life, your property,

and all that you possess; but you are henceforth a stranger among your people. . . . Your fellow creatures will shun you like an impure being; and even those who believe in your innocence will abandon you, lest they should be shunned in their turn. Go in peace! I have given you your life, but it is an existence worse than death. (pp. 337–339)

Hypothetically, among the motives for forming groups is protection from one's own aggression and that of others (Freud, 1912–1913). Political theorist Judith Shklar (1989, p. 27) suggested that the proper subject of politics is to protect the weak from the worst depredations of the powerful. But the weak might remain unaware of their need for protection and the reality of their disempowerment. Gramsci (1971) propounded how mass media and popular culture indoctrinate the citizens of society, via "cultural hegemony", fostering a complex system of domination by one group or class.[30] The status group threatens alienation or exile for non-compliance with its norms. Redl (1980; also, Horowitz, 1983) described the process of "role suction", in which members get drawn into the rigid roles and ideological positions seemingly required by this gang dynamic.

At the prospect of innovation and change, large groups, such as psychoanalytic, political, or religious organisations, may become "paranoiagenic" (Kernberg, 2000), and take conservative or counter-revolutionary stances. The political history of psychoanalysis includes many instances of bipolar thinking: bullying, exile, and secession of dissenters. "Correctness permeates and envelopes psychoanalysis . . . This rightness and propriety are nowhere more prominent than in the efforts to practice according to a prescribed and proscribed method" (Goldberg, 2001, p. 123). Some individuals, rather than attempting to change from within the system, retaliate by devaluing membership, or simply by participating passively. While endemic schisms might lead to creative, break-away groups, the new institutions, like the old, tend to be organised hierarchically around iconic figures, and enforce allegiance with the threat or actuality of excommunication.

The psychotherapist's tasks include protecting group members from mindlessly submitting to the polemic ideas, but our job is complicated since, as I have emphasised, we, too, maintain deeply ingrained loyalties. Establishments exist inside as well as outside the mind. To effect change in the external world and one's affiliations requires awareness and modification of what Menzies Lyth (1988) referred to as an "imaginary institution", an internalised social system, consisting of conscious and non-conscious images, fantasies, self and interpersonal roles and relationships.

Grossman (1995, p. 889) described an underlying hallucinatory level of mentation, connected to the psychoanalyst's professional identification and affiliation that has "a status analogous to shared daydreams". The teachers, texts, supervisors, and therapists who have contributed to the clinician's expertise and sense of professional identity could create an imaginary institution of ideal objects exerting internal pressure, enforcing polemic ideas at the expense of the new and experimental.

Assuredly, institutions consisting of good rather than ideal objects also exist in the mind, and they may be used constructively. In a stressful Tavistock group, one member reported protecting his mental freedom by forming a group in his mind, which consisted of historical and contemporary figures who stood up unbroken to intolerable social forces.

Clinical anecdote: disapprobation in the mind, or, also, by the institution?

A senior psychoanalyst invited a younger colleague (and also my analysand) to contribute to a symposium on "Women and Anger". She was complimented by, and interested in, the offer to present at a major psychoanalytic conference. However, she was afraid to broach her idea, which was to explore transference–countertransference configurations of anger as they varied in her individual and group analytic work. She was relatively comfortable acknowledging and exploring her responses to several "difficult" patients, but could she disclose the reality of a combined practice to an audience of members of a prestigious psychoanalytic organisation?

In her psychoanalytic sessions, we had no difficulty exploring the personal roots of her anxieties. The organisation was her religiously conservative family, the senior colleague, her mother, who could be warm, but easily wounded, and she herself, the little girl, "afraid of upsetting my mother and making my father angry". And, she knew that she could be the "worst combination the two of them", histrionic and reactive, "holding grudges and critical".

With regret, she declined the invitation: "I may be paranoid, but I'm not crazy." She was not eager to entertain my thought that being courageous and presenting was worth the risk.

Discussion

I have argued for the validity and power of combined psychotherapy (Billow, 2010a). Combined treatment would seem to be a logical extension and natural fit with relational theory, which attempts to destabilise bipolar thinking involved in the "one person" psychology model and, thereby, reduce patient–analyst asymmetry, and foster a mutual, egalitarian process (O'Leary & Wright, 2005). Group members are witnesses to the combined treatment of others, as well as participants, and their voices may be as authoritative, informed, and psychologically evolved as their therapist's. Even more than dyadic relational psychotherapy, then, combined treatment advances Racker's (1968, p. 132) call for "social reform" and demolishing of the traumatogenic "patriarchal order" and "inequality in the analyst–analysand society."

Of course, combined dyadic–group analytic psychotherapy is not "establishment" psychoanalysis, as defined by such traditional extrinsic features (Gill, 1994) as the dyadic setting, session frequency, use of the couch, and so forth, all of which may be conceptualised as therapist-induced enactments, expressing polemic ideas. Nevertheless, combined therapy is psychoanalytic, given that "the wide scope of the current forms of psychoanalytic therapy allows room for many ideas, which do not even have to be restricted to the field of psychoanalysis in the stricter sense" (Thoma & Kachele, 1994, p. 188).

Freud himself introduced the possibility of combined treatment in describing the two intrinsic features of psychoanalysis; these are key factors also for psychoanalytically orientated practitioners of combined therapy.

> The theory of psycho-analysis is an attempt to account for two striking and unexpected facts of observation which emerge whenever an attempt is made to trace the symptoms of a neurotic back to their sources in his past life: the facts of transference and of resistance. Any line of investigation that recognises these two facts and takes them as the starting-point of its work has a right to call itself psycho-analysis. (Freud, 1914d, p. 16)

The combined modality offers the opportunity to study multiple as well as mutual influence, the multiple including social, cultural, economic, and political forces.

However, neither psychoanalytic nor group analytic organisations are friendly to the idea or practice of combined psychotherapy. Dalal (2000), for example, excoriated Foulkes for not taking the group "seriously", to the extent to which he was not sufficiently group-centric. Indeed, while Foulkes suggested that individual analysis, if needed, take place after completion of group treatment, later in his career he practised a "back door" combined approach. Group members were seen individually in turn, one per week, and so, approximately bi-monthly (Hobdell, 1991, p, 137).

The iconic leaders and journals of the respective psychotherapeutic organisations promulgate polemic ideas: party-line theory, technique, and professional initiation rites. Their thinking is bipolar, and they do not publicise, surely not valorise, combined psychoanalytic points of view.

For the young psychoanalyst in this example, the combined psychoanalytic mode, which she valued, also existed as a heretical "bad object", both in the reality of the respective establishment gangs, and, possibly, in her own mind.

Motives for power and recognition engulf the group and its leader in bipolar scenarios

It is not possible to engage in a relationship with another (or others), where there is total equality. That is, human interactions involve shifting positions of power and, therefore, I suggest, the experience of polemic indoctrination of the weaker by the stronger, anticipated or real.

To some degree, the structure of therapeutic relationships fosters polemic thinking and enaction, since it promotes the exalted position of professionals and the ascendancy of their ideas. "Both metaphorically and actually the therapist sits in the most comfortable seat, controls the time and place of meeting, receives payment, and is protected from discomfort" (Michels, 1988, p. 55).

Implicit polemic ideas are conveyed when therapists adopt the "stereotypic, stylized posture of psychoanalytic hyper-unperturbed calm" (Hoffman, 2009, p. 621). Racker (1968) referred to this façade as supporting the "myth of 'analyst without anxiety or anger'". In my reading, while intending to "replace submission by co-operation on equal terms between equals" (p. 65), Foulkes (1964) advocated a mythic façade of benign superiority. He strove to exert

> an important influence by his own example. The conductor represents and promotes reality, reason, tolerance, understanding, insight, catharsis, independence, frankness and an open mind for new experience. This happens by way of a living, corrective emotional experience. (Foulkes, 1964, p. 57)

Foulkes' polemic idea, while unstated, fosters an equation of mental health with an unreachable ideal of equanimity and wisdom.

Similarly, Bion's oracular style of "taking groups" reflected allegiance to polemic ideas of neutrality, abstinence, and anonymity. Bion's austere, aloof self-presentation, as well as his group theory and technique, probably contributed to a static, "hierarchical arrangement of [leadership] power and privilege" that Gerson (1996, p. 626) characterised as typical of the classical tradition. In my opinion, conceptions involving "me" *vs.* "them", the leader *vs.* the group, reflect bipolar thinking, and iatrogenically generate basic assumptions. As in the following example, a frustrated therapist might refuse to engage emotionally and become impassive, yet analyse the patient as withholding, spiteful, or unconsciously resistant, or the group as involved in a basic assumption such as fight/flight.

Relational theorists such as Hoffman (1992, 1996) have proposed that, ultimately, it is the therapist's avoidance of ritualised roles that establishes the conditions for self–other understanding and mutual growth. The therapist's authenticity—genuine interest and concern along with an awareness (and perhaps acknowledgement) of personal and professional limitations—becomes an emotional reference point, a ground for the development of nuclear ideas (Part III).

Clinical anecdote: diagnostic classification as polemic idea

A therapist reported casually in supervision: "We [the group] were trying to reason with George [a member]. I got really annoyed. He batted away what anyone said. I realised how disturbed a compulsive personality could be, with his obsessive defences. I felt it better to sit back and let the group give up on its own."

Discussion

The therapist's irritation was understandable and perhaps even a necessary component of the transference–countertransference, which needed to be opened up for discussion. (For instance, the therapist could acknowledge feeling that he was being controlled and/or ask George if he felt he was being controlled.). However, the therapist's reversion to bipolar thinking transformed George to a "disturbed personality disorder", from subject to diagnostically coded object: "Once you label me you negate me" (Kierkegaard). The therapist's polemic "nosological truths" paralleled the patient's obsessive defences, each used to out-power the other.

Hegel's dialectic of mutual recognition asserts that power is sought not for its own sake, but to compel recognition that would not otherwise be forthcoming. In this example, the therapist probably felt wounded, his expertise rejected, and at risk of being experienced by the entire group as ineffective. "Sitting back" was a strategy to disempower George, as the therapist withdrew from the supportive, introjective–projective exchanges that gird empathic human relationships.[31]

Freud (1916, p. 315) himself had implied a symmetry between patient and analyst: "We all demand reparation for early wounds to our narcissism". Reactivity to challenge and defiance, investigative and interpretative pacing, tact, empathic gestures and bonding efforts—all these verbal and non-verbal variables and more—represent the group therapist's tendencies towards securing or sharing (usually both) power and control. In banishing George from the intersubjective space of contemporary relational thinking, the therapist had to have had an impact on all members of the group.

The leader of the gang: self, superego, member, group

Freud (1921c, p. 129) theorised that each individual, "bound by ties of identification", builds an ego ideal (later called superego) consisting of "numerous group minds"—those of race, class, nationality, and so forth—all of which become embodied in a leader. "The primal father is the group ideal, which governs the ego in the place of the ego ideal" (p. 127).

As a member of the various groups that exist in one's mental life, the individual wants "to be ruled and oppressed and to fear its master" (Freud, 1921c, p. 78). The leader or master may be an aspect of oneself then, that is, the "superego", which seeks power and control over other aspects of one's personality and bludgeons with the "should books" of psychotherapy, or the leader might be another group member, the group as a whole, or a socio-political organisation (such as psychoanalytic or group). These "masters", creations of child-ish, bipolar thinking, convey polemic ideas.

Case example: castigated by myself

I was struggling to eliminate a midweek evening group from my prac-tice, yet how could I even introduce the subject? Three of our long-term members announced their leaving and I would not break into their termination processes. Then, Stan changed jobs, but he juggled professional assignments and continued. No opportunity there. While Alexa and Elliot, two senior members, grumbled about being in group too long, I could not force them out. I had to do something soon: I would malnourish the group if I did not feed it with new members, yet to announce my intention would be to plunge a knife into its heart.

Six months passed, each week entering with a plan, but then recoil-ing, and surrendering to group process. Finally, I spoke.

> "I need to bring something up that has been very difficult, about ending our group. I want to reduce my workload. Several of you have said you are getting ready to leave, and I have space for anyone who wants to continue in another group."
>
> Ann: "I can understand. You want to leave more time for writing, and being with your family."
>
> Alexa: "When will this happen?"
>
> "I have never done this before, and I would like us to work this out together."
>
> Stan: "A month, longer?"
>
> Alexa: "Feels too short."
>
> I agreed: "Why not let the idea sink in and see how we feel?"
>
> I expected the group to turn on me, justifiably, but:
>
> Ann: "I can imagine how hard this is for you."

Alexa: "Sophie's choice."

"Exactly." I absorbed the members' caring, making no effort to hide my sadness and discomfort, which would not have been possible, even if I had tried. When gathered sufficiently, I said, "You must have other feelings. Aren't you angry with me too?"

Alexa: "Not yet, although I am feeling: 'Why us? What's wrong with us?'"

A feeling close to terror descended on me: where would the other members take this thought? What harm was I inflicting?

Stan teased, "Yes, Alexa, it's because of you."

Ann: "I thought that too for a second, why not another group, then I decided it was because we were the last group of the week—Richard must be getting tired."

Stan: "I reviewed the group and felt that we were OK. Although I wondered why Ronnie and what's her name didn't stick [two recent, short-term members]."

I turned to those who had not spoken: "I can't be 'OK' with all of you."

Elliot: "You're entitled to spend your time the way you want. You haven't done anything to be mad at."

Barbara: "I feel like I'm a rat leaving a sinking ship, but I had been talking about leaving group with Richard."

Ralph: "We know that, Barbara. You spoke to us too."

"I'm afraid that I am the rat, sinking the ship," I iterated, but neither in that session nor in the three months leading to our moving termination could I elicit the anger that I believed existed, and felt was deserved.

Then, from members continuing individual treatment:

Ralph: "You must have heard that we have been meeting."

"Yes, I had." I was touched by the members' bonding, but had also been feeling vague discomfort that I could not at first identify.

"Last week was an Italian restaurant, too noisy. Next time we will pick a quieter place. We work around Stan's schedule."

From Alexa (three months later): "Ann called Barbara [who had terminated before the group ended]. She's going to come to the next meeting, although I'm ambivalent about her."

From Ann (nine months later): "Everett joined us [a long-term member who had terminated two years earlier]! So great to catch up."

Stan (two years): "You should feel very pleased. Everybody came. And Everett said he was going to call you, he really needs some more individual work."

Now they are a group of seven, meeting quarterly. Pleased? Yes, and troubled, too. "Ye brook of conscience – Spectres! That frequent / The bad Man's restless walk, and haunt his bed" (Wordsworth, 1839). I rehearsed and anticipated polemic ideas conveying moral superiority, guilt-inducing accusations, and disparagement; instead, I receive "punishment in thanks" (Shakespeare, 1961: *Measure for Measure*, I, 4, l. 379). Since the members do not rebuke, I castigate myself with a gang of self-critical taunts.

Discussion

A polemic idea propels or quells action. I intended to end the group, but for months I was paralysed by self-critical variants of "me" (Part III), the "bad Man" (Wordsworth), a "rat", sinking the ship. When I had gathered myself sufficiently to initiate termination, I offered my person and behaviour as something to be felt and thought about: "You must have other feelings." "Aren't you angry with me too?"

In my mind, the group punished by refusing to consider "me" with the dimensionality I thought appropriate, refused to terminate as a group, and refused, by their ongoing presence, to permit my guilty ideas to recede to the comfortable past. Perhaps I disarmed a nascent gang-up by presenting myself as vulnerable, open to the member's administrations and co-leadership. Also, in playing that card, the members would have endangered their leader—which I remain *in absentia*—and risked splintering off from each other. Preserving "me" as an ideal object of thought helps safeguard the goodness of the group and its holding power.

We gravitate towards bipolarity, particularly when afraid, anxious, or perplexed, as I was with the thought of ending a long-term group. The individual projects and colludes to set up other individuals ("spectres") to broadcast polemic ideas, and acts both subordinate and superordinate. Each person remains perpetually in intrapsychic conflict, struggling with, submitting to, and rebelling against a superego that justifies itself by its encyclopaedia of polemic ideas.

I have suggested the value of subjecting polemic ideas to thinking—the goal being the development of nuclear ideas. Writing this example is a step on the way, but I have not fully achieved the transformation. An enduring, easily accessible guilt signals that the polemic idea is still cathected and operating. The weight of a polemic idea can linger, even as it develops into a nuclear idea. Tension between the two so often holds sway.

The press to bipolar thinking remains

A question remains about the extent and ease with which mental independence and thoughtful self-governance is sustainable. For an aspect of the thinker is driven by polemic ideas, and attempts, consciously or otherwise, to likewise control others. A type of drive-dominated thinking emerges immediately and unmediated in situations of emotional intensity, for example, frustration, anxiety, threat, challenge, and competition. Polemic ideas may interfere even as they coexist with the development and use of nuclear ideas. They play out in societies, groups, families, and dyads, and in the enactments in which one entangles others (see next chapter, on inveiglement). Each individual is perpetrator and target, seeks to be the master and the slave, and an aspect of mutual recognition resides in acknowledging the pleasure as well as the pain in our participation.

In social as well as psychotherapeutic relationships, we strive for and enjoy moments of subject–subject relationships. Sustaining the depressive position (Klein)—existing democratically and interdependently with others—is an achievement on intrapsychic, interpersonal, and political levels. However, we are "group animals" (Bion, 1961) with an "archaic heritage" (Freud, 1921c, p. 127). Particularly when interacting in groups (which is always), there is a press to revert to bipolar thinking, and polemic ideas: to that which is "very simple and very exaggerated . . . [with] neither doubt nor uncertainty" (Freud, 1921c, p. 78).

CHAPTER SEVEN

Inveiglement

"Inveiglement" describes a mode of interpersonal influence, in which the individual or group becomes bound by mental parameters imposed by an other. The intended effect is to divert knowing, believing, thinking about, or acting on thoughts that exist mentally, or that could be generated. Inveiglement, thus, serves as companion to, and sponsor of, the polemic idea, which, in turn, contributes to the effectiveness of inveigling as a means of domination and control.

Chapter Four provided the clinical example of "hostage taking", and illustrated how inveiglement works to take over the mentality of its targets. A departing member attempted to convince the group of her entitlement to attend post-session dinners. In thought, word, and deed, Miranda personified the bipolar thinker. I paraphrase the variants of the essential polemic idea: "You love me, so you should do what I propose." "I am very hurt by any disagreement and need compliance." "I explode violently when challenged to think about my ideas." "Anyone who doesn't agree with me is a bad person." "If you don't fulfil my wishes and wants, I fill you with dread." Her convincing manner of self-presentation intruded into the minds of the group with such emotional force as to constrict freedom to think and behave independently, leading to acquiescence or reactive rebellion.

As with this example, inveiglement often involves a potent combination of emotional and cognitive flooding and induced dissociation, stimulating and directing ideation that cuts off further thinking and that leads to actions that might operate against one's or the group's best interests. A polemic idea or set of ideas is proffered, which might be false and deceiving, but stated, implied, or insinuated as "fact", and is emotionally convincing.

I underscore that polemic ideas are not, *per se*, thought inhibiting, antisocial or antigroup. To the extent to which they *inveigle*, that is, control thinking and behaviour, they interfere with the development and utilisation of nuclear ideas. Referring again to the clinical incident described in Chapter Four, "hostage taking" could coalesce and develop into an effective nuclear idea only when I could interest the group (and myself) in thinking about what was occurring, reviewing the enactments and finding commonalities with coincidental and antecedent group and personal interactions.

Hostage taking is often a dimension of inveiglement, which is a broader concept, and a phenomenon, I suggest, that pervades clinical situations and, perhaps, all human interactions. It has been written about from many viewpoints, but rarely appears in the psychoanalytic literature and perhaps never in group theory. It is worthwhile to be aware and study the effects of inveiglement on individuals, groups, and larger socio-political entities since, as perpetrators and targets, we remain subject to its influence.[32]

One of the great literary works of Western culture may be appreciated as an epic of an inveigler:[33]

"Sing to me of the man, Muse, the man of twists and turns"
(*The Odyssey*, Book 1, l. 1, Homer, 1996)

In obstructing or diverting ideas that the individual or group depends on to make an independent and accurate assessment of reality, inveiglement might lead to fateful consequence: Ulysses blinds and misguides the Cyclops, lures and vanquishes the Trojans with the enticing horse, and lulls and then slays Penelope's suitors via a beggar masquerade. As a lethal master of inveiglement, he is able to inveigle others while resisting the Sirens of inveiglement.

In this chapter, I describe four broad subtypes: toxic, neurotic, communal, and presentational inveiglement.

Introduction to four types of inveiglement

"I'm their product, it's vital you sell me / So Machiavell me, make an Argentine Rose" ("Rainbow High", Lloyd Webber & Rice, 1976). Like Evita, all of us are actors, fixing setting, appearance, and manner to "sell" our personal brand of polemic ideas: versions of our self that stimulate and guide impressions so that others will act voluntarily to comply with our own wishes and plans. The face we present to the world—often including one's inner world—veils, may divert or obstruct receptivity to a full range of ideas, including those that might be in conflict with our immediate wishes and goals.

Presaging contemporary thinking and writing regarding the multiplicity of self-states (e.g., Baars, 1992; Bromberg, 2009; Lampl-de Groot, 1981), Goffman (1959) proposed that individuality is neither inherent nor permanent, but a sociological construct of persuasive interaction (Trevino, 2003). Although he did not use the term, Goffman informally classified different types of inveiglers and inveiglement. On one extreme is the cynic, who sets out to defraud, confuse, mislead, or antagonise to achieve "a kind of gleeful spirited aggression from the act that he can toy at will with something his audience must take seriously" (Goffman, 1959, p. 18). (Ulysses would seem to fit into this category, although a heroic variation; Richard III, the antiheroic.) I refer to this type of interaction as toxic inveiglement.

Occupying a less pathological position is the sincere individual, "taken in by his own act; he can be sincerely convinced that the impression of reality which he states is the real reality" (Goffman, 1959, p. 17). Such individuals promulgate neurotic inveiglement.

Goffman proposed that individuals conspire to act as "teams", stabilising the groups of which they are members by preserving certain defining features and conspiring to conceal or play down others. Bion (1970) referred to a similar social process as structuring a falsifying "Establishment", which draws in the susceptible by offering mind-stultifying but comforting ideas. Socio-political influence may be assessed, then, in terms of communal inveiglement. Consensual "truth" is presented as if with a capital rather than small "t" and, hence, functions as a polemic idea.

Finally, Goffman called attention to "the presentation of self in everyday life" (the title of his classic book)—referring to common and even prevalent interactions involving self–other enticements. I

consider these as intersubjective processes of presentational inveiglement, pertaining to the inveiglements of everyday life.

Toxic inveiglement

Shakespeare's *Richard III* dramatises how toxic inveiglement provides
a structural bulwark to certain extremely pathological personalities,
with severe consequences to self and others. Richard aspired to
"deceive more sly than Ulysses could . . . And set the murderous
Machiavel to school" (Shakespeare, 1961, *Henry VI, Part III*, III, iii,
ll. 189, 193). He took particular pleasure in fakery and persuasion:
"[to] wet my cheeks with artificial tears / And frame my face to all
occasions" (*Henry VI, Part III*, III, iii, ll. 184–185).

Richard revelled in his ambition—not just or even primarily for the
throne, but for taking over the minds of others. Richard triumphantly
woos the widow of the man he murdered: "Ha! Hath she forgot
already that brave Prince, / Edward, her lord, whom I some three
months since, / Stabbed . . . Upon my life, she find . . . / Myself to be a
marvelous proper [i.e. handsome] man" (Shakespeare, 1961, *Richard
III*, I, ii, ll. 240–241, 254). He discards Anne upon marrying, aiming for
new targets to dominate and destroy: "this earth affords no job to
me / But to command, to check, to o'erbear such / As are of better
person than myself" (Shakespeare, 1961, *Henry VI, Part III*, III, iii, ll.
165–167).

Unloved and unwanted, Richard felt less than human, destined
to "snarl and bite and play the dog" (*Henry VI, Part III*, V, vi, l. 77). In
toxic inveiglement, hatred and envy, characteristic of the paranoid–
schizoid position (Klein), energises the "gleeful spirited aggression"
that Goffman described. Underlying feelings of inadequacy and
meaninglessness propel compensatory polemic ruminations and
monothematic behaviour. The restless and agitated Richard leaves a
bloody trail of the conscripted; the parasitic activity itself provides
tenuous self-organisation and purpose "Since I cannot prove a lover
. . . I am determined to prove a villain" (Shakespeare, 1961, *Richard III*,
I, i, ll. 28, 30).

Toxic inveiglement implicates early and severe developmental
trauma, as with Richard, who was treated inhumanely and rejected
by his own mother: "Love forswore me in my mother's womb"

(Shakespeare, 1961, *Henry VI, Part III*, III, ii, ll. 153). Richard displayed no evidence of secure loving attachment: "I am like no brother; / And this word 'love,' which greybeards call divine, / Be resident in men like one another, / And not in me. I am myself alone" (*Henry VI, Part III*, V, vi, ll. 80–83).

Richard reveals the self-hatred and inner turmoil behind toxic inveiglement: "Alack! I love myself. Wherefore? for any good / That I myself have done unto myself? O! no alas! I rather hate myself / For hateful deeds committed by myself . . . 'Guilty! Guilty!' / I shall despair" (*Richard III*, V, iii, ll. 186–190, 199–200). Increasingly reckless and unheeding of consequences, Richard stages his own downfall, betraying and acting out a dissociated need for retaliation, attack, and punishment. In effect, his outrageousness brings others to their senses, frees them from toxic inveiglement, so that they could think and plan a realistic course of repair.

Case example: discovering and exposing a toxic inveigler

Allan, a successful accountant in his early forties, tearfully and convincingly described to the group his tumultuous marriage to an irrational, raging wife. He was charming and convincing, and it took effort for the members to free themselves from his polemic rants against Ella, his wife, to call attention to some of his contributions to the marital difficulties. Ella, finding Allan's new therapy encouraging, scheduled a series of marital consultations.

With some good humour, Ella let me know that she found me "difficult and unfair", but that since Allan seemed to feel the same way about me (and about her), she wanted to pursue her own individual and group therapy with me. Of the two, Allan ostensibly appeared the better group citizen. He verbalised appreciation of negative feedback, and could diverge from marital preoccupations to become co-operatively involved in group life. Ella remained fixated on her husband. His faults and her maltreatment coalesced into an unshakeable polemic idea; the frequency and intensity of her venting made the idea, and Ella herself, seem extreme and unreasonable.

Over the next three years, however, Ella began to refine and modulate what remained her overriding focus on Allan. Her polemic began to make sense to us and she detailed, with increasing alarm, financial and legal crises brought on by Allan's professional behaviour that had led to the dissolution of his partnership in the accounting firm.

In his group, Allan tendered a new bipolar idea: he was a changed man. His infractions, professional, marital, and otherwise, were pre-therapy, he insisted, while Ella remained suspicious and confused. Allan could not believe Ella would carry through her divorce threats, and only after legal pressure did he leave home. Allan vowed never to abandon his children, or desert our group that had given him so much support and guidance throughout his stormy marriage. However, once in separate residence, Allan had to readjust his budgeting, and this meant eliminating individual sessions. He then began to delay payment of group fees, with the excuse that formerly his wife had paid the bills. The pattern continued, with increasingly lengthy intervals between payments, and a mounting unpaid balance.

Not wanting to embarrass Allan, I spoke to him after the group sessions. Several small cheques bounced, and then a larger one. With trepidation, I alerted him that I had to discuss these developments in group. He assented, and greeted the group discussion amiably. As a professional himself, he understood the issue of settling accounts, particularly since many of his own clients were in arrears. He did not expect me to carry him indefinitely. Everyone knew of his legal hassles, complicated by divorce proceedings with the insufferable Ella, a stock market "bust", a sports car lease that he was renegotiating, and the expense of a child-friendly apartment, "the kids come first, before me or Rich."

He was so agreeable: understanding my predicament "as a professional" while explaining the economics of his adverse circumstances. However, he denied and diverted attention from the ethical significance of his financial transgressions, or from acknowledgement of what was transpiring within him, and between us, that endangered his group membership. I was struck that not one among Allan's affectionate group members protested when—after another month of promises and non-payment—we agreed that Allan had to take a leave of absence. He left a cheque that evening to cover a portion of what was now a large balance. As the reader might have predicted, it bounced.

In the session that followed, I anticipated the group's disapprobation, both for evicting Allan, and for prolonging his stay. I found instead a supportive group far more ready to view and review reality

than I was. A sense of guilt and failure (see Chapter Six, on the bullying superego) inhibited my memory and thinking, and I momentarily
relied on the group for leadership. (Perhaps I am not alone with the
self-inveigling therapeutic fantasy that I can, and should, "cure"
everybody.) As in *Richard III*, Allan's increasingly alarming behaviour—his histrionics, exaggerations, and rationalisations—had
brought members to their senses. They began to talk about their
ambivalent experience with Allan and individuals like him, developing a nuclear idea.

Discussion: toxic inveigling

Allan inveigled by "gaslighting" (Calef & Weinshel, 1981), subtly
changing the rules of interpersonal engagement so that he appeared
as a blameless victim and not a ruthless victimiser. Like Richard III,
who could "seem a saint when most I play the devil" (Act I, iv, l. 338),
Allan's disarming polemic of self-righteous innocence tended to
confuse and undermine the mentality of those whom he took advantage of and who would otherwise challenge his mendacity.

   Allan convincingly masqueraded as a good citizen, adjusting to
our group by becoming one of its vocal leaders. As long as he could
live undisturbed in an omnipotent mental world of his self-creation,
Allan could be perceptive, genuinely caring, and behaviourally
responsive. However, he did not modify his dependence on toxic
inveiglement, projecting and transferring mental conflict to others.
Faced with his deception, he responded with further deceit. Confronted with truth that he could not undermine, Allan killed the messen-
gers, his accounting partners, Ella, and the group—perhaps also his
sane self. In forestalling reality, Allan effectively inveigled himself and
was blind to his path and its consequences. Disbelieved and deprived
of a parasitic dependence on an audience, Allan came to exhibit the
turmoil and chaos that he had stimulated in his wife and others. He
eventually filed for bankruptcy and never regained professional or
personal footing.

   Like Ella, I remained conflicted, unsure, and even guilty for generating ideas in conflict with his self-presentation. I hesitated and
questioned the validity of my doubts about Allan's sincerity regarding
the bounced cheques, even my right to discuss the issue of payment.
I did not want to use my privileged position as therapist, what I knew

about Allan, including his not paying my fees, to retaliate by counter-inveigling, unduly influencing group process and Allan's relations to other members. Yet, it would have been another form of inveiglement to cloak myself in a therapeutic shroud of being understanding, non-judgemental, and lenient.

The group witnessed Allan's behaviour and monitored its effect on my response and on me. To function with integrity (Billow, 2010b; see Chapter Four) and not promulgate falsity, I could not spare Allan, others, and myself exposure to the realisation that he was making unfortunate moral choices with meaningful consequences. Without challenging and then expelling Allan, I would have colluded in damaging links among thinkers—our group members—and, hence, along with Allan, endanger the truth-seeking that defines a function-ing work group.

Neurotic inveiglement

Freud (Breuer & Freud, 1893–1895) located "proton pseudo", the "first lie", as the heart of hysteria. In effect, he understood the aetiology of neurosis as related to the individual inveigling oneself, interfering with thinking and reasoning capacities. Cure was achieved by the individual uncovering and accepting the "shameful" truth—that is, an integrating idea, emerging from the nucleus of the therapeutic rela-tionship. In neurotic inveiglement, dynamics involving the depressive condition (Klein) predominate, revolving around desires/fears to love and be loved and protection against anxieties involving shame and guilt (related to aggression, actual or imagined).

In her anthem, "Think" (Franklin & White, 1968), Aretha Franklin declares her "freedom" from being victimised by an inveigler: "It don't take too much high IQ's to see what you're doing to me . . . / Tryin' to make other people lose their minds". Yet, even the master group clinician, most definitely a person with "high IQs", Louis Ormont (2001), acknowledged vulnerability to neurotic inveiglement: "An attractive woman inadvertently smiles when I am about to confront her regarding her lateness. My mother would always do that. . . . Now my patient's smile disarms me, and I hesitate to confront her" (p. 192). Others follow suit with captivating smile responses. "Taken in" and "neutralized" (p. 192) by his fear of harming his symbolic

mothers, Ormont felt a loss of mental freedom, and the group's disre-
spect, presumably for being inveigled.

Excessive projective identification has been implicated (Bion, 1961)
as the mechanism by which psychotherapy patients and groups
attempt to "make other people lose their minds". While, Bion (1961,
p. 149), like Ormont, did not use the term "inveiglement", he described
its effect: "[to be unknowingly] manipulated so as to be playing a part
. . . in somebody else's phantasy . . . being a particular kind of person in
a particular emotional situation".

I add excessive *introjective* identification as a co-instigating mechanism, for the individual, group, or socio-political entity has to be
receptive to inveigling influence, willing and able to be baited and to
swallow the bait, too. Given the hints Ormont supplied regarding
the oedipal configuration of his inner life, Ormont was primed and
ready to be "blinded" by a pretty smile. Another therapist might
have responded differently. While other group members "teamed"
(Goffman, 1959) with the smiling perpetrator to control Ormont's
behaviour, it is possible that they themselves were not inveigled.

Ormont, in keeping with contemporary therapists, accepted the
inevitably of vulnerability to mental influence and control, and looked
outward, to the group, as well as inward, for support in identifying
and working his way out of the resulting enactments. As a well-
trained group analyst, he was able to "shake . . . [himself] out of the
numbing feeling" (Bion, 1961, p. 149).

Because introjection is as powerful as projection and complements
it, inveiglement is contagious. It is even common, as in the formation
of basic assumptions, a mind-numbing dimension of all groups in
which the individual member is both victim and a co-perpetrator with
other members.

I believe that the neurotic inveigler—a category that includes us
all—intuitively appreciates the personal and interpersonal cost in
such distortions of self. In doing effective psychotherapeutic work,
members are made aware of polemic ideas that underlie and propel
tendencies to inveigle and become inveigled.

Case example: working with neurotic inveiglement

> Rachel (angrily, to me, in an individual session): "You ruined things, why
> did you have to bring *her* in group. Don't you think about the effect on
> others before someone new comes in? Now I have to leave. I can't stay—

besides, I have a lot of business appointments coming up. A new job. What's the point of even going back?

"She comes into group late, her first session, then she offers advice and she doesn't even know what's going on. And everyone defends her, and she's a mess and lets everyone know and doesn't even feel that bad about it. What is she going to offer me? Nothing. She's a walking disaster, and she knows it. Can't control her eating, sleeping—ruining her marriage and her kids, and can't get in control. Yes, she's open and admits it. Good for her. I didn't get such a warm reception when I came into group."

When I suggested that she discuss her predicament with the group, Rachel offered a polemic idea that reflected her fear of her aggression and reverberating guilt: "I have to be nice, or else I'll break things. Everything will break apart, my relationship to Mary and Deb [other members], the whole group; my relationship to you. Building will fall down."

"Are you that angry that you won't be able to control yourself?" I ask, dubiously.

Rachel: "Look what you made me do in group. I couldn't [control myself]. I had to say something critical, and then I got criticised [mocking others]: 'Rachel, this is her first session,' so what! I've built a framework being supportive, seeing the best. I'm genuinely caring. What's wrong with that?"

I wanted to make sure I understood what I was hearing: "So, you 'outed' yourself by 'outing' her?"

Rachel: "I guess. No, *you* outed me by bringing her in group. And everyone came down on me. Deb and Mary."

I attempted to introduce some reality, to modify her paranoid and depressive reactions: "I thought they cautioned about your timing, and others complimented you for calling it right, for being unusually direct and not so 'nice'."

Rachel: "I didn't hear that."

"Too terrified in being real?" I suggested, and reminded her that I had called her "our country club lady", now a group soubriquet that she both hated and found useful. Her mother played that role in the family, maintaining a pleasant but brittle persona and spouting bromides throughout a troubled marriage and divorce. Rachel had taken the role of the well-behaved child, attempting to protect her mother, younger siblings, and herself from her commanding father's outrageous behaviours. "Everyone was fake, trying to convince each other that they didn't see what was going on, his temper, gluttony, no boundaries."

Rachel nodded when I commented, "The emperor's new clothes."

A few more tears and protests, and we began to make connections: "So you feel that she inveigles the group—blinds them by 'copping' to her weaknesses, and either I'm blind too or too afraid to deal with her act."

Rachel: "Well, you need patients for your group. [sarcastic] You're such a 'group person'. Why did I ever join!"

"Is the group ever going to see this?" I asked.

Rachel became apologetic: "I have to take my anger out at someone."

I responded: "Must feel good not to have to inveigle me by being 'nice'. You convince yourself that what people see is the 'real you'. You deny and act so reasonable, but still suffer and rage."

Rachel (defeated yet pleased): "I want to be real, I hate people who put on an act and I hate doing it by acting nice all the time."

Discussion: neurotic inveiglement

In a classic *Seinfeld* episode (No. 78, 1994, full text available on the internet), George is chagrined that Jerry told the "it" girl from college that he had become a marine biologist rather than offer George's preferred pretence of being an architect: "It's one thing if I make it up . . . I know my alleys." Inveiglers often know enough truth to make sure their communications are untrue, and have a good enough sense of others to mentally disarm them for what they perceive as personal protection or advantage. For Allan, inveigling shored up a chaotic identity, for Rachel, an endangered identity, and for George, the *Seinfeld* character, perhaps an inadequate identity.

Rachel allows us insight into the desperation, confusion, and ambivalence that might motivate neurotic inveiglement. The combined individual–group work revealed compelling resistances underlying Rachel's overt but disguised refusal to modify her façade and move towards greater authenticity (Billow, 2010a,c). For the very structure of group symbolically represented and, thus, induced inveigling: "I don't like revealing myself," she acknowledged in one group session. "I love group, don't get me wrong, but the circle. It is like all the dinners with my family, at a big round table and we were supposed to tell about our day, but a big act. Couldn't talk about anything real, too scared of being judged. Not to say that you [other members] don't, but I'm not ready."

Rachel was primed to see, speak, and be spoken to with only the positive, and conveyed a feeling of being hurt and damaged when challenged. The press of inveiglement was a means of complying with a beloved family, and inveigling was a strategy of social protection: "Everyone had to convince everyone else that they were having fun at the dinner table and engage in interesting conversation. It didn't matter that ten minutes before my father could be humiliating my mother or brothers. My mother didn't protect us, she needed protection, and she joined with him too. But it *was* interesting—my father always made it interesting. I still like family gatherings, even though I realise now they don't know me, and I don't want them to."

The entry of the new member had unforeseen but therapeutic consequences. For, as Rachel raged against me, she found her combined inveigling father–mother not only in the new member, but in herself as well. Relieved and refortified by these emotional revelations, she felt more comfortable sharing with me frank opinions—incipient nuclear ideas—that she "dares not" bring into the group. In effect, Rachel bullies the members, for they remain fearful of offending her and only cautiously confront her disarming "helpfulness".

Every family inveigles its children. Lacan suggested that the first inveigler is mother (the maternal other), who draws upon desire for her wish to shape the infant's identity and mould behaviour. The inveigler-father, the signifying "lure", "seduces" the child into language, separating it from the symbiotic maternal relationship (Lacan, 1977[1953], p. 213; see Chapter Eleven).

Inveigling may be understood as a type of covert bullying, while the specific tactics and consequences are different. The bully attacks, face first; the inveigler wins trust and misdirects away from truth by presenting and representing false ideas about the self and the relationship. Bullying is an overt and forceful move, in which the bullied are made to think about their powerlessness and hopelessness. In being inveigled, the mind is bullied, sometimes to the degree that one does not realise one's loss of identity and purpose.

President Nixon (or his aide, Chuck Colson) is reputed to have said, "If you grab them by the balls, their hearts and minds will follow." While also genuine and caring, Rachel still works to "grab" her cohorts' hearts and minds to constrict group interactions. While Rachel presents a maternal façade, broadcasting a polemic of excessive nicety, hints of underlying anger also transmit a sense of her father's mesmeric control.

Communal inveiglement

Communal inveiglement refers to a dimension of group and societal life promulgated by individuals, in conjunction with socio-political organisations, and by their dissemination of polemic ideas. The effect is to unify and direct individuals and groups to follow predetermined modes of thought and behaviour. Le Bon (2002), Freud (1921c), Bion (1961), and many others have written about the dynamics of the crowd and crowd mentality and vulnerability to manipulation. As discussed briefly in the previous chapter, Gramsci (1992) put forth the influential concept of cultural hegemony, through which the dominating class manipulates the beliefs, explanations, perceptions, and values of the culture, such that its worldview is imposed as common sense, a *status quo* masquerading as beneficial to all while mainly serving the interests of the few. For example, television and other media might be exploited by its corporate owners and sponsors to attract, penetrate, and pressure the mass of viewers and listeners to believe in and promote polemic ideas disguising political agenda (Schiller, 1989).

Hogget (1998) emphasised that all groups have inveigling propensities, a facility "of being able to get its subjects to lie to themselves" (p. 21), "drawing upon its subjects' willingness to be 'taken in' . . . [and on] their desire not to think too much" (p. 22). To some extent, a group's identity rests upon forms of "organized deception" (p. 20), designed not only to mislead others, but also the group itself, to protect itself from the threat of change. As Freud (1921c, p. 118) observed, "the herd turns away from anything that is new or unusual".

Polemic ideas are endemic in sociopolitical life, limiting freedom of thought in national and international negotiations, affecting relations between genders, races, religions, sexual orientations, and so forth. Haidt (2012) proposed that, given our "tribal" nature, individuals gather around and cohere into groups by adopting certain symbols, ideas, ancestors, books, or gods, and treat them as sacred. In effect, groups construct and fight and even die for competing value narratives, blinded by the "rightness" of their own polemic ideas.

As therapists, we try to be aware of inveigling and being inveigled by polemic ideas. Still, in moments of stress and uncertainty, we might cling defensively to our particular establishment "tribe" and over-value its ideas, forcing clinical phenomena to fit preselected theory (Britton & Steiner, 1994).

Case example: communal inveiglement in a training group

The candidates in an advanced group training programme had been together for six months, each bi-weekly meeting consisting of a mix of didactic and clinical courses, and a three-hour experiential group. Phillip had been the first to form his own private practice group, and, at my request, he was scheduled to be the first to present at our case conference. However, Sam surprised us by declaring that he had gathered together six of his clinic patients and also started a group.

"Something embarrassing occurred and I almost didn't!"

We shared his delight, and then I asked whether he could tell us about the session, and about his embarrassment, unless he was too embarrassed. He hesitated, and then: "I might as well. You know that the stomach flu was going around. Right before the session, I barfed on my clothes! Maybe I was nervous, but I was pretty sick during the weekend [that followed]. Anyway, I didn't know what to do—people were expecting me to begin. I went to the men's room, washed my shirt and pants as best I could—I took them off and used the hand dryer. I opened the window and hoped they [the prospective members] wouldn't smell puke."

"So how did it go?" I asked. "Great, as far as I could tell. It was pretty wild; some of them are borderlines. I've seen them all since and they're coming back. I loved it!"

After some appreciative comments directed to Sam, we moved to Phillip's most recent group session in which he skilfully worked to integrate a chal-lenging new member. Phillip's relaxed and confident non-judgemental style had much to do with the session's success, and, after discussing the new member's psychology and group dynamics, the candidates turned admiringly to Phillip: "I wish you would be here like you are in your group. So direct." "He's direct here, blunt." Phillip: "I am? Too blunt?" "No, I like that you tell it as you see it." "Sometimes you're too quiet." "I can't tell when you're anxious. Not like me, I can't contain myself, as you all have noticed."

At one point, I asked the candidates to compare Sam and Phillip's groups to our training group. All three were relatively newly formed, they agreed, and integrating ambivalent members remained an ongoing task. But "Are we a real group?" one candidate asked dubiously.

"Why not?" I countered.

Janis: "I think about us during the week when I try to lasso my patients to form a group."

Thomas: "Even though I get tempted not to give up a whole day with my kids [for the programme], I'm glad to be here—this is me being enthusiastic."

"Sam's new members reported the same [a sense of enthusiasm]," I observed.

Keira: "No one likes to miss one of our sessions."

Phillip: "That goes for my group too, I must admit."

"But how honest are we with each other?" Burt challenged. "There's a lot I don't say."

Keira: "Yeah, but there's a lot you do say, especially to me!"

Charlotte claimed to "walk on eggshells" in our programme, but several candidates disagreed, saying that she was honest and forthright: "careful, not hostile". From other candidates: "Well, we don't act obnoxiously to each other, like Phillip's new man in his group.'" "I've had lots of helpful feedback." "Eggshells mean that we've been making omelettes."

Phillip cautioned me that while his group worked with the new member's aggression, the members had not dealt fully with their own. "And neither have we here." My suspicion that Phillip was insinuating that I was out of touch with an aspect of basic theory, and our group process, too, was confirmed by Burt's explicit "Remember, Rich: 'formin', stormin', normin'." Another candidate reminded me of the "3 R's", implying my being out of touch with myself.

It was not difficult for me to "shake" the "numbing feeling" (Bion, 1961, p. 149)—a fantasy, perhaps induced by the group, of being the novice, and the candidates, my tolerant instructors, before enquiring, teasingly, "Not stormin' enough?" Several more reactions: "Well, Felix [one of our faculty] said that we're not even a group, but he didn't explain and no one asked."

Charlotte: "I felt offended, but thought maybe because we have rotating leaders [of the experiential group] and we don't get into basic assumptions."

Amanda: "We're not developed enough even to be regressed."

No one seemed satisfied when I commented about our group, "Well, people like and respect each other, are relatively truthful and think about what's said during the week, and they come back." I asked Phillip and Sam whether their members liked them.

Sam (embarrassed and beaming): "They call me 'God'. The way I think of you [laughter]."

Phillip: "They haven't turned on me yet," and then, again rebutted me with what I evaluated as an "overvalued idea" (Britton & Steiner, 1994), "the way they're supposed to."

"What are you doing while you're waiting?" I enquired sardonically. "I'm starting another group," Phillip replied sheepishly, "it's been the highlight of my week." Amanda lobbed affectionate disapproval in my direction: "That's it?" and she teasingly sang the Beatles' refrain "All you need is love". Smiling and nodding along in rhythmic agreement, I emphasised: "That's a lot," and added, "but not everything. We're 'stormin'' by struggling with a difficult emotional idea."

Discussion: communal inveiglement

Therapists work from love. We like people, are drawn to them, and stay enduringly curious. It seems a first principle to acknowledge—not necessarily in words—the loveable qualities of those we work with (and of the group as a whole) and, especially, to keep these qualities in mind during the ruptures and disjunctions that occur in every worthwhile session. So, I admit to a degree of mutual captivation: I tend to be charmed by clinical collaborators, such as the candidates in our programme, patients, and group members, and expect and enjoy that they find me appealing, too. Assuredly, such intersubjective dynamics pertain to the "unobjectionable positive transference" that Freud (1912b) described, and the co-participating unobjectionable positive countertransference (Racker, 1968).

In working with novice group therapists, I attend to the "matrix of love" (Moeller, 2002), in my opinion an expectable and necessary formative and sustaining process in all constructive psychotherapy groups and in training groups as well. The class was well versed in the theories of group cohesion and the importance of bonding; they had read about and discussed the concept of *passion*, and the fluctuations of "L, H, and K" (Billow, 2002). Why were they blinded to "L"?[34]

Freud (1921c) himself had suggested that individuals group because of an inborn need to love and to be loved: "A group is clearly held together by a power of some kind: and to what power could this feat be better ascribed than Eros, which holds together everything in the world" (p. 92). Preferring Eros or "libido",[35] Freud tended to avoided using "love", a word circumvented by almost all in our community of clinical theorists and practitioners, perhaps to shun allusions to seduction and physical contact. Even now, our colleagues are often more uncomfortable with positive feelings, such as sexuality, love, and dependency, than with negative feelings, and make tacit agreements with patients to avoid them (Jacobs, 2001).

No wonder, then, that these novice group therapists could be made anxious by emphasising the warm feelings existing in the room. Primed and intimidated by the texts and the professors (me included) that had assigned them, they launched a polemic of the "sacred" (Haidt, 2012): enshrined ideas relating to aggression, basic assumptions, barometrics (Bennis & Shepard, 1956), incohesion (Hopper, 2003b), and so forth.

The "clinical facts" (Britton & Steiner, 1994) were irrefutable: Sam found his first session as leader "great . . . wild . . . I loved it!" Phillip acknowledged that his group was his week's "highlight", and he was planning on doubling his pleasure with a second group. In terms of our candidates, I trusted and enjoyed my feelings of mutual embrace, and could feel their loyalty and steadfast, if cautious, caring for each other.

However, as if in one voice (typical of a basic assumption group formation), the candidates ribbed, disparaged, and gently scolded me, to lure us away from a nuclear idea that they undervalued. As the candidates momentarily "hated" and mildly rebelled against my approach and rendering of emotional truth, they fulfilled their own criteria of what constituted a "real" group. As expectable in a group with love, we were living through a "barometric event" (Bennis & Shepard, 1956) and learning from it without anyone being unduly "hostile" or "obnoxious".

Our group was "stormin'", fuelled by the beginner's anxieties dealing with therapeutic entitlement, the leader's right to assert power and influence, to feel part of the group and separate, too, and to feel and be worthy of love and gratitude (Billow, 2001). As the creator and prime mover, every leader serves as the god of the group, as Sam served for his, and I for the programme. In each of the three clinical situations, involving Sam, Phillip, and the group programme, a relatively truthful group provided nutritive experience for members and leader— "omelettes" of recognition, challenge, support, and guidance.

Presentational inveiglement

In *Resistance, Rebellion, and Refusal: The 3 Rs*, I placed into a relational and group context Bion's (1970) assertion of an ineliminable screen of protective falsity existing in all human relations and, to some degree, in any thought or communication. In forestalling reality, falsity shields the psyche from too much revelation achieved too quickly (see Grotstein, 2004). Only a certain amount of truth may be introduced into experience, and truth must be considered in terms of its emotional and social impact. In "Tell all the truth but tell it slant", the poet, Emily Dickinson (1960), wrote, "The truth must dazzle gradually / Or every man be blind". Like inveiglement, truth possesses "blinding" capabilities.

All individuals and groups regularly mislead and misinform others and themselves regarding what they think and feel. To avoid stimulating anxiety and pain, individuals and groups practice concealment and lying. In the myths, rationalisations, and denials that occupy everyday life, we attempt to blind ourselves even to ourselves, along with inveigling others. However, while we succeed in deceiving ourselves, it is likely that our deceptions are more transparent than we imagine.

In this section, I will concentrate on the therapist as participant in the inveiglement of everyday group life. For, as leader, the therapist also participates as member, and so contributes to, and remains an inveigled subject of, an "invisible group", the collective and "unanimous expressions of the will of the group, contributed by the individual in ways of which he is unaware" (Bion, 1961, p. 65).

No matter how sincere (Billow, 2010c) the therapist's feelings and intentions, and how directly expressed, he or she cannot be fully conscious or certain of motivation, meanings, interpersonal consequences, and therapeutic effects (Frank, 1997; Greenberg, 1995). We might be offering polemic when we believe we are developing nuclear ideas. Pragmatic meaning, that is, paralinguistic signification revealed by subtleties in timing, tone, and cadence, might contradict what is verbally spoken and what the therapist believes to be true (see Chused, 1991; McLaughlin, 1991). The therapist's words sonically and lexically communicate his or her felt need, and exert pressure on the group to potentiate the therapist's projective identifications and respond to the therapist's will.

Despite one's best conscious intentions, then, the therapist often is more and less truthful, and more and less certain, than he or she strives to be. Anxiety, exaggerated or deficient empathy, personal blind spots, loyalty to outdated and ill-advised establishment principles, or to those which merely are current and fashionable, and unavoidable ignorance and human limitation influence what the therapist perceives as the truth, and how and when the therapist approaches and evades it, bringing others along in an inveigling intersubjective process.

Clinical vignette: everyday life disturbs the presentation of the professional self

A young analyst reported in supervision that she felt "unmasked" when one of her patients in combined treatment saw her in a restaurant with her husband and preschool children. "Now she knows I'm just a person," she exclaimed. "I've lost my specialness."

I thought that if the patient saw her as special, as indeed she might, it was because of her personal qualities, not in spite of them. I advocated an investigation, preferably in the next session, which was group. Gathering her courage, the supervisee took an opportunity to enquire about the chance meeting. The patient, also a young woman, admitted feeling awed by what she discovered in the unexpected encounter. The patient's fantasy was confirmed: her therapist was a well-rounded human being with a career and a family. The woman wished such a reality for herself.

The therapist had felt protected by her analytic persona, and felt vulnerable when she feared loss of its capacity to screen the patient and group from the "real" her. Ironically, until their discussion, both the specific member and therapist had felt unconfident *vis à vis* each other, whereas afterwards, they both felt enhanced. The patient seemed relieved of some of her suppressed feelings of inferiority by simply expressing them in the accepting group context. For her part, the therapist also experienced self-assurance from being seen, literally, as herself. She felt relieved of her imaginary mask of anonymity that, she had convinced herself, gave status, power, and influence. She tolerated a discussion of her loveable qualities, which the group developed into a nuclear idea via their associations and comparisons to other figures in their lives: parents, mates, each other, and themselves.

Discussion: the tension between inveiglement and authenticity

As therapists, we function with and propagate contradictions. "Be real" is an unstated message. Yet, therapists and group members wear masks, that is, presentations of self, adopting roles that are social and mutually contracted. They allow, but also constrict, the types of possible discourse and, therefore, the range of potential nuclear ideas that we may co-develop. Communication is bounded by congruent and competing needs of the participants, by constraints of time, and by the limited accessibility that even the most self-disclosing therapist has or is willing to provide regarding his or her psychic life.

The therapist, in being professional, takes on different, seemingly contradictory roles; to maintain a disruptive–creative influence, he or she must function as both conservator and challenger of group process. At the same time, in striving for authenticity, the therapist eschews role-playing and affirms the personal. This involves attending to the influence of our own regressive tendencies to bipolar thinking and reliance on polemic ideas. A nuclear idea that bears developing and reconsidering involves the fictions and disguises—the inveigling self-presentations—that, to a greater or lesser extent, each of us feels we must adopt to preserve sanity, good spirits, and interpersonal comity.

Inveiglement is a fundamental aspect of relating

"You have shown me a strange image, and they are strange prisoners."

"Like ourselves," I replied; "and they see only their own shadows, or the shadows of one another" (Plato, 1973).

Plato allegorises the Socratic journey from establishment certainty to the exploratory attitude—one that also characterises the thinking group. Still, given that we are born into the social world, there is no escaping illusion; unencumbered mental "freedom" serves as a lyrical ideal, but it is not a reality. We absorb polemic ideas from our birth into the commune of family and culture and transmit them presentationally in character, movement, and language by how we group, in what and how we say, and do not say, and do and do not do.

Not only physical perceptions then—the social process itself tends to deceive and sway thinking. Hoggett (1998), following Winnicott, characterised each group as creating its own story, a "hallucinated" or illusionary dimension that is a source of creativity, but that hardens into a consoling myth in the face of challenging ideas. In other words, it is an aspect of group life to inveigle. The group sponsors polemic ideas of itself, "designed not only to mislead others, it is also designed to mislead the group itself" (Hoggett, 1998, p. 20).

Perhaps, at best, individuals and groups present and are capable of seeing "shadows" of truth, approximations that are not necessarily acts of conscious will or intentionality. Inveiglement may be considered, then, as a fundamental aspect of being—of relating and being related to—impinging upon, yet also contributing to, the sense of identity. Yet, a vector of the self inveigles the sense of identity the moment it declares itself and, in conspiring with others, we remain constrained by our fictive intersubjectivities.

PART III
ITS ALL ABOUT "ME"

CHAPTER EIGHT

The therapist's psychology as nuclear idea

"With what fear and avoidance does the analyst write about his own method of coming to conclusions, about his own thoughts and impressions! The devil himself could not frighten many analysts more than the use of the word 'I' does in reporting cases. . . .

Analyst, analyze yourself"

(Reik, 1983, pp. 147–148)

A prevalent, if often submerged, nuclear idea concerns the influence of the therapist's psychology, the "me", which the therapist, along with other group members, monitors with varying accuracy. To some extent, we have freed ourselves from the hegemony of classical psychoanalysis (Wallerstein, 1988), and its polemic formulations regarding the well-analysed therapist's alleged neutrality, objectivity, and emotional disengagement.[36]

The therapist's "irreducible irrational involvement" (Renik, 1993)—cannot be eliminated, and this is not even a desirable goal. For it is out of our full participation that we bring our own dissociated experience into relationships, potentiating key interactions related to the participants' difficulties in living (Harry Stack Sullivan's phrase) that would not otherwise be discovered. While the therapist's conflicts, character structure, and misunderstandings lead to inevitable resistances, rebellions, and refusals in the group and its members, they also provide vehicles for learning and transmitting information.

Kierkegaard is believed to have said, "Life can only be understood backwards, but it must be lived forwards". We characterise the therapeutic process similarly. The basic premise of the relational approach is that psychoanalytic data are mutually generated by therapist and patients, co-determined by their conscious and unconscious organising activities, in reciprocally interacting subjective worlds (Stolorow, 1997).

Relational theorists (e.g., Chused, 1992; Renik, 1993; Spezzano, 1996) presume that patients and therapists do much of their thinking non-consciously and intersubjectively, each affecting the other. Neither therapist nor members can be aware of many of the important group activities that are co-determined in these subterranean intersubjective exchanges. Therefore, the participants may learn only retrospectively—and partially—about what has been going on mentally, when the derivatives emerge. By that time, words and actions have produced enactments (Boesky, 2000; Ivey, 2008; McLaughlin, 1991), co-created symbolic and behavioural scenarios that are learnt about with the benefit of insight, hindsight, and, often, with mutual feedback.

Self–other awareness is the linchpin of any psychodynamic approach. The therapist's mental relationship to him or herself—to the therapeutic/personal "me"—has the potential to be an ongoing, evolving, and primary nuclear idea. Part III is devoted to the proposition that the therapist's increasing understanding of one's own (inter)subjectivity—and its impact—is a driving force of group process and the group members' development and growth.

The therapist shares the basic human conflict regarding emotional thinking

Aristotle (1998) declared "all men by nature desire to know". Bion emphasised a relational dimension. He reasoned that we share a particularly human need to learn about our psychology and the psychologies of others.[37] (Contemporary theorists might refer to this type of emotional learning as involved with "mentalizing" (Fonagy & Target, 1998), in which self and others are recognised as thinkers.) The aspiration is existential and operational: to discover meaning and, thus, provide options to direct our actions towards those that are personally and interpersonally significant.

The desire for psychological knowledge motivates people to group: to seek and live in groups, and to accept the invitation to participate in group psychotherapy. However, the kind of thinking that leads to psychological learning often hurts, since the process may be confusing, anxiety arousing, and disturbing. Its truths might feel "not nice", judged as primitive and irrational (which is, indeed, what they often are), socially inappropriate, and personally embarrassing.

Emotional thinking leads to the possibility of growth and change in the personality, but what we discover has the potential to disorientate and reorientate the thinker to past, present, and future. The person who bears to think and to learn risks ever greater separation from established, conventional relations with others, as well as with one's previous ideas. Again, there is the likelihood of anxiety and mental pain. Freud and Klein emphasised that self-knowledge brings forth the primacy of self-integration over repression and splitting; hence, self-knowledge brings inner peace and social harmony. Bion emphasised that integration entails the capacity and the courage for even greater levels of emotional turbulence, existential risk, and personal and social disharmony.

No one is exempt from a basic conflict between thinking and avoiding pain, and the therapist, along with other group members, might detour, delay, and obstruct learning from experience. Thinking and its evasion are psychological dimensions of all group members' consciousness and non-consciousness. Groups generate their structure, process, and meaning from the interactions among the ambivalent, conscious, and non-conscious "desires to know" of all participants. The defining characteristics of group life—its progressive and regressive influences—are co-created, maintained, and processed intersubjectively.

The therapist is not a blank screen, or sole arbiter of psychological truth or the methods of reaching truth. Patients form valid and significant insights regarding the group and, particularly, the therapist's personality and the complexities of their therapist's psychology (see Gill, 1994). The dynamic factor involving the group leader's psychology—the "me"—is always prominent and influential, and often apparent to members, although not always articulated consciously or publicly as a nuclear idea.

All about me: two broad principles

When I declare, "it's all about me", I am asserting two broad principles. (1) Every intervention the therapist makes (including silence) is filtered through one's (inter)subjectivity, a shifting, but also relatively stable idea of the therapeutic/personal self. Given the leader's importance to what occurs and does not occur in group, the therapist needs to keep a "third ear" acutely attuned to "me".

Then, there is the old joke: "Well, enough of 'me'. Let's hear about you. What do *you* think of me?" We have imperfect knowledge and limited access to our own non-conscious, character, and reactivity, so we need to hear about "me'" from other group members. The members respond directly and indirectly, through what they say and do not say, via symbolic derivatives (metaphors, dreams, jokes, enactments, basic assumptions, and so forth), and by participating in individual, subgroup, and group resistances, rebellions, and refusals.

(2) The members' individual and collective ideas of who the therapist is have an impact on everything that takes place in group. We have been meeting as reader and writer. Although existing in different time and space, we are linked in a relationship, defined in part by our mutual "desire to know" and reconfigured as you formulate, develop, and modify your idea of "me".

I think about my own idea of "me" in planning to "go public": that is, to introduce and present my psychic truths, whether in print or in a group. I try to anticipate and, to some extent, influence your emotional as well as intellectual response to "me" in what you read (see Chapter Seven on the presentation of self).

However, while I state that it is all about "me", it is not only about "me". I do not negate or minimise other influences and effects on member–member, subgroup, and whole group interactions. In demonstrations groups, such as I describe in Part III, in-group–outgroup differentials are likely to be particularly influential, since they most often consist of admixtures of people from different agencies, professional status, and power, position in organisational hierarchies, and so forth.

In any group, all individuals, not only the reality and fantasy of the leader, exert pressure. Likewise, the group exerts pressure on the mentality of each member, including the leader. Nevertheless, at those very moments when a group seems to attend to anything and anyone but the leader, he or she is likely to be of prime interest. In my groups, whatever is being talked about, whoever is reacting to whom or to what, the group's focal conflict, predominating basic assumption, developmental level or stage, its regressions and progressions, dyadic interactions, subgroupings, and so forth, I have come to assume that, on one level, it is all about "me".

I illustrate this process of how being mentally involved with "me" can work by providing a clinical example of it not working the way I believed and wanted until the group's interventions. Something about "me" emerged unexpectedly when my psychology became a developing nuclear idea during the course of a day's conference offered during an annual American Group Psychotherapy Association (AGPA) meeting.

Clinical example: talkers and non-talkers

As is my custom, I asked the attendees—about thirty—how they would like to spend the day, and what they wanted to accomplish. This process allows me to present myself and to make eye-to-eye contact with individuals, and for the whole group to bear witness to the ideas presented and the persons behind them. Not everyone took opportunity to talk, of course, but there was general agreement that I would present some didactic material that would address some of the members' questions and interests, do a "fishbowl" demonstration group in the morning, and spend the afternoon conducting a full-group process experience, and end with a return to concepts and a debriefing.

The morning's interactions confirmed my impression that this was a lively, interactive group, with some large personalities dispersed through the wide range in age and clinical training. However, as we resumed after lunch, I realised that some of the attendees had spoken minimally or not at all. I had tried to involve them, such as inviting participation with a welcoming smile, picking up on body language, and "bridging" (Ormont, 1992), such as by having one member translate another's feelings about a third member's feelings.

Now I addressed their lack of verbal participation specifically: "You will get more from this afternoon's meeting if you say something. Even one comment gives you a new sense of the group." The room remained quiet. Then I said, 'It's OK even if you grunt or groan." My humorous intervention met with some success.

One person said, "I've been wanting to talk, but I've been afraid. Thanks for noticing." The member then filled in some biographical data, as did several others who followed. Some of the active members made appreciative and encouraging gestures, but the process ran out of emotional steam, and the group turned to other interactions.

Still, I felt unsatisfied, and curious, and near the midpoint of the afternoon, I said, "There seem to be two groups here—the talkers and the non-talkers." That drew the group's eyes to the verbally non-participating, and then I felt anxious about scapegoating them by applying peer pressure.

Someone came forth: "In my family, I was always very quiet. At home, I let my mother speak for me until I left for college."

"Who reminds you of your mother?" I asked. My purpose was to encourage more individual participation and member-to-member involvement, and also, to introduce transference analysis and intrapsychic exploration in the group setting.

"I don't know . . . maybe anybody who dared to speak."

I had found a useful angle to extend participation: who reminded someone of whom, and why, and how did it feel. I was feeling relaxed and successful, until an attendee broached what seemed like a change of direction:

"If I were running this group, I'd want to know what I did to cause the 'two groups'."

I felt embarrassed, as if accused of not practising what I preach about considering the impact of "me", but the comment was delivered respectfully, and I answered in the same way.

"What do you think I did to cause subgrouping?"

"You like people who talk."

Several members came to my rescue: "Well, Richard was faced with a new group, of course he wanted people to talk." "He tried to bring people in, he's doing it now [and to the person who posed the challenge], you tried, too."

But I thought the comment deserved a fuller consideration and, in thinking about it, I felt inspiration in the question I had posed a few moments earlier: the topic of family relations and intragroup transferences. I shared an insight that felt sudden and intense: "Well, I was the first-born in my family, and I maintained my position by doing a lot of talking."

In conducting groups, I do not make a habit of intentionally self-revealing, but here saw no reason to be evasive. Now other people— including some of the formerly quiet—pressed to talk, and I kept further introspections to myself.

"This is my first workshop as a member. I did not know what to expect. I never heard of you but I liked the topic [the *3Rs*]. Since I'm going to start working with drug addicts next month, I thought I better learn about refusing. I'm learning a lot anyway. Am I resisting, rebelling, or refusing? I don't know yet."

"I'm here because my professor is here, and [humorously] she threatened to flunk us if we didn't come. She didn't say we had to talk." "Yes, me too, we read your papers in her class. They were really good, although I can't say I understood them or this group [laughter]."

I reflected that it takes courage (see Gans, 2010) for the students and teachers to mix it up in this group setting, with expanded boundaries and rules of exchange.

A woman spoke up: "I must come out of the closet. I'm the 'mean' teacher. I've been so impressed by your writings, Dr Billow, that I guess I feel intimidated."

I lightened the atmosphere by saying that other people must be a lot less impressed because they seem comfortable calling me "Richard" and challenging me to think about what I have been doing.

More people took chances with themselves in reflecting on the "two groups":

"I was the 'golden boy' in my family. Talking, but not talking too much. I want to be the golden boy in your group. Just me. [Humorously] Am I being it now?"

"I was the second fiddle. I feel like that here, and that's why I haven't revealed myself. I have to think about my responsibility. You welcomed me, several times."

"I was my parents' 'joy,' their 'ray of sunshine'." And with irony, "See how I always smile."

A young man volunteered, "Maybe I've been Cinderella here, waiting to be invited to the ball. I need to man up, I got my own balls."

We turned to the professor self-described as "mean", who was crying. "In my family, I was the oldest, and my job was to take care of my siblings, as they arrived, one by one. But I liked it. My parents weren't close, I was afraid of my father and my mother wasn't very warm either. I wanted to have my students here. [Turning to them] I felt you would make me feel safe and secure. Thanks for coming . . . You all get an 'A'," she said, smiling between visible tears.

One of the members who had tried to shield me from criticism joined in: "I had to protect my mother. She has 'issues' and gets depressed. When you blamed Richard for creating the 'two groups', I worried that he would fall apart. I'm always worried that my patients are going to fall apart, and then my psychotherapy group that I run. I see that not happening here."

With some sadness, we drew the group process to a close. During the debriefing and evaluation, one of the members complimented me for the day, but wondered, "Could you have obtained the same results if you had stayed out . . . and not worked so hard?"

Discussion

"Me": a fratricidal leader

> Cain said to his brother Abel, "Let's go out to the field." And while they were in the field, Cain attacked his brother Abel and killed him (Genesis 4:8).

To illustrate the effect of intersubjective factors on group formation and process, I share some personal thoughts.

Freud (1921c, pp. 120–121) traced the development of our inclination to group (gregariousness) to the reaction against the initial envy and aggression an older child experiences to the arrival of a younger sibling, who now is a rival for the leader's (i.e., the father's) attention. Whereas this hypothesis seems not applicable universally, it might partially explain my own interest in groups and my style of leadership.

I could easily justify my technical approach to the silent members: after all, people unfold at different times, and not always verbally. Besides, some of them had asked questions at the workshop's beginning and I kept in mind and addressed the questions throughout the morning. But I came to realise that projection, envy, rivalry, guilt, and reparation were among the emotional elements I utilised—for better and worse—in conducting the workshop.

As we know, silent members and subgroups exert power, and may even hold a group hostage, demanding special attention by their very quietness. In terms of my psychology, of which I was not conscious at the time, such individuals represented my younger brother.

I felt envious of the attention he received, and interested in him, too. His emotional unavailability was irritating and intriguing, and both stimulated and frustrated my curiosity. I provoked him to respond, teasing, wrestling, socking him when necessary, which was often. (I think now of Dylan Thomas's (1954, p. 12) description of brotherly love: "It snowed last year too: I made a snowman and my brother knocked it down and I knocked my brother down and then we had tea".)

In my reflective, adult consciousness, I know (and probably knew as a child) that he wished to isolate himself from any unpleasant intensity of our family. Selective withdrawal seemed to be beyond my emotional capabilities. In my ongoing non-consciousness, he was (and is) a rivalrous model of a "better" type of individual, one self-contained and without need.

In the group, the quiet members became rivals too, competing with the talkative ones, which included me, for my attention (as father-leader) and for the group's attention (my "parents"). I could easily express curiosity, fight and embrace the talkative ones. Whether they were friendly or hostile, I knew who they were, and I "liked" them. In terms of infantile narcissism, they were reflections of "me". I resented the quiet ones, the "better than us", who deigned not to participate in the intensity of our group. Caught between deciding to kill or love the quiet ones, I tried both.

The group reveals "me" before I find myself

Self-disclosure is inevitable and continuous in any human interaction. Even classically orientated psychoanalysts, such as Ralph Greenson (1967, p. 91), have acknowledged that, as therapists, everything we do or say, or don't do or say, from the décor of our office, the magazines in the waiting room, the way we open the door, greet the patient, make interpretations, keep silent, and end the hour, reveals something about our real self and not only our professional self.

The lines between intentional and unintentional self-disclosure are ambiguous and fluctuating. The therapist's behaviours may range from spontaneous exclamation to measured revelation, from those that are seemingly consciously determined to those non-consciously enacted. Levels of meaning, revealed by subtleties in timing, tone, and cadence, might contradict what is verbally spoken (Chused, 1991; McLaughlin, 1991).

Group members see a therapist-in-action, responding to intense group, subgroup, and dyadic situations. The perspectives are multiple, and members might not be in agreement with each other, and much less with the therapist. Still, the therapist learns about "me" by attending to these various perspectives. In learning about the members' ideas, expressed in feelings, fantasies, symbols (e.g., metaphors, jokes, dreams), thoughts, behavioural reactions, the therapist reflects on how he or she affects the culture and process (e.g., as in co-creating and sustaining "two groups").

In the development of human attachment, a prolonged period of mutual "eye love" (Beebe & Stern, 1977) between mother and infant occurs, involving not only the visual sense, but also touch, sound, and movement (exteroception–interoception). In this "dance", each partner enjoyably takes into account and makes moment-by-moment adjustments in response to the other's shifts in behaviours (Beebe & Lachmann, 2002; Beebe & Stern, 1977; Stern, 1971; Tronick, 1989).

So, who did what to "cause the two groups"? It was not I alone who decided whom I "danced" with, and when. Signs that I "like people who talk" were many and obvious to certain members, yet not all of them are evident to me, then or now. My "liking" was co-regulated, encouraged by some (the talkers), and held in abeyance by others (the non-talkers).

Like the mother, the therapist needs to maintain relaxed but intense interest, empowering the members to seek and avoid engagement, without anxiously "chasing" after them. I believe that even with my inevitable clinical and personal shortcomings, my behaviours of "liking" were sufficiently well distributed to propel bonding, mutual recognition, and the development of the group's identity.

In being (selectively) self-revealing, I took responsibility for "me", for my contribution in "sucking" (Horowitz, 1983; Redl, 1980) members into their respective roles, as best I could understand. But whether or not one self-discloses, keeping a focus on one's mental relationship to the therapeutic/personal self allows the leader to more easily understand, acknowledge, and expand on the group members speculations and beliefs, to bring out and develop their nuclear ideas of group, self, and other.

My self-referential behaviour encouraged members to take responsibility for their "me's", too. As the nuclear idea of "me" developed for the members, various individuals explored their respective psychologies and personal histories, discovering the emotional equipment for the part they played and their influence on others. In our group, then, the technical decision to concentrate on "me" as a nuclear idea seemed to have facilitated self–other awareness, greater openness among members, and furthered the development of group cohesiveness and individual autonomy.

The therapist cannot expect to be aware and in control of all, or even of many, of the group members' varied and variable transferences to the leader, other members, and to the group situation itself. Still, this group gifted me with a vital and ever present nuclear idea: I am now more acutely aware of the possible differences in enthusiasm in which I invite, meet, and sustain the gaze of various group members and, also, more aware of their visual and bodily reactions to me and the transference–countertransference potentialities behind these responses.

Emotional co-participation: loving, hating, and being curious in the group

As I emphasise in my writings, psychoanalytic treatment is not about cure, but about transforming pain into the richer capacity to "suffer" meaning (Billow, 2003a; 2010a; Bion, 1962). To drive change and stimulate creative growth, the therapist needs to provide an ongoing sense of security, but also must encourage a breaking down of pre-established and safe emotional attitudes. Leadership entails aiding the group and its members to tolerate, communicate, and eventually integrate a wide range of emerging, contradictory, and intense

emotional thoughts. In effect, the leader works to create a group motivated to generate and respond to nuclear ideas: mind-sets reflecting
experiential, personal, symbolic, affective, and metapsychological
aspects of the ongoing group experience (Chapter Two).

However, often our group members come to treatment to be
relieved of pain, and they initially might display little toleration for
increasing the range of felt feelings, or for understanding and integrating them. It is often left to the therapist to suffer mental pain, to
think about the feelings of the group, including one's own, and
those operating and those denied. Eventually, they form the basis of
nuclear ideas—emotional "truths", presented with an empathic
"slant" (Emily Dickinson, 1960).

Our emotions derive from affects, drives, or instincts involved in
loving (attachment or bonding), expressing frustration–aggression
(hating), and exercising curiosity. Bion (1962) provided a shorthand,
L, H, and K: respectively, the drive to love, to hate, and to know about.
While these drives, LHK, are basic, they do not operate in pure form.
Like everyone else, it is difficult for the therapist to "know" what he
or she feels, or to be certain about the source, extent, or purpose of
one's curiosity. Feelings hide behind their opposites, fantasies remain
submerged and disguised—defence mechanisms of denial, dissociation, reaction formation, and projection are to be expected, particularly in situations of anxiety and conflict.

I function as leader with a sense of apprehension, co-existing with
confidence, that something unknown about myself will emerge, and
that I will learn and grow from each group session. I attempt to monitor my affects, and to be open to the feedback from others. How loving
and empathic do I feel? How frustrated, impatient, angry, or hateful
do I feel? How interested am I in myself and in the group? How am I
utilising these affects to link up with the patients and with the group
as a whole? Thinking about my affects brings some self-awareness to
the therapeutic realities of the group, as I experience them. I now have
an option to introduce and test out nuclear ideas with the other
members.

In the group under discussion, one simple sentence jarred me out
of the complacent fantasy of being in full command of how I felt and
what I was doing. "You like people who talk." My "not nice" feelings
were exposed, and I felt guilty, personally and professionally deficient. For the group member was implying that I did not like people

who did not talk (H), and did not embrace them with full curiosity (K). The communication had a ring of truth, and "suffering" the meaning-making process provided access to my love and compassion (L) towards these same members, toward my brother, and toward myself as well.

I had believed I was working with professional ease and competence, eliciting involvement from a significant segment of the attendees. I do not think too many observers would have disagreed with this perspective. But other perspectives jarred me out of any tendency to rest secure in my relative comfort zone: "You like people who talk"; "If I were running this group, I'd want to know what I did to cause the 'two groups'"; "Could you have obtained the same results if you had stayed out?"

I cannot say I found these remarks pleasant—but they were on point and deserved to be respected as legitimate thoughts about "me" and my impact, and not prematurely interpreted as "transference", "resistance", an expression of a basic assumption, and so forth. My functioning as a clinician became a nuclear idea: in the public setting, I had to re-evaluate my feelings, technical actions, and even my very way of "being".

Becoming aware of avoided feelings allows the therapist some control over expressing them, and to function with fuller emotional co-participation. I did not wish to banish my negative feelings towards the non-talkers, but I wanted to know where they came from, and how they affected my group relationships. Then I would be able to use a fuller array of feelings, and with greater clinical acumen.

Freud (1912e, p. 112) counselled the analyst, "It must not be forgotten that the things one hears are for the most part things whose meaning is only recognised later on". During the interval of the group, I could only come to understand some of my feelings, and my understanding was partial. Most difficult to sort out and bring to meaning were probably the very reactions that had the most "causal" influence on the group.

Racker (1968) suggested that a neglected aspect of the Oedipus complex was the analyst's wish to be master or king, not only of other people, but also of his or her own unconscious. The best the therapist can do is to eradicate, as much as he or she can, not anxieties, resistances, wishes, and fears, but their repression. In being receptive to the infantile, primitive, and neurotic aspects of one's own personality, one may more fully experience one's own experience, and this is, I believe, the precondition that allows the therapist to help the group members do the same.

We are humbled by the awareness that our words and actions are partially derivatives of an unfolding (and evolving) conscious–non-consciousness, and that we cannot fully understand ourselves before, or even after, we communicate. Authentic communications represent the therapist's most profound insights and powerful intentions. Our own ideas remain only "best guesses" of emotional truth—what we feel, think, and decide is appropriate to express—to be re-evaluated and revised as we offer ourselves as a nuclear idea. In reconsidering the therapeutic–personal "me" in the context of the here-and-now clinical experience, all that we have felt and believed to understand about that "me" might undergo a far-reaching revision.

Activity level of the relational group therapist

Of all the comments, questions, criticisms directed to me during our six-hour group, one rankles in my retrospections: "Could you have obtained the same results if you had stayed out . . . and not worked so hard?"

I heard my mother's voice behind the questioner: "Why can't you behave like your brother!"

Who was this questioner, I wondered, a junior colleague or critical competitor, friend or foe? Given my emotional involvement with my family of origin, I could not be sure of the accuracy of my judgement.

As much as I hated the comment and the commentator, I took it and him as sincerely curious, and I respectfully replied that my way of working was something he and other people could think about. The nineteenth-century poet, William Blake, penned these cautionary lines:

> The questioner, who sits so sly,
> Shall never know how to reply.
> He who replies to words of doubt
> Doth put the light of knowledge out.
> (Blake, 2008, "Auguries of Innocence", p. 492)

I did not wish intellectually to reduce the experience and provide premature closure. Besides, a didactic rationale would have felt defensive. But here I will offer my point of view, which situates "me" as a centre of action.

The major group theorists have described groups as organic entities, evolving through stages, rebounding from one defensive position to another in accordance with developmental conflicts consequent to group membership. According to their theories, successful groups depend on the therapist's effective performance in pre-therapy tasks such as patient selection, composition and preparation, and in negotiating the novice group through its formative stages of boundary formation, structuring, resistance, and goal direction. It follows that the mature group more often treats itself, coming to appreciate the therapist as a consultant rather than as the continuing mesmeriser of transference (Agazarian, 1997; Ettin, 1999; Foulkes & Anthony, 1965; Rutan & Stone, 2001).

Foulkes (1964, p. 61) wrote that the group therapist "does not step down but lets the group, in steps and stages, bring him down to earth . . . [the group] replaces the leader's authority". Along this line of thinking, Yalom (1995, p. 216) presented the maxim,

> Unlike the individual therapist, the group therapist does not have to be the axle of therapy. In part, you are midwife to the group: you must set a therapeutic process in motion and take care not to interfere with that process by insisting on your centrality.

These classic contributions in theory and in descriptive phenomenology are fundamentals of every group therapist's thinking and practice. However, the emphasis on member-inspired dynamics seriously underplays the impact of the therapist's psychology, observed by both therapist and group members, but often left undeveloped as a nuclear idea.

Therapist-influenced dynamics supersede the clinician's theoretical or technical orientation, and we sometimes achieve more, or less, in our practice than that which we preach. Being "active" and leader focused might eventuate in being attentively quiet. Bion wrote about non-verbal containment: how the therapist's capacity for "reverie" (dream-like, internal free association), patience, and inner security communicates something crucially important, and supports the group members' containing: their capacity to tolerate powerful affects and develop emotional thoughts.

A group therapist's respectful silence or brief appreciative acknowledgement in the face of an apprehensive member's challenge might be a powerful, even decisive, intervention. Conversely, verbal formulations that reach into the realm of non-conscious phenomena, involving constellations of fantasy, desire, anxiety, character, and defence, rightly might be valued for their effort and concern as much as for their acuity and depth.

Our amiable, sincere, and patient efforts to reach the group count for a lot, and we fumble and are forgiven for our fumbling more than we know. No school of thought owns exclusive or automatic rights to empathy, or to understanding of the self and others. And, in our striving for depth, clinicians of all theoretical persuasions might miss what is timely and most relevant.

Whereas the focus of this chapter is on the leader's affects, thoughts, and behaviour, and their influence on the minds of the members and on the interactions of the whole group, subgroups, and individuals, I appreciate that change flows not only from the efforts of the therapist. A restrictive focus on the leader, or, for the matter, any predetermined theoretical–technical orientation, comes to serve as a polemic idea, deflecting attention from other important group, subgroup, and interpersonal factors, other ways in which experience may be generated and understood.

Indeed, although I conceptualise leader or therapist-inspired dynamics as a prevailing influence behind group interactions, I appreciate that the force of these dynamics are modulated by the nature of the group situation. Inter-member interactions are multiple and complex, and may be directed to individuals other than the leader, and to dyads, subgroups, and the whole group.

Members and leaders derive benefit from multiple factors of group participation; each group is unique and its constituents provide a wide range of interpersonal options and therapeutic effects. Important, too, are cultural, ethnic, and political factors that contribute to the group's organisation, functioning, and goals (Hopper, 2003a).

We think about the question, "Could you have obtained the same results if . . .?" without concluding that there is only one way, or a best way. This brings us to the question of "truth"—the timing, relevance, and effectiveness of one's interpretative thoughts and interventions. We cannot be sure of all the factors that drove the process of the group under discussion, the accuracy of my evaluations of the interactional dynamics, or even the emotional realities that I have described. The therapist cannot neatly separate self (the "me") from others and from the group at large.

Emotional reality is not a concrete, unchanging something, from which truth can be derived with certainly or finality, but an ever-incomplete process of learning and becoming. The group therapist's and members' communications are intersubjectively constructed; their intent and effect remains highly personal, and no final, or fully objective, assessment is possible. Group leadership involves holding the tension of truth as best as one understands it, and deciding its "slant": how, when, and how much to convey, and to whom. To lead well, we must live with inconsistency and paradox, attempt to find balance without definitive solutions, and accept the non-existence of the perfect option, flawlessly applied. Growth remains possible and likely, if the leader remains thoughtful, invitational to feedback, and self-critical as to what is achieved.

I attempt to be personable, maintain a light touch, and not function as a mysterious figure, invulnerable to feeling or feedback, or a know-it-all. When I am confused or unsure, which is often, I might seek clarity from other group members, although I do not necessarily agree with, or follow, their guidelines. In the group under discussion, I asked for help and achieved insight, which inspired me to develop the thoughts regarding the influence of the therapist's psychology that configured into a nuclear idea, and which came to occupy our attention and to develop together. For these efforts, I received several jolts of productive pain; their effects linger.

Revealed: the therapist's dynamics

The therapist's "me"—a characterlogical complex of basic affects, feelings, thoughts, and fantasies, many of which remain out of self awareness—affect how we comport ourselves, how we relate to our groups, and how they relate to us (see Kite, 2008, for a recent review of the impact of the analyst's character). I have illustrated how unresolved oedipal and sibling dynamics were involved in my perceptions, theory, and technique—perhaps in every micro-action and interaction that comprised the group experience.

Groups—small and large—intuit their leader's orientation, both technical and personal, and, to some extent, respond accordingly. As in this example drawn from an experiential workshop but applicable to psychotherapy groups, members adapt to the leader's personality characteristics and *vice versa*. When groups function constructively, participants learn from each other how to tolerate difference and, also, to come together to function as a working unit. They negotiate, compromise, and "match up" to assure efficacy.

The "me" is observed and awaits development as a nuclear idea. The group therapist's activity, internal and interpersonal, exposes the qualities of care and establishes authenticity. By personality as well as behaviour, then, the "me" to some extent defines the working group culture: how group relationships and experiences are to be regarded, and to the metapsychological depth to which exchanges may be considered.

All psychoanalytic psychotherapy is grounded on Freud's belief that the understanding of others is based on self-understanding. However, self-understanding is an evolving, affective process, stimulating strong and often painful emotions that influence, and are influenced by, others. Self-awareness remains tentative and uncertain, and is revised according to the shifting currents of present-day reality. Inspection, introspection, retrospection, the longevity and stability of a group, these factors do not vouchsafe objectivity or inoculate therapists from the tendency to rationalise "me": who we are, how we feel, and what we are doing.

Whatever the therapist is attending to, he or she is also reflecting upon and revealing him or herself, influencing other members—and you, the reader—in this process. Contemplating one's evolving mental relationship to one's own self, and its influence on the group, brings layers of meaning to the here-and-now clinical situation, however conceptualised. All benefit from a group therapist unequivocally and openly involved in "me", in personal discovery and growth.

All groups have the potential to develop core nuclear ideas of itself and its leader

This six-hour experiential workshop provided opportunity for a median group to reveal and develop core nuclear ideas of itself and its leader. A subject had stimulated my curiosity; it represented both my clarity and lack of knowledge. The attendees had organised into two subgroups, talkers and non-talkers. I waited to discover if my observation would garner interest, and where it would take us. To my surprise and apprehension, it drew attention to my behaviour and psychology, rather than to that of others.

Two interrelated core nuclear ideas developed. The one that pertained specifically to "me" emerged from an attendee's assertion that I "like people who talk". Thus, my psychology was offered as an idea, which I acknowledged as truthful and extended by introspection and self-revelation. It became critical in terms of the clinical decisions I made in how I would continue to run the group.

The other idea pertained to the group's bi-dimensional structure and process, composed of individuals who felt "liked" or "not liked". The distinction, once revealed, had significant personal relevance for many attendees, some of whom spoke up for the first time. "Two groups" cohered into "one".

In their containing function, the core nuclear ideas of the leader and his influence on the group allowed us to think and respond to each other authentically. The experiential, affective, symbolic, and metapsychological dimensions (Chapter Two) of the enactment of "two groups" now made sufficient sense. We were able to do productive work together, undeterred—in fact stimulated—by the anxiety aroused by the revelation of uncomfortable psychological truths. The psychology of, and in, the group changed through our attending to the leader's therapeutic/personal self: feelings, fantasies, and thoughts by and about "me", and about the two subgroups I had unknowingly co-created.

CHAPTER NINE

The group beholds its leader

C hapter Eight stated two broad principles: (1) every intervention the group leader makes (including silence) is filtered
through his or her subjectivity, of which the leader has limited
and imperfect knowledge; (2) the members' convergent and divergent
nuclear ideas of who the leader is have an impact on everything that
takes place in group, and, to some extent, determine group structure
and process. A case example and an extended discussion described
how the group identified a common point of reference—"me". My
psychology served as the experiential dimension (Chapter Two), an
axis of self and group reflection, clarifying that which was central to
the here-and-now of our group process. Additionally, the nuclear idea
of the leader, revealed and developed, served as a bridge to the
psychology of others, to building intrapsychic and interpersonal
meaning.

When these core nuclear ideas of the leader and the group
emerged, I found direction, and, despite the revelations of my vulnerabilities and limitations, enhanced confidence in my leadership. The
group progressed in an orderly, understandable fashion, even before
many of its determining influences were revealed.

Certainly, the leader or therapist's expanded consciousness of his or her personal/professional self and its influence—the "me"—is a driving force in the group. But the leader cannot expect to be aware of all, or even many, of the members' varied and variable subjective reactions to him or her, or to the group situation. Also, in workshops such as I shall describe, an organisation's conflicts, politics, and subgroupings are likely to be enacted and might remain outside an invited presenter's awareness, even while being apparent to the rest of the room (Gans, Rutan, & Lape, 2002).

The group beholds its leader: a looming figure of fantasy, an emerging figure of reality. Psychic patterns that play out in group cohesion, culture, conflict, and process are rooted in interaction with this combined object, the "me" that enters into the mentality of all the members.

We may agree in spirit with Bion (1961, p. 149), who held that identifying the roles we play, "no matter how difficult to recognize, in somebody else's phantasy . . . is the prime requisite of the analyst". However, bringing forth and unravelling the intertwined psychic material to identify the threads of the leader's impact that could materialise as a containing nuclear idea often cannot be accomplished immediately, and never entirely, or with certainty.

As in the example that follows, the very impact of the leader—the collective mass of projective and incorporative forces—might disrupt and distort the truth-seeking process. The group becomes flat, or fervent with thoughts and feelings. The leader experiences painful intervals of mental blankness; he or she might be flooded with anxiety, or oppressed with countertransference feeling and fantasy. Yet, nothing seems cogent as a containing nuclear idea. All must be endured, coped with without retreating to silence or resorting to polemic formulations.

A two-day workshop on relational group psychotherapy

The meeting was sponsored by several professional organisations of a central European country. I had no prior knowledge of the professional composition, affiliations, or interrelationships among the attendees. There were twenty; Eric, the conference's organiser, explained that two registrants cancelled, one only minutes ago, due to illness. I threw open how to proceed. All members wished to partici-pate experientially and we settled on moving among lectures, median process group sessions, and discussions involving debriefing and didactic feedback.

I said I would prefer keeping our remarks during the lectures and discussions directed to group theory and process, and not to specific individuals or interactions of the experiential segments. However, I acknowledged that we could not neatly separate one set of experi-ences from another, and that everything surrounding the experiential segments would relate to those encounters, and *vice versa*. Nothing anyone said or did could be unrelated to the larger context; in effect, we were already immersed in a self-reflective, self-revealing median group.

My intention was to sustain an experiential format that most closely paralleled that of a psychotherapy group. Even short-duration "fishbowl" or demonstration groups—and certainly a two-day median group—may be utilised to illustrate key principles and processes of long-term groups, as involved in opening and establishing group cohesion and trust, unfolding of symbolic derivatives (including horizontal and vertical transferences), and individual and group conflicts and defences, and terminating (Gans, Rutan, & Lape, 2002).

The conference was structured as four half-day sessions.

Day 1, morning

Introductory lecture and discussion. I began with an anecdote and ques-tion: I arrived several days ago, taking an hour's flight from another European capital. A young mother and seven-month-old girl had occupied the next seat forward. "What did the little girl do?"

The members' responses included cried, squirmed, screamed, fed, and slept. I said she was "truthing". She had spent the hour turned to my wife and me, staring into one set of eyes, and then the other, until we prepared for landing. Her scrutinising compelled attention, and we put aside our reading to smile and make sounds and hand gestures, participating in her quest to find interpersonal "truth". That is, she was attempting to make sense of us, and presumably, of herself, and in relationship to us.

I noted that I had been scrupulously avoided during this morning's pre-conference coffee hour, and how, arriving late to a lecture I had offered at another institution the day before, a woman sat in the one empty seat, next to mine. When my gaze met her, she whispered loudly, "Don't look at me!"

I concluded by asserting that group leader fosters "truthing", that is, the process of making sense of group experience, by responding to needs both to seek and refuse engagement. Everyone came to be informed by the guest leader, but, as an object of interest, I would have to regulate being taken in according to others' needs, wishes, and fantasies and not just according to mine. I predicted my falling short of this ideal, and the group would need to decide what to do with that reality, too.

Experiential session 1. The two absent individuals became a topic of concern; they were well known by many. "I spoke to Margit yesterday, she was looking forward to coming." "I hope she is all right, she had been suffering from . . ." "Jerzy told me he had commitments at the hospital and wondered if he would be able to make the trip." "I know he had planned to stay in town." "A lot of traffic this morning."

The talk moved to positive expectations and enjoyment of the lecture. Several acknowledged having attended workshops with me, here or in other countries; then there was an expectant silence. I said, finally, "Do you think the two missing members know something we don't?"

There was relieved laugher, and then Yuri spoke. He was a tall, athletically built, middle-aged man: "I had a dream last night, of being chased, by a woman. This is a dream familiar to me [laughter] . . . I mean, of being chased. I was afraid of what would happen when I was captured, and I was trying to escape."

Yuri barely acknowledged the good-natured quality of the laughter, which influenced other members to offer their comments solemnly, so that they became intellectual hypotheses.

A woman: "Perhaps you are afraid of the group, which is what Richard suggested—our two missing members represent a part of all of us."

Yuri: "Perhaps, but I know many of you from the Society, and taught some of you at the Institute, I doubt it."

Carl: "Yes, you are a very confident and handsome, man, Yuri, I doubt that you are afraid of us."

Yuri: "I think more [afraid of] myself, that seems familiar, my own aggression."

Egon: "That probably goes for many of us."

Katrin: "Me, for sure, my aggression. I am the woman from his [Richard's] lecture who wouldn't let him look at me." [Laughter]

Several others: "Are we so afraid of being looked at by each other?" "I am." "Perhaps we are." "But this is what we wanted."

Another woman, Anita: "Maybe the woman [in the dream], is a lover, and Yuri is chased by love." She went on to recount her positive experience with me at an international conference.

Several other members attested to my worth, based on our contacts, either during this week where I had lectured at other institutions, or before. I expressed appreciation and said that I had my own emotional limitations. Perhaps I had trouble with all the love, too, and would try to be open to Anita's interpretation. I admitted to being unconvinced, however, and wondered if Anita might be creating a wave of idealising the leader.

Anita was intrigued: "You mean I'm being Polly . . ." She struggled with the word, "Pollyanna," and Egon clarified its English usage.

"Hi, I'm Kurt. We group analysts say that Yuri is 'holding' the ambivalent feelings towards you, and perhaps [towards] each other too."

Yuri seemed impassive. I turned to Carl, who had revealed himself as Yuri's colleague: "Kurt thinks Yuri is 'holding' everyone's ambivalence." With his first of many laughs that seemed uncomfortable and disconnected to the context, Carl replied, "Maybe."

Kurt became irritated. "I think you are too, Carl, ambivalent towards the leader. You like to lead."

Carl laughed in Kurt's direction, "Of course, so do you." The men had traded accusations, and coldness passed between them.

Yuri stayed non-committal and addressed me: "I really don't know who you are, when you say that you may have your own difficulties with 'love'. You don't seem anxious or take things personally."

"Well, now we are meeting each other personally," I replied. But we, too, did not seem to connect with any warmth.

Yuri: "I can't tell if you are interested in connecting, or just using technique."

"Both," I replied.

Egon: "Richard is being himself, trust me. Eric and I have been to some of his other workshops—it's what he writes about. He's trying to connect to all of us, so we can connect to each other."

Several women followed: "I was a little bit confused during your lecture, and maybe it was not about the language. [Laughter] Your point of view, so different."

"I'm intrigued, I like the way you insert yourself."

And from the previously avoidant Katrin: "I'm ready to look at you." I invited her to continue; she smiled: "That's all for now!"

Kurt: "I am pleased to have someone with a different point of view, but I detect some sarcasm in your reference to 'holding'. I can tell that you take issue with group analysis."

I replied, "I think it is better when a person takes ownership for 'holding', rather than refer to the whole group."

Kurt agreed, but when it became apparent that we were beginning to become embroiled in a debate regarding group analytic *vs.* other types of interventions, Egon objected: "Why don't you wait and see how Richard works." The conversation drifted away, and then Kurt turned heatedly to me: "I'm angry, I feel ignored and minimised by you."

Katrin: "I'm angry with you, Kurt, I was talking,"

Egon: [to Kurt] "You're minimizing Katrin, and also Tamar was trying to speak, finally."

But Anita turned back to Kurt: "Kurt is very upset." Others agreed: "I haven't seen you this way before." "Perhaps he ought to speak."

I asked several individuals if they were frightened by Kurt's anger at me. "He's taking a chance with me, and with us," I added, and then to the group, "A lot of you seem to know each other, and this meeting could allow you to know each other in deeper ways, although it also could be upsetting."

Anita nodded. "Yes, I like it when a man comes forth and speaks for himself. I like when you disagreed with my interpretation of the dream and told me." Katrin, Tamar, and several others encouraged Kurt to continue.

Egon: "I'm envious of the way Kurt can draw everyone's attention, and I think he wants Richard all to himself. I think we are all greedy for Richard."

Marina (apparently a colleague): "Kurt expresses himself strongly, in all situations."

I said to Marina, "Can you help Kurt come forth, as Anita suggested?" She seemed at a loss, but others succeeded in prodding Kurt, who told us (and me, in particular), how he worked as a group therapist. Then he thanked me for not turning the group against him. "I felt you wouldn't connect with me—our 'different theoretical orientations'—but now I feel you are genuinely involved and interested." Unexpectedly, he began to cry: "I haven't mourned my mother since she died." It took a while for Kurt to explain the connection between what occurred between us and his history of conflict with his mother.

As the session drew to its close, Anita commented: "I am touched by how much we've connected to Richard—not only Kurt." I acknowledged that this morning's process seemed to support her interpretation that we might run away from something good—from connecting not only to me but to each other, too. And, referring to Yuri's dream of being chased by a female, I ended with, "I might have been enough for Kurt, this morning, but I wonder if I can be 'woman' enough for Yuri, and for this group. Let's see."

Debriefing. Attendees commented favourably on the leader's activity level and insertion of self, and its impact on our cohesion and the intensity of group process. Kurt sparked the discussion of observed similarities and dissimilarities with the group analytic approach, emphasising the former. I suggested that, in a productive group, member-to-member bonds and meaning-building connections radiate from, and depend on, member–leader bonds (Billow, 2003a,b). The morning was intense: unpredictable, unsettling, and unresolved; I felt we were off to a good start.

Day 1, afternoon

Lecture and discussion. We reviewed concepts concerning basic drives to love, hate, and seek knowledge (Bion, 1962), and how they applied to bonding and to taking chances with self and others, as exemplified by the morning's experiential session. In "truthing", learning from experience, something unexpected should be expected in every group session as members become informed by their *passion*, the developments, shifts, and reintegration of their basic affects and attendant fantasies and thoughts (Billow, 2003a).

Experiential session 2. After some cursory back and forth, Victor spoke up. He was a large bear of a man, aged by a lined and bearded face, and had seemed depressed, perhaps troubled by the morning. "I find this all very interesting. Your approach has something in common with existentialism, you think?"

He occupied the seat to my left (the seat to my right remained empty), and we faced each other: "I am glad you spoke, you seemed distressed this morning." Victor seemed surprised and gravely shook his head. I then responded to his question, affirming similarities between an existential and relational approach, such as the focus on developing meaning as a commitment to the lived present, as in the here-and-now of our group.

Victor's beatific smile lasted until Carl's disconcerting laugh caught attention. Carl, turning with an amused familiarity to Yuri, "I've been trying to make sense of what occurred this morning. I was wondering if perhaps all of us are like you [in the dream], running away from something." Carl did not respond to encouragement to express his own feelings, and we meandered about.

Then Victor addressed Carl: "You laughed when I spoke and ignored me, as if my comments were not worth taking seriously." Several individuals attempted to dissipate the tension by reassuring Victor that Carl's laughter was directed at me and not him.

> Anita: "I've noticed that you have been laughing a lot, Carl; do you think you are anxious?"
>
> Carl: "Perhaps." And then he addressed Victor: "Your comments are naïve, as if you are not connecting."
>
> Victor: "No, I listen very carefully and I connect to many subjects."
>
> Yuri joined Carl: "But not always to what is being presented."
>
> Victor: "That seems to be the opinion of the faculty."

I directed the participants to stay with what is occurring here in our group, rather than draw on their histories with each other. But the conversation drew further away. Eric, apparently another of Victor's teachers, launched a lengthy debate on the didactics of presenting a single *vs.* multiple model of theory and technique. "We teach group analysis in depth, but we are open to other points of view. That is why we invited Richard." As if providing evidence, Eric invoked the names and orientation of some former presenters.

I broke in and thanked my host for including me on the list of such prominent guests. "Eric, you not only invited me, but are providing case material for tomorrow morning's lecture: as the group's Refuser, you are doing a great job of forming your own subgroup of refusers."

Eric smiled broadly, but, as if he did not hear my message, continued, "I think it important to clarify the training institute's philosophy regarding learning."

"You're doing it again," I smiled, and Eric remained friendly, although unconvinced. Elisabeth and Lise, who had not spoken, affirmed that they wanted to get back to our group. And, they liked hearing their own voices! Marina seemed disconnected from the women's delight, and turned to Victor: "You seem dismissive."

> Victor: "No, the Institute dismisses me. Now I am asking Carl to address me and tell me why he has no respect for me."
>
> Marina: "But this seems to be your attitude." We heard Carl's nervous laughter in the background.

I asked Marina if there was something Victor was doing here, in our group. She seemed to ignore me; her impassivity made me wonder whether Marina was displaying a characteristically European hauteur, or did not like the question, or the questioner. I turned to Elisabeth and Lise; they were in close proximity to Marina, and they seemed to know her and tried and failed to intercede.

> Marina (to Victor): "When you say that you feel people don't respect you, I feel that from you. I feel you are laughing at me when I try to supervise you." Her tone unexpectedly softened to hurt and vulnerability and Victor responded similarly: "I did not know that. I'm not [laughing], I'm trying to understand." The group paused appreciatively.
>
> Lise: "I felt I was taking a risk with you, Marina, you can be so severe." Marina smiled at both women and seemed poised to respond affirmatively, but Yuri and Carl interjected: [to Victor] "You asked Billow about existentialism," one of them scoffed. "It was off topic, that's what you do at the Institute."
>
> Victor: "I know you don't want me here. I could quit. I joined the Institute training for pure knowledge. Perhaps it is that you don't like my religious orientation, or my political background. All of us practise religion of one kind or another. I may not have groups the way of the Institute, but I have much to offer, even if you don't think so."

No one missed hearing the veiled threat in Victor's "I could quit", even though the suppositional remarks were directed elsewhere. The room became unpleasantly tense. I said that Yuri and Carl were "double teaming" Victor. Egon and several of the women—all of whom seemed to be Institute connected—made half-hearted attempts to reassure Victor that he had a place. I emphasised that their comments also applied to our group in progress.

> Eric: "I think it is important to clarify the Institute's position and its relationship to the Training Programme and the Society."

> I asked him to bring in his own voice as a group member. "No, I will remain 'the Refuser', and try to clarify," he said playfully.

> "You can't do both. You're not clarifying your own feelings or letting us know the basis for your refusal." Although agitated by what I took as Eric's obstructionism, I attempted to reply in a similarly playful tone. I hoped that our struggle displayed safe combat. And, although shaken by the unresolved hostilities and threat of secession, I attempted to close lightly: "Many elements of the group situation need to be 'clarified,' and Eric is not the only person refusing my directive to 'stay in the room'."

Debriefing. During the fifteen-minute coffee break I gathered a few notes and gathered myself as well. Like an exasperated teacher, I wanted the antagonists to shake hands, and to chastise the whole group for abandoning the wounded warrior, Victor. The conference's organiser, Eric, had revealed himself to be stubborn and doctrinaire; I wondered whether he harboured the intense hostility towards me that I now felt towards him. What could I say to cool the situation sufficiently, yet uphold my point of view with *integrity* (Billow, 2010b; see Chapter Four), which meant staying within the boundaries of the debriefing?

I began with an aphoristic line from William Blake (1977): "A truth that's told with bad intent / Beats all the lies you can invent". I wanted to draw attention to the use of "truth" as a weapon and, also, as a defence against openness to fresh experience, without blaming the antagonists or group. A dynamic tension exists between truth and falsity, and to make war or peace, individuals and groups tend to use the former (truth) in the service of the latter (falsity) (Billow, 2004). The profusion of dialogue involving Institute relations—however "sincere"—reaffirmed and hardened pre-existing attitudes and relationships, and, hence, obstructed rather than furthered "truthing".

Authenticity is more complex than *sincerity* and requires mental fortitude (Trilling, 1971): its truths are more difficult to emerge and accept—they disturb the persistent fiction we hold of possessing a unified, coherent, and moral self (Billow, 2010a,c). We were fortunate to be able to continue to think and feel about the day and return, perhaps with fresh dreams that could lead us to "truths" less known, less obvious, and less false.

Eric graciously thanked me and closed the day. He had arranged my transportation with his colleague, Egon. I was surprised when Eric introduced our driving companion as Egon's wife, the outspoken Anita.

The group—Victor particularly—haunted my mind during the evening and I was a distracted dining companion. Had I averted or orchestrated a slaughter? I reviewed some reading material before sinking into a troubled sleep. With no dreams remembered, I awoke with a different outlook. But who would be present to hear it?

Day 2, morning

Lecture/discussion. It was my turn to scrutinise, surreptitiously counting heads until each seat filled with yesterday's occupant. I began by quoting another poet, on the scapegoat: "happy beast, / From every personal sin released . . ., hidden apart, / Dancing with a careless heart" (Warner, 1985, p. 46). All were implicated in the careless dancing: the combatants and the vicarious witnesses. (Evidently, me too, for I had been "dancing" solely with the identified scapegoat.) All participants derive some reward—pleasurable or not—from the roles they play: victims and victimisers, rescuers and those rescued.

Victor seemed disappointed and alarmed: "Do you mean you were playing a role in group?" I said yes, but that is not the same thing as "role playing", meaning being intentionally artificial and false. He was relieved when I referred to Nietzsche's aphorism that "every profound spirit needs a mask" (in Trilling, 1971, p. 119). We take roles in group as member and leader, allowing a type of sophisticated dialogue, in which we balance what we are ready to reveal with what others are ready to hear, knowing, too, that our assessments are subjective, partially determined by non-conscious, partially irrational, self/other/group vectors, and represent both truth and falsity.

I said I was distrustful of proscriptive models of therapy, such as classical psychoanalysis or Tavistock; however, any model, including group analytic and relational, provides structure and direction, and places the therapist in a certain mind-set that unavoidably makes less likely certain paths and potentialities. I acknowledged having trouble with certain Foulksian admonitions, which I now classify as polemic: for example, "the conductor does nothing for people in the context of the group that they can do for themselves and one another". Groups do more—and less—than we may anticipate. There is no neat divide between "they" and "I", those that choose to speak (the "holders") and those that let, stimulate, or inveigle (Chapter Seven) others to speak for them. Being in the matrix with other members, the therapist or leader cannot assess with objective certainty who is doing what and to whom, or the "that" which is being "done".

Experiential session 3. Egon expressed his satisfaction that everyone had returned, a feeling echoed by several others. "Why is that important to you?" someone asked. Egon replied "I like taking care of people," and Anita retorted, "Even when the person doesn't want to be taken care of." Egon blushed and remained silent in the face of implied marital discord, while others laughed uncomfortably.

"Are there other pairs that I do not know about?" I asked. Ada raised her hand. "I'm married to him," pointing across the spacious room to Victor. I reflected, "Yesterday's workshop must have been especially difficult." "Yes, but Victor is very strong and can take care of himself," she asserted. I suggested that she take care of herself today. Ada: "I will try."

Victor said he had no thought of not returning, and, turning to Carl, "We talked briefly this morning before the session, when we had coffee, that made all the difference." Carl assented, but as Victor continued to speak, teacher–student nastiness reasserted itself, as if nothing pleasant and personal had just transpired, and as if my evening and morning's palliations about staying in the present and in the room had fallen on deaf ears.

Victor said, "I'm finding a different model here, one that I have been looking for, and that must irritate you, and others from the training programme."

Several members attempted to arbitrate, which set off a chain of further irritations, opinions, and disagreements—some friendly, some not—involving Egon and other men. At one point, I turned to the women: "This is what males do with each other. We stick our dicks out. It's sort of like making love, if we don't kill each other first." The room exploded in laughter; members supplied apt translations for the few who needed them. I had created an opening, but the women were slow to take my invitation, and several men backtracked.

As the morning's midpoint passed, I enquired whether "the men were 'running' [referring to Yuri's dream] away from the women, and vice versa." Egon took issue: he was taking a chance and opening up personally. Anita suggested that Egon was trying to protect her by protesting my intervention, and that she did not need it. She thought I was right [yesterday] about Yuri's dream: people were running away from their aggression and that the women, in particular, were angry with her. "I feel this happens because I come on strong, like the men. Maybe I'm just projecting, I can't be sure. I probably should shut up now." That seemed to please some of the women, who began to talk about themselves, and to profess "confusion" about what another said or was feeling.

I said that Anita had taken a chance and was being ignored. Were the women angry with her? Now several women came forth: "I know I shouldn't feel this way, I admire how you get in, but I do feel jealous when you talk." "You have a lot of interesting things to say and you get the men's attention." Lise: "You have courage, and it makes me feel inferior."

I said that it took courage for Lise and the others to acknowledge their mixed feelings and, to Yuri and Carl, "Doesn't it take a load off us when the women 'hold' their share of aggression?" For the first time, I felt the two men warm to me; they seemed to enjoy my humorous allusion to group analysis and not take offence. I then addressed Anita: "So your sense of being envied is not just in your head, but real. Better to be hated than to think you are crazy." The group had followed certain stereotypical gender patterns: men "stick out" their aggression, particularly to each other, while women often keep inside similar feelings towards their same-sex peers. The women had been running away from aggressive feelings towards each other.

Anita came to speak movingly about her relationship to her competitive mother and beloved father. Now she knew something about her "ambivalent relationship to the Society, with all you women," she declared. Her last remark stirred Eric to speak supportively about her participation "there" (within their Institute). I asked if anyone would help him deal more personally with "here", perhaps regarding ambivalences to not-so-beloved fathers, such as me. My interpretative foray did not seem to register with Eric, and I vowed playfully that before the conference ended, I would attempt to repay him for his kind invitation to his country by "cracking" his refusal to analyse his refusal. "You can try," Eric replied, with unmistakable delight.

Debriefing. Egon wondered why I had interrupted him, and I said I was being "diplomatic" (Billow, 2010b; see Chapter Four). I trusted our good feelings would allow him to bear with me, and that I had to take care of the "truthing" difficulties of the whole group. I had asked members to stay focused on feelings as they related to our group; mostly they refused, and, typical of *refusal*, refused to explain why. Did they object to me, personally, my leadership, or my focus? Unlike in a constructive rebellion, no one offered a rationale for preferring what I evaluated as truth-evading interactions.

Diplomatic is not synonymous with non-interventionist, "polite", supportive, democratic, or non-confrontational. I felt that I had been both political and strategic in my assertion of therapeutic influence. The group began to distribute its power—and its aggression—so that both the men and women were participating and taking chances with each other. I commented that we had succeeded in bringing group process to "the room", and that, perhaps in the afternoon, we could begin to make sense of the underlying individual and group *resistances*—the symbolic dimensions of our conference.

Day 2, afternoon

Lecture/discussion. Yuri asked about the use of my own feelings. He said it was difficult to believe that I had a personal reaction to everything that had taken place. Was I being "dramatic" yesterday when I said I had my own emotional difficulties? We arrived at a better footing when I suggested that we shared similar subjectivities. His dream expressed paranoid and depressing feelings in anticipating the conference and a group configuration. Did he not believe I could have similar anxieties? Carl seemed to bless our coming together, with an approving rather than patronising smirk. I wondered to myself if facial expression was a major dimension of Carl's "language".

Final experiential session. My leftward seating companion, Victor, smiled in my direction, and I was not sure if it was aimed at me, or my rightward companions, Carl and Yuri. Across the room was Ada, his wife, and I said to her, "He seems in an improved mood." "Yes, this is easier. We come from a different part of the country . . ."

Good-natured laughter followed from the group, and she continued, "and we do different types of group work, as Victor explained." Another woman interjected, "Where do you work?"

The simple enquiry provided entry to other introductory questions directed toward several attendees: "What's your name?" "Where are you from?" "How did you get here on time! [from a distant community]" "You haven't spoken very much." "I have been thinking of you."

So, some persons were strangers to each other, and not only to me! The mood of the room had changed dramatically. Was the group "doing" for itself, and should I do nothing? It took a while for me to understand what was transpiring and formulate an intervention: "This seems to be the first time in two days that people seem friendly—genuinely interested in each other."

I expected my remark to be controversial, but it met immediate understanding. We were nearing the end of the last experiential session, and I thought it could be a useful dimension of termination to include a focus on an *idea* about the group and our interactions during the entire conference. Egon iterated that everyone had been greedy and competing for the leader. "Me especially," he acknowledged. Anita suggested that members could be interested in each other because all had had a good feeding. Another woman: "You have been woman enough for us!" Envy did not seem to have currency as a potential nuclear idea and I did not pursue it.

At one point, I turned to Eric and said that he might be fed up with me, but that I felt unsatisfied, and needed to learn more about who he is.

"I told my wife you called me a 'refuser' and she knew what you meant." Another Eric emerged, touchingly vulnerable and self-revealing: the care-giver to ailing parents, younger siblings, the Institute and Society, the conference, and, I realised, to its leader. I thanked him for inviting and hosting me, and for being my "textbook case". I do not remember if I was quick enough to extend the metaphor: one purpose of the conference was to provide a living textbook, to learn about a different model of group psychotherapy. If we were successful, all of us would be rewriting our texts and moving forward to new ones.

Debriefing/closure. We reviewed group process. "Everyone got engaged, very quickly," several commented. A woman said, "Even though I didn't talk until you provoked the women, I was processing a lot." Kurt thought a turning point occurred during the first morning. "I could attack you without your attacking back."

"And you would survive," Anita added. Eric smiled devilishly: "Billow can take care of himself." Egon suggested that I had given the group the freedom not to be "friendly": "We could be real with each other."

I admitted having been concerned by the intensity of the exchanges Victor had with Carl and Yuri. But the three men seemed unperturbed, and my self-disclosure met mild surprise but little apparent interest. No one seemed to realise—or care—that I had been unnerved by yesterday's altercations and refusals and that I had not quite recovered.

Members re-engaged with Eric, to express affection and emphasise his value to their community. They thanked him for securing the time, meeting place, and publicity for the conference, and inviting me. In turn, I expressed gratitude to Eric and all the members, confessing to being puzzled by much of what took place, and troubled—and that was preferable to walking away thoroughly satisfied. Others expressed their take-aways, and their goodbyes.

Discussion[38]

From the first session and onwards, Egon had circulated the idea of envy. Certainly, I knew what he meant. To covet others, their possessions and achievements—I live with these feelings every day. Also, I have studied, interpreted, and written about its dynamics. But even in moments of fear for the safety and survival of our group, I did not comprehend the extent to which envy, in tooth and nail, with devouring hunger, tore into every aspect of our mentalities. Under its catabolic force, I was captured and I could not yet articulate to myself a pertinent nuclear idea, until the group shifted and released me from envy's intersubjective captivity. It had seemed too early—too abstract and yet too obvious—to introduce envy as a group idea, and then, it became too late to pursue it.

An assemblage had beheld "me", a visitor with gifts of knowledge, welcomed with collective expectation and acquisitive desire that set group process in motion and undergirded what followed. In professional conferences such as the one under discussion, the attendees are motivated, in part, by desire to expand professional and personal *being*: "to become the *Other* and still be himself" (Girard, 1965, p. 54).[39] As with the infant on the aeroplane, I came into sight as that *Other*, to turn toward and away, to learn from, imitate, emulate, and incorporate.

Confronted with "me", the representative, messenger, even embodiment of truth, a group must deal with feelings, fantasies, and thoughts that are "not nice". Covetous desire and rivalry threaten the comfortable relationships and alliances the participants—leader included—make with self and other.

Surely, there were premonitions of envy's mythic power—an injunction, omen, and oracular dream. "Don't look at me!" Katrin's forewarning had stayed in my mind. And we began with Eric's report of two sudden absences. I asked humorously, when the cohering group had become ominously quiet, "Do you think the two missing members know something we don't?"

Yuri then presented a dream of being chased: "I was afraid of what would happen when I was captured and I was trying to escape." Yuri (and Carl) denied any suggestion that the dream could be about the leader and the group. "I know many of you from the Society . . . Institute . . . more [afraid of] myself, that seems familiar, my own aggression." An oracle deals in general phrases and indefiniteness; "the more impressive the diction, the greater vagueness in the statements made" (Jastrow, 1898, p. 343). The debate over the dream's meaning amplified its relevance: "Are we so afraid of being looked at by each other?" "But this is what we wanted." "Are we fearing aggression or love?" "I think you are . . . ambivalent toward the leader. You like to lead."

The members prepared to face "me": "I really don't know who you are." "Richard is being himself . . . trying to connect to all of us, so we can connect to each other." "Your point of view, so different." "I'm ready to look at you now!" The heated debate between theories and styles of leadership provided a way for Kurt—and all—to observe, taste, and test me that first morning.

Egon acknowledged being "envious the way Kurt can draw everyone's attention . . . he wants Richard all to himself . . . we are all greedy for Richard." In my understanding, anyone who actively comes forth covets both truth and its symbolic representative "all to himself". But the reality of envy and greed does not preclude reparative generosity and interest in others as well (Klein, 1952). During the first morning, usual beginning group themes were brought up, symbolised, and enacted, involving dread, excitement, danger, and security—issues of trust in the leader and among members—and were dealt with constructively. Beholding "me" seemed "enough" to set in motion a desire for a truth-seeking group. I saw no need to rub "envy" in the group's face.

In the afternoon, a religious man approached, seeing in me a self-reflection that made him my emissary and martyr. Our philosophies had much "in common", Victor declared, and, like me, he did not "have groups the way of the Institute". In ostensibly challenging the prevailing establishment of my hosts, Victor offered himself as sacrificial lamb, naïf, receiver of God's wisdom, and my apostle. However, in threatening the group's cohesiveness, he was also a most formidable opponent.

As Victor and certain members of the Institute staff (Yuri, Carl, and Marina) became more intensively combative, professing dramatically opposed points of view, they became more alike, united in their treatment of "me". The object of covetous regard was "carelessly" disregarded. The antagonists no longer imitated each other's desire for "me", but each other's antagonism. There was little I could do to ameliorate the hostilities, and no one else seemed concerned about protecting Victor and preventing scapegoating, or even making sense of the transactions in terms of here-and-now group process. I found myself, alone, in the neighbouring region of fear and trembling; throughout the evening I could not shake off feeling ineffective, and I worried about being inadvertently harmful.

However, as his wife declared the next morning, "Victor is very strong and can take care of himself." And here he was again, in our second morning (and third session): "I'm finding a different model here, one that I have been looking for, and that must irritate you, and others from the training programme."

Now I found myself amused rather than alarmed by his "sleight of hand"—typical of the scapegoat who draws out his victimisers—and which had drawn me in, too. He worked the faculty, the whole group, and me, in an attempt to become the other Other, and to triumph over the Other ("me"), commandeering fear and everyone's attention, mine particularly. "I know you don't want me here. I could quit. I joined the Institute training for pure knowledge." As a victim of "scandalised innocence", he thereby reversed polarities of scapegoating: the accused becomes the accuser (Tricaud, in Anspach, 2004, p. xxvii).

I could understand why he was such a provocative and compelling source of interest and irritation for the faculty, and I sympathised with them. Victor cared not at all about my directives to stay in the room, my feelings, or how the consequences of his threatened self-exile and martyrdom could affect the group or me personally. He had found "a different model here, one that I had been looking for". My most sincere admirer was "torn between two opposite feelings toward his model—the most submissive reverence and the most intense malice. This is the passion we call *hatred*" (Girard, 1965, pp. 10–11, original italic). He loved and hated "me". Consequently, he was a force to stimulate thinking, and enviously damage it.

Victor was not innocent, but not completely or uniquely guilty, either. Guilt rarely concentrates in one direction, and no one is pure. I had stepped unknowingly into a pre-existing impasse between Victor and the Institute faculty. Victor envied me because I was allowed to have a different theory, and attempted to use me as an ally to get at the Institute faculty. The faculty—as represented by Carl, Yuri, and Marina—envied me as a foreign expert, but attempted to neutralise my differences and me.

While Victor took himself too seriously, so did his faculty (as had I). Each blamed the other for disrupting a harmonious relationship to learning and knowledge. Neither side turned the other cheek, or approached the other with empathy, humility, or humour. Neither showed interest in learning about the other's truths, or increasing their own. I realised later, the group as a whole suffered from a dearth of curiosity and mutual interest.

The contagion of scapegoating had affected me, too, and while I had worried about Victor, I had harboured during the evening less benevolent feelings towards my host, Eric. But by morning I had regained sufficient equilibrium not to be unduly concerned by the varying expressions of feelings and thoughts—contentious, angry, loving, self-revealing—and concentrated on their distribution between sexes and among all the participants, myself included. For a painful interval, I had been caught up in the contagion of rivalry and opposition. Now I had freed myself from the imitation and mirroring, and withdrew from the *mêlée* of antagonisms, no longer siding with any antagonist or remaining antagonistic myself. I felt comfortable following my own frustrations and irritations; my curiosity fell, unsated, on Eric.

Unlikely to be coincidental, Eric relaxed his refusals and revealed himself when the group—and its leader—became genuinely "friendly". "Billow could take care of himself." Eric's behaviour had belied his assertion. Defying my directives to stay in the room, and instead clarifying and reaffirming the Institute's boundaries had been Eric's attempt not to fight me, but to avoid or, at the very least, smooth over disagreements and controversies. "We are open to others' points of view. That is why we invited Richard." My truths and establishment truths could be contained in our conference. In his compulsive, but sincere and heart-warming manner, Eric had been "care-taker" of the entire group.

When the leader is beheld, a contagion of adversarial relationships is to be expected; one member imitates another's desire and the group is "plagued" with envy. "If any two men desire the same thing, which nevertheless cannot both enjoy, they become enemies" (Hobbes, 1996, p. 83). Kurt and Carl, Victor and Yuri, Egon and Anita, Eric and I, the men and the women—we were antagonists, foils, and gifts for each other: "It's sort of like making love, if we don't kill each other first."

This is not to suggest that anyone behaved badly. All were good citizens of our group, expressing themselves and participating at the edge of their self-knowledge. In our maturity as well as our infancy, we behold an object of interest and for moments, or even intervals that dominate a phase of a lifetime, everybody and all else is ignored, willed out of existence, and possibly destroyed. If the leader is adequate, and maintains the position of a thinking subject, the group will come to imitate the Other's desire for self–other recognition. Some, many, or all the members will seek the meanings motivating envious fascination, to love, and to grow (see Adams, 2000; also Garrels, 2006).

Returning to the oracle, Yuri's dream, the puzzle remains: who was chasing whom, and for what purpose? I was correct and so was Anita: the members were running away from me, from each other, and from the group experience; they were running away from hatred, and from love. But neither of us was correct: Yuri was not running away, but dreaming about—wishing for—someone and everyone to run after him. A group wishes to be caught, to come face to face with the Other, to learn about the nature of interpersonal being, and to be enhanced.

Earlier in this chapter I acknowledged that I knew about being a subject of my own envy; and now I knew much more about the process of "becoming" (Bion, 1975) envy's object. As a subject experiencing the group members' envy, the leader suffers through intense and ongoing incorporative–projective processes that represent attacks on his or her mentality and sense of self (Bion, 1967).

In attempting to contextualise envy in terms of "me" (its effect on me and my effect on the group), I found myself flooded with sensations of pleasure and pain, intense love and hate, and a with restless desire to know.[40] In retrospect, I realise that in my concern about the others, I could not make it sufficiently about "me". My attention scattered from participant to participant—Yuri, Carl, Victor, Anita and Egon, Eric, from interaction to interaction. I was here and there, with the participants who seemed to be running away from love, and those who seemed to embrace it. Reference points to envy were experientially close, affectively intense, and full of dramatic significance. Everything seemed salient, and yet I could not settle down and address the theme of envy in a sufficiently "friendly", non-accusatory manner. When I was ready to develop envy as a nuclear idea, the group had moved away from its here-and-now relevance.

I have described, then, my trajectory of deepening understanding of what it means to be a leader, experiencing the others' envious desires, and the impact on my thinking and behaviour. If I had known then what I know now, I ask myself, would I have attempted to move the group along by making different interventions? Might I have responded to and developed, early in the group process, Egon's initiation of the idea of envy? If I had, perhaps the conference might not have worked out so well.

To contain the group, the leader maintains the position of a thinking subject, always willing to put forth, respond to, and test potential nuclear ideas. To function *authentically*, by which I mean to pursue salient emotional truths, those that are relevant to one's own "being", the therapist must be relatively comfortable with the limits of his or her knowledge. Envy and jealousy, greed and reparation need to be contextualised in the here and now group and not merely elaborated theoretically. Even more so, these powerful emotional experiences must be contextualised in the psyche of the subject of the group leader, him or herself. To some degree, a group learns and grows by witnessing and imitating "me": an individual "listening to oneself listening" (Grotstein, 2009). *Being* in this group, with these members, in this time and place, predominates as a nuclear idea that lodges itself in the minds of the participants. For this to happen, envy had to become all about "me".

The nuclear idea may develop post hoc

Of course, an invited group trainer from another country and with special knowledge would stimulate heightened interest in the leader, but I maintain that the dynamics I have written about—the centrality of the leader—applies to all groups, and not only therapy groups (Alford, 1994, 1995). In invited workshops such as the one I am describing, an introductory or phasic period of struggle often emerges (Bennis & Shepard's (1956) "barometric event"), as the group resists, rebels, and refuses. We come to understand what some of the contextual issues are, such as involving my leadership approach to "truthing", as well as expectable and typical defences against experiential learning. I am usually able to co-regulate our process with sufficient diplomacy to establish constructive, leader–member, member–member alliances, so that meaning gradually reveals itself. Even when not immediately efficacious, I begin as soon as possible to work with symbolic issues, the underlying individual and group *resistances*. I share my thinking (Aron, 1996), acknowledging the limited basis and hypothetical nature of my interventions.

As in this workshop, I observe and participate in the group's struggle, without any expectation that I would be able to articulate—concurrently, or even *post hoc*, as in this report—its symbolic and metapsychological dimensions. I came to the conference with certain ideas I have developed in my career, and presented and contextualised them in the here and now of the ongoing group experience. These ideas, while not superfluous or extraneous, did not capture an essence of the group culture and process, specifically, nuclear ideas related to the group's envious mental relationship to the leader, and its effects on the leader. The group became "friendly", and that realisation freed me, so that I could break out of the intellectual framework of pre-established ideas. I began to understand in my "guts" what I had just been through, as witness to, and participant in, the group's fantasies, conflicts, subgroupings, and scapegoating. A nuclear idea now made *sense*; I had a sufficient experiential basis for me to behold "me", anew.

CHAPTER TEN

The invited presenter: outrage and outrageousness

Through years of training, my professional practice, and my own individual, group, and self-analysis, I have cultivated a mode of communication that I believe has served me well in public presentations and in clinical practice. *Contra* Salvador Dali (2007), who strove to live by his declaration that "The one thing the world will never have enough of is the outrageous" (entry for August 30, 1953), I never try to be outrageous, as a person or therapist, but sometimes, people see me that way, and appreciate, disapprove, or, on occasion, react with outrage.

As mentioned earlier in this volume, a group leader functions in the mode of *diplomacy* (see Chapter Four), exercising authority and power to establish and maintain an exploratory culture that values nuclear ideas. Patience—timing and tact—would seem to characterise therapeutic diplomacy, but also, humour, linguistic play, affective openness, challenge, and confrontation may further leadership goals. In my opinion, it is a matter of professional *integrity* to risk being perceived as outrageous, for the effective leader must challenge and break down the boundaries that obstruct, or even preclude, emotional learning. Without such leadership, a group—whether in formation or ongoing—is more likely to be marked with conventionality or stalemate, or submission to, or rebellion against, authority. As the eminent American judge, Learned Hand (1927), opined, our dangers, as it seems to me, are not from the outrageous but from the conforming.

The two faces of the group therapist

As leaders, we introduce principles and practices that normalise group relations and provide a sense of continuity and regularity. To establish cohesion, we encourage bonding among members and monitor each member's bond to us. Conforming to group norms provides an important sense of identity, regularity, and security for the therapist as well as for other group members. Yet, we risk creating a stultifying establishment,[41] becoming too comfortable in the overt and covert alliances and compromises we make with other group members and our self, and we might avoid thinking about and investigating these arrangements.

There needs to be, then, dialectical tension in the roles of group leadership. In order to preserve a well-working group, or attend to the difficulties of an ineffective one, the leader must wear "two faces", being constructive and deconstructive (Billow, 2005, 2010a). Bion (1966, p. 37) challenged the therapist to function with "the impact of an explosive force on a preexisting framework", the goal being that the group "should thrive or disintegrate but not be indifferent". To foster nuclear ideas, the leader must disturb the very status quo that he or she works to establish, dislodging group members from the state of basic assumptive "groupishness" that all participants, including the leader, reflexively settle into (Caper, 1999). This stimulates anxiety, of course, provoking personal and group psychological upheaval, and, precisely, it is this upsetting of the apple cart of now-comfortable polemic ideas that leads to the perception of the leader as outrageous.

Masters of the outrageous

Certain therapists use outrageous behaviours technically. I have been fortunate to have had direct contact with some of the masters, as observer, group member, supervisee, or co-therapist. Showmen Carl Whitaker, Elvin Semrad, Harold Searles, Jay Haley and Chloe

Madanes, Lou Ormont, and Bernard Frankel have modelled using unexpected small talk, puzzling *non sequiturs*, paradoxical metaphors, non-reassurance, biting humour, sarcasm, in-your-face verbal confrontation, and indirect communication with difficult group situations, uncompromising family constellations, and even floridly psychotic individuals. I do not attempt to imitate their tactics, yet, because of their influence and my respect for them, sometimes my moves as leader shade in that direction. However, for me to use outrageousness intentionally would feel inauthentic.

While in pre-doctoral training, I found myself leading a demonstration group of unco-operative clinic patients, while my co-therapist read the newspaper. At one point, he sat on a patient's lap. Many levels of meaning were packed in Carl Whitaker's artful madness: "Let's break mental set." "See me as the mirror of the group's avoidance." "I can non-participate and out crazy the best of you." "I can tolerate failure and will work no harder than any other group member." His "inappropriate" behaviours stirred things up sufficiently to create the rudiments of a cohesive group. On a symbolic play level, the therapeutic relationship became an interactional metaphor (Whitaker & Bumberry, 1988), driven by the force of the leader's presentational self. In effect, an unspoken but powerfully effective nuclear idea of the leader contained the participants and propelled participation.

The self-described "hayseed from Nebraska", Elvin Semrad, could seem "either brilliant or so vague, general, and simplistic that I wondered if he had lifted [his remarks] . . . directly from the *Reader's Digest*. Was he a guru or fake?" (Mazer, 2003, p. 14).[42] Yet, it worked. In view of an audience of psychiatric residents and trainees, Dr Semrad "[talked] with [psychotic] patients more effectively about more difficult material than anyone else I have known" (Rako, 2003, p. 17). Talking directly and intuitively, Semrad risked being perceived as outrageously mundane, glib, or corny to a censorious observer.

I have danced with Bernard Frankel, as a group member, supervisee, co-leader, and friend and colleague. Bobbing, weaving, turning towards the individual or away to the group, Frankel listens, reflects, and speaks with body and tone, adding "tenor"—layers of impacted meaning—to what is said, as it is said. Frustrated with my cohorts in a training group, I morphed—according to Frankel—into its "nose", or "bullshit detector". These epigrammatic remarks—were they complimentary or not?—connected me to the group (and *vice versa*), interpreted aspects of my character and defence organisation, supported the reality of my criticisms and blunted their toxic edge. Frankel emboldened me as leader to be perceived as outrageously empathic (or not): to echo, play on words, tease and frustrate, and call people unpleasant names, "labelling" and (seemingly) make fun at their expense. How could I not have made him a part of "me"?

I do not consider as outrageous—in the positive sense I use the term—mere action, drama, humour, sarcasm, or a style of dress or addressing. These are communicative tools, and should be evaluated in terms of their effectiveness in carrying the freight of thought, feeling, empathy, and therapeutic strategy.

The therapists and therapeutic manoeuvres I have described might be perceived as outrageous because they go beyond the comfortable norms of the prevailing clinical establishments. The goal: breaking boundaries in thinking and feeling, freeing the individual and group from personal and social polemics, to allow for fresh experience to emerge, and vital ideas to develop. Moments of frustration, confusion, anger—even outrage—may be part of the process. If the leader retains sufficient confidence and security in him or herself, and in the group, perceived outrageousness—and even a response of outrage—might signal the possibility of the new idea, inviting curiosity and the adventure of learning.

A conference on "Loving, hating and knowing— working with the 3 Rs: resistance, rebellion, and refusal"

The conference, sponsored by a regional group organisation in the USA, started almost twenty minutes late. As is my custom, I asked the group what they wanted from the day. This gave me a preliminary sense of the eighty participants—and them of me—and how to frame my ideas and respond to theirs. We agreed to shave off a few minutes from my prepared lecture, and reduce the time of the planned demonstration "fishbowl" to one hour.

The morning "fishbowl"

Concluding the informal lecture and discussion, I asked for seven or eight volunteers and placed my chair in the centre of the room.

Quickly, ten individuals appeared, with several more approaching as the circle closed. I indicated that this seemed like a large group for an hour, and with a shrug suggesting "whatever", continued by addressing both groups—volunteers and onlookers.

I said that I would try to work within an hour's time frame, but reserved the option to extend if I felt we needed more time to reach the conference goals. I also said that I was going to put aside theory and suggested we all do the same. I commented that I would like the audience not to interact with the demonstration group, except by yelling out "louder" if we could not be heard.

Shari began by saying she was the first to join the circle:

> "Hollie [the conference organiser] instructed that people who usually volunteer for demonstration groups should give others a chance. But I like to volunteer and be part of the group, and so I decided to rebel."

She received an approving welcome from other members. Ari, who had centred himself directly across from me, said that, as President of the organisation, he did not want to join the demo group and be in the centre, but he professed, oddly, that not enough people had joined, so he decided to "save the situation". The audience—perhaps sensing some competition for leadership in his choice of seat as well as remarks—laughed along with our group.

Other people offered their own motives for joining the circle, the common denominator being that they wanted to get something for themselves. When the group became silent, I suggested that, given our brief time frame, the best way to get something personal was to connect to another person directly, rather than to address comments to "the group". "We don't have time to slowly unfold," I added.

Ari said that he had been disappointed in my opening lecture. It was not as clear and organised as he would have liked. Robert disagreed.

> "I like the way you fielded questions and responded spontaneously." Looking at me, as if to test my response, Ari disagreed with Robert's positive evaluation. I said to Ari, "I like the way you come in to 'save the situation'."

The room erupted in laughter, and Ari joined in: "Yes, anything I can do to help." Several other group members returned to the theme of my lecture, either echoing Ari's criticisms or being positive about my presentation.

Jimmy attempted to join the two factions:

"I thought it was informative, but you could have given us a hand-out or done PowerPoint."

I said, "Jimmy, I have a hand-out which I plan on distributing before lunch. I want you to tell me what you think of it." Jimmy seemed taken by surprise: "I like that. [Audience laughs.] Also I like that you answered me."

Robert, sitting to my right, interjected to the group, "I said I wanted to get something personal and we've spent enough time talking about the lecture, which was fine and clear if you had listened."

I said, to Ari in particular, "I couldn't have said this better." [Laughter]

Shari, sitting to my left, asked Robert what he wanted to get out of the group, and when he did not answer, she pressed: "I'm curious as to what you mean by 'personal'."

Robert retorted, "You're 'curious'?" As if she did not hear his sarcastic tone, Shari repeated herself, and Robert iterated what he had communicated non-verbally: "I don't like the question."

Shari rushed forward: "I'm trying to get to know you, I don't understand why you can't tell us what you want. Is that something that happens with you?"

I dramatically put my hand to my face and shook my head in Shari's direction, to give her the cue to think about what she was doing and to let Robert know that I was not supporting her interrogation.

Robert: "What don't you understand, sweetie?"

Shari: "You call me 'sweetie' but I'm not clear what you mean."

Robert reddened and I put out my other hand slightly and said gently to him, "Back up." I turned to Shari.

"Shari, you said you join these demo groups all the time. Don't you know that whoever acts like a therapist is going to get killed? [Laughter] Relax, let me be the scapegoat. Our president is doing such a good job at trying to kill me off."

The group and audience laughed with relief; Shari's laughter followed, but she also seemed confused and I asked if someone could explain.

> Carol connected to both combatants: "Robert wants to express himself without being pushed to explain. You needn't keep pressuring him." I turned to Robert and asked him if Carol had done an adequate job and he said "I'm fine . . . for now."

> Jimmy piped up, "I'm not fine. It felt safe the way you intervened. I was scared that you would let things get out of control but you didn't. But you like Robert the best!" [Laughter]

> "I do, but you're coming up strong." [Laughter]

Several other members agreed with Jimmy's positive assessment of my handling the tense Shari–Robert interaction: "I like your sense of humour." "I feel I can trust you."

> Shari: "I'm still confused. [To Robert] What happened, what did I do?"

> I turned to Robert: "Let's get other people involved." Carol gently explained to Shari that she was trying to analyse Robert rather than express her feelings. When it became apparent that Carol was doing the same, I intervened, "Are you going to be the group translator?" [Audience laughter]

> "You're right," Carol said, "I'm going to resign from that role."

Other people made tentative forays into the group, until everyone had spoken except Enid, to whom the group turned expectantly.

> "I'm totally confused."

> I smiled encouragingly, and with a dubious tone, said, "Are you?"

> "Yes, this is a very strange situation. We're trying to talk personally and there is a room full of people looking at us. I want to participate but I don't know what to say other than this is difficult and that somehow I feel connected to you [the group], but that I have all these eyes around us that I'm trying to ignore." She continued timorously, until I said to her that she was expressing with clarity the situation that all of us found ourselves.

> "Perhaps this is a confidence issue for you—taking a chance with your feelings and thoughts," I continued. Enid nodded and I did not wait for her verbal response. Given the time constraints and purpose of the group

demonstration, I wanted to keep an interpersonal as well as an intra-psychic focus. "Who could help you practise [taking a chance]?"

She turned across the circle to Carol, who had been Shari's "translator". "I've been looking at you, you've been quiet but very sensitive and involved. I've known you a bit from other conferences and always wanted to get closer. I wish I could change my seat."

Gabe volunteered, Enid voiced appreciation, and they began to rise. I intervened: "Could you both wait and you, Enid, put your feelings in words?" My request was ignored; Enid and Gabe were in motion and seats were exchanged. Rather than express disapproval or rebuke, I said in a resigned tone that brought laughter, "A rebellion! OK, this is your organisation, you do things your way."

With their chairs adjoining, Enid patted her receptive partner: "This feels so good to be sitting next to you." "More action!" I exclaimed, in mock disapproval. "Try to talk about what you're feeling. It's very positive, sisterly." A moving interlude passed between the two women, each shared a bit of personal history and then Gabe spoke with some pain: "I'm glad for both of you, but I'm sorry I moved so quickly. I'm too agreeable. I should have held my ground, not try so hard to take care of people."

Enid (getting ready to move): "You can have your seat back, I got what I needed."

I groaned: "Try to hold on to your seats. Let Gabe work on his feelings. [To Enid] You [also] seem very ready to take care of people."

Enid nodded tearfully, and she elaborated on her isolated, "help-ful" role her family of origin and her need for "sisters". The group continued with lively interactions and some personal revelations, punctuated by several of my interventions that brought laughter to the room.

Towards the end of the session, Ari and I reconnoitred affection-ately; Jimmy noticeably monitored our interaction and I turned to him while communicating indirectly to Ari.

"Ari stays too much in his head and we don't know what he really is feeling, but you show your feelings."

Ari acknowledged that he could be "bullheaded" and not communicate directly. "Maybe it is from my position and responsibility . . . and maybe it is my personality."

"Yeah, 'maybe'," I teased. [Laughter]

I was surprised when Jimmy turned on me, saying that I and the group had ignored one member, a young woman from an Asian country who had spoken haltingly at several intervals. She thanked him and struggled to explain that she did not feel ignored at all. Jimmy seemed to have an agenda, perhaps an identification with outgroups. But this was not the time or the place to launch an investigation into his personality or into the seeming alteration of his mood, and I asked whether anyone else was feeling ignored. The woman thanked me for understanding and not "pushing".

Several members reached out to Robert, who had become quiet. They said that his "intensity" had made a big impact, and helped the group. He said he had done something important for himself and was pleased to have volunteered. Shari stirred and as she began to mouth words in his direction. I spoke over her: "Don't start." She laughed appreciatively along with the room. Other people expressed thanks to each other and to me, and we closed with applause from the onlookers. A break followed, which extended so that we had an abbreviated debriefing and discussion before lunch.

The afternoon

Introduction of concepts. We again got a late start, and I attempted to move quickly through the lecture and discussion without sacrificing key ideas relating to the conference topic and, specifically, to the demonstration group. At some point, Jimmy volunteered that his mind was beginning to wander. "Not as alive as before."

I replied, somewhat defensively, "Sure, lectures aren't as gripping as experiential groups." I had planned on continuing my presentation when a second person called out, "It's time to move to the large group process", another person called out, and, from a fourth, "We already have."

The natives were restless, why the rebellion? And then I saw that it was the actual time that the large group experience was scheduled to begin. I felt there was no point in extending the lecture, and hoped that I would get a chance to round out concepts, but we moved in a different, and unsuspected, direction. My mode of presentation became the afternoon's focus.

Large group experience. The large group—the attendees now seated in several concentric circles—began with a round of compliments: the participants and onlookers agreed that the fishbowl was "totally engrossing". They found the use of humour striking, and surprising that it did not to detract from the give-and-take of the group process. From one participant: "I was aware of the audience, and the laughter, but I was totally engaged in the [demonstration] group." Other comments from fishbowl members included, "The humor seemed to make things safer"; "If people were attacking each other, or you, you made it no big deal"; "Same when people were doing things that you didn't want them to, like change seats or touch each other"; "You set up firm boundaries, like between Shari and Robert, but with confident ease"; "Even when you said things that could have been hurtful, they weren't."

From Warren, a senior therapist, "I was in one of your groups before, and when I came back, I was 'doing' you for a few weeks." From others: "Is it 'you' or some technique?" "Could I learn it?" [laughter] "Are you always 'on'?"

I said that I don't "do me" in my practice. Sometimes, being "on" means listening quietly, or connecting non-verbally. I reminded people that I had said I work more actively in a demonstration than in a long-term group to get, and keep, things moving. I stated my belief that the same principles and practices could be applied to any group.

Several demonstration group participants reported that humour was helpful but inconsequential in terms of what they experienced and received. I asserted that having a sense of humour is a plus—referring to Lou Ormont, Bernie Frankel, Jerry Gans, Scott Rutan, and other well known mentors who use humour artfully in their demonstration groups—and acknowledged that even in the most serious of my group sessions, a moment of humour is not unusual.

After a while, I enquired whether continuing to focus on "me" and "doing me" might be in the service of precluding other types of exchanges. The intervention received some agreement, mild interactions among participants, and then silence. One of the organisation's elders, Sidney, spoke aggrievedly: "What is going on here! What are we supposed to be doing? Is this a discussion, didactic, psychotherapy, a training group? "Yes! A group"; "It's in the programme"; "In the brochure", several called out, to laughter.

After another silence, Warren spoke up again:

"I don't mean to be critical, but I question whether your use of humour precludes other types of exchanges."

Given the previous discussion regarding the judicious use of humour and the testimony of some of the fishbowl members, Warren's "not meaning to be critical" felt like a condemnation, and I wondered to myself if Warren's "doing me" could involve "doing me in". Another senior member, Wilma, continued,

> "I too am wondering about your interventions. When people asked you for feedback, you slid away from answering them. I couldn't get a sense of what you were saying, what you were thinking. It wasn't very clear."

> "What would you like me to clarify?" I asked, surprised, since I had just attempted to clarify my use of humour.

> "I notice that you did not answer any of the questions addressed to you, and now again. Is that your style?" she continued.

I replied that I had just addressed some questions, and that I had invited and attended to questions during the morning's presentation, which I had designed as a discussion rather than a lecture. Wilma shook her head disapprovingly; I felt myself tensing up and being defensive, and tried to relax.

From Miriam, also a senior member:

> "Your style reminds me of the technique called 'fogging'. You don't argue or represent a contrary point of view, you sort of agree with the other person but not really."

I had not heard of the term or technique, and asked Miriam if she thought I was being foggy, fogging other people, in the sense of clouding their criticism. She tried to explain further, correcting my misunderstanding, and offering a compromise: legitimising the technique as a recognised type of therapeutic communication, but, at the same time, she seemed to be criticising it.

At one point, Wilma burst in.

> "You're doing it again."

> ""Fogging?" I said, somewhat bewildered. [Laugher]

> "You're not answering Miriam."

I explained that truly, I was not familiar with the term. I felt I was being direct and sincere, but I did not get a warm response from Wilma. "I feel like you are playing, circumventing me."

"What are *you* asking me?" I accented the "you" in an attempt for a more direct and feeling interaction.

"I'm just trying to understand," Wilma said, with an undertone of disapproval.

"Me too," I said. My tone was tinged with intonation, too, and it conveyed awareness that we were involved in an antagonist exchange.

"You really don't answer questions," Wilma reprimanded.

"Sometimes questions aren't questions," I replied pointedly.

Wilma: "I feel you are being critical."

"I am, as are you."

I had experienced an upsurge of cold anger toward Wilma, which I tempered internally before responding. But, while I wanted to be open to criticism, I did not want either to masochistically submit to, or shunt off, the reality of her implicit outrage. I believed I had succeeded in responding in a sufficiently matter-of-fact tone to invite further conversation. The room fell silent, as if waiting for Wilma's response, which she withheld.

Sidney, who had seemed aggrieved earlier with the idea of an experiential large group process, now spoke with unconcealed outrage:

"I am aware that there are many first time attendees, the young students. They haven't said anything and I am wondering what they are making of this and what kind of model this is for doing group therapy?"

There was no pretence in Sidney's remarks about not "meaning to be critical". His unambiguous condemnation, while unpleasant, clarified what I took to be a subgroup organised around attempts to bring down the leader, along with his "teachings". There was no need or reason to address him directly: either I was a danger to the profession of group psychotherapy, or I was not. I wondered if an onslaught would continue. Most probably, I would survive; I anticipated carrying away my own bad feelings—not for moral lapses, but for failing to represent myself adequately.

Sidney's remarks had unexpected consequences, for they succeeded in drawing out a large segment of the non-talkers. An older woman first spoke up:

> "I'm not a student, a newly minted therapist or anything else. But I am from out of town and I am so glad to be attending. I find the day riveting."

Now the students and new professionals spoke: "I am in the processes of being 'minted', and I am so glad you [the last speaker] disagreed with that gentleman [Sidney]." "I haven't understood everything, but I'm going to buy your books after the conference, if there are any left." [Laughter] Sidney's outrage mobilised a significant number of the previously quiet attendees to disagree with his appraisal.

To be exonerated—by the next generation in particular—felt sweet, too sweet.

I reined in my sense of triumph sufficiently to thank everyone for being open with their reactions and closed the segment by suggesting that after the scheduled break we could revisit and relate the afternoon's group process to the conference's theme.

Debriefing. During the final hour's debriefing and summarising of concepts, Miriam observed that I seemed different in the large group than during the morning's fishbowl. Her perception gave me a chance to clarify the difference between *resistance* and *rebellion*. The fishbowl typified the former: we made use of verbal and enactive byplay to encourage, unfold, and express emotional truth that had been unformulated, suppressed, dissociated, or repressed. The group process promoted thinking and feeling—tension, suspense, and surprise—and also, intimacy.

The large group exemplified rebellion: intersubjective tensions arose from differences in beliefs in how groups should operate. Who was this leader? It became all about "me". My therapeutic premises, methods, and personal qualities were at the centre of attention. Here was a nuclear idea ripe for development.

To extend the discussion, I invited anyone who had not verbally participated for most of the day to come forth if they thought they represented the mode of *refusal*. A senior member spoke up: Allan said that he did not feel a part of the day's activities and certainly did not feel clarity about the 3 *Rs*. I wondered if Allan was an envoy of the Sidney–Warren–Wilma–Miriam faction, and had been outraged. But his sincerity encouraged me to ask if I could treat his remarks as the substance of resistance, rather than primarily of rebellion or refusal. He assented.

I said I did not know if this interpretation applied to him, but that sometimes people feel envy towards those participating in the fishbowl or who successfully compete for attention, and enact their defeat by withdrawing. He might be inhibited and need a push. He followed my suggestion to engage directly with someone who had touched him emotionally; a warm exchange with the woman who asserted that she was not "newly minted" produced a marked difference in his posture and facial expression. When I suggested that he seemed happier with the conference and with me, he readily agreed. I reflected that people feel better when they get a chance to express themselves, for they satisfy a deep desire to "know" about their psychology, to learn about and reflect on what they think and feel.

We were approaching the end of the day, there was more to be said, and more people to be heard from, but little time. Another of the elders came forth and commented that the exchange with Wilma was one of the most powerful he had ever witnessed and the high point of the conference. "I know it couldn't have been easy for you, but it was truly a moment of 'mutual recognition'." I thanked him for his insight.

Attention focuses on the leader

In Shakespeare's *Henry IV* (1961), Glendower brags, "I can call spirits from the vasty deep". Hotspur taunts, "Why so can I, or so can any man; But will they come when you do call them?" Leadership is a "performance art"; its inherently social nature involves influencing others to follow, by establishing a direction for collective effort and managing the collective activities accordingly (Bennis, 2007; Zaccaro, 2007).

"Patients come to group because of the therapist's importance . . . as an object of cathexis and dependence" (Slavson, 1992, p. 179). "[The group conductor's] influence on the therapeutic group, quite particularly from unconscious sources, is hard to overestimate" (Foulkes, 1964, p. 179). While the therapist sits in the seat of power in the centre of the group process, he or she must earn this position. Likewise, a consultant is counted on to attract attendees, to stimulate and maintain their interest, and to draw enthusiasm for the host organisation and its future conferences.

In short order, I had to encourage sufficient cohesion to form a "group", really, several groups with shifting memberships: a small demonstration group and the bigger group of observers, preceded and followed by the large discussion group comprising all attendees. I had to establish norms and create a safe enough culture to take risks, to learn, and to seek help. Events occurring in both the larger and small groups were to be utilised for the benefit of the individuals and the groups themselves, to make the experience interesting and sufficiently compelling, to teach the basic principles promised by the conference's theme, and to demonstrate technique. To advance emotional truth as well as intellectual learning, painful, aggressive, even destructive processes were to be tolerated and contained, while averting dysfunction or negative consequences.

I had to deal with two somewhat overlapping and somewhat differentiated tasks. I wished to comply with the implicit organisational mandate to provide a good conference experience, but keeping the customers happy could not be at the expense of providing *authentic* (Billow, 2010c) small and large group experiences. My intention was to invite my hosts to consider different perspectives, to different types and levels of meaning, all represented by the person and activities of a presentational "me". To make the ideas I wished to develop with the group salient, learning had to invite an emotional experience for all present.

Activity of the group leader

A demonstration group is most interesting and successful when it models aspects of an actual group therapy session, which involves establishing and maintaining "as if" working alliances—the split between the observing and participating ego that marks the psychoanalytic enterprise (Sterba, 1934). A fishbowl requires establishing a double "as if": the volunteers interact "as if" they were in the "as if" group therapy situation—in front of colleagues.

Special opportunities for learning exist when the demonstration group is part of a larger workshop or conference that has an explicit purpose to study that group. For, the *in vivo*, unrehearsed fishbowl group magnifies interactional dynamics that, I believe, occur in all groups, but often remain ignored or unpublicised. However, certain risks are prominent as well, since the demonstration group is most often composed of a leader and participants who know and trust one another to varying degrees (or not at all)—professionals exposing themselves and interacting in view of colleagues.

The group process must quickly establish and safeguard appropriate boundaries and modes of interaction. Still, based on my various experiences as leader, observer, or member, what is most at risk to the vitality of the group is too little self–other exposure, rather than too much. I have no trouble sitting back and letting themes develop, but a slow opening group with a too passive leader heightens anxieties, distrust, and provokes a long interval of typical and all too predictable themes: how safe is this group? who is the leader? what should we do about the leader's lack of participation? Rather than being enriched by the "as if" dimension, associations tend to be reality based, literal, and flat, leading to pseudo-symbolic expressions, for example, metaphors that are self-conscious and contrived.

An interactive approach sets process going in unexpected ways and encourages associations, verbal and interpersonal. Even though the leader is perhaps more active in a demonstration group, the intensity and variety of interactions closely parallels a long-term group. When a demonstration group becomes bogged down, I usually do not wait too long for what could develop or ask why the group seems stalled. I actively intervene and attempt to focus on specific individuals, dyads, subgroups, or happenings. In this group, I said, "We only have an hour, we will get things going if we address each other, rather than 'the group'."

It is not unusual for attention to land first on the leader, of course. Indeed, I believe that it *always* does, no matter what else might be happening simultaneously. The members separately and collectively, openly and covertly, build, modify, destroy, and resurrect varying features of the idea of the leader.

I welcomed the controversy regarding the opening lecture, for it provided continuity and a bridge to the unknown waters of a soon to be cohering small group. This much became known about the leader: that he could tolerate the fishbowl participants attacking, praising, or questioning him. He would survive, respect the reality-based, literal level of communications, but also, through "personal action" (Sterba, 1981[1934], p. 305), function metapsychologically, calling attention to affective and symbolic levels, too.

I operated with forethought: some conscious awareness of my idea of the personal/therapeutic "me". Yet, I preserved a freedom to be spontaneous, appreciating that what I observed, said, and omitted saying had elements of the "not known", to be discerned during the day with the large group and afterwards, too. I monitored interactions throughout the demonstration group and inserted my presence, providing interpretative opinions, directives, even prohibitions. Unsurprisingly and thankfully—for who wants a merely compliant group?—some of them were ignored.

The demonstration group had become quickly immersed in creative processes of resistance, and I encouraged its varied symbolic derivatives and manifestations and, when possible, brought out underlying meaning. I was confident that the observers and participants could learn about "me" and develop their own ideas from this live, shared experience.

In reconvening as a large group, I—"me" as the leader—continued to be the focus, but controversy had turned contentious. Several of the conference attendees expressed outrage, and others were questioning and critical. While processes of resistance were not absent from the fishbowl, rebellion and refusal predominated during the afternoon session. Leadership required altering my communicative style and the nature of interventions to address shifting interests: that is, to respond to questions about my leadership and my character.

Pathways of group process: resistance, rebellion, and refusal

Resistance, Rebellion, and Refusal in Groups: The 3Rs conceptualised group organisation and activity as a series of pathways—each with moves and countermoves—directed to express, redirect, modify, or block the search for emotional truth. Traditionally, all efforts to forestall or counter psychotherapeutic work have been captured under the umbrella term, resistance. However, the assumptions, methods, and goals of therapeutic work may be challenged metapsychologically, philosophically, ethically, pragmatically, and politically. Hence, rebellion and refusal.

Resistance. I assume that when individuals risk volunteering for a fishbowl group, even when partially exhibitionistic, they want, like Robert, "to get something personal". What could that be other than a metapsychological encounter with self and others and the opportunity to learn about it? An "as if" frame that simulates group psychotherapy allows members to become symbolic foils, playing off one another and the leader. As ideas emerge, they may be mere intimations, "foggy" and vague and not fully translated into verbal language. The putting-into-words process often displays its own limitations, functioning best as poetry, condensing and refracting meaning, opening up rather than resolving discourse.[43] I thought the fishbowl reached those objectives.

For some observers, however, my use of language became a source of irritation, and perhaps contributed to outrage. Still, the fishbowl became emotionally gripping, and the volunteers entered into our minds, both as themselves and as mythic representatives—metapsychological archetypes—of various aspects of our social–personal selves: Shari, the invasive rebel; Robert, the angry one; Ari, the challenger/son; Carol, the mother; Enid, the sister; Gabe, the sacrificial lamb; and Jimmy, the contact hungry, ambivalent baby.

Rebellion. While the volunteers in the morning's demonstration group wanted to learn about themselves via the leader, the participants in the afternoon's large group wanted to learn about the leader and his theories and methods of leadership. Our process came to centre on the question: what kind of group leader is this and is his leadership acceptable? The interpretative approach I first tried— suggesting that exclusive interest about me might be defensive and self-protective, precluding member–member exchanges—did not move the group and educational process. Rather, eventual silence and the outburst from Sydney, "What's going on here!" heightened attention to my leadership and, even more, to myself as leader.

Several anonymous members unceremoniously hushed Sydney, but I suspect that his indignation emboldened the rebellion that followed. The most vocal challengers were Warren, characterising my use of humour as excluding other types of interventions, Wilma, evaluating me as not being clear, "sliding away" from providing feedback or answering questions, Miriam, portraying my style as "fogging", and finally, Sydney again, denouncing me for leading youth astray. We had entered into an interval of tension that arose, although only in part, from differences in beliefs about how experiential groups should function. More to the point was the developing nuclear idea of "me", my therapeutic–personal self, and I had to tolerate, respect, and make sense of the unfolding insinuations and accusations directed to my character and personality.

I felt that dealing with the rebellion as legitimate and attempting to explain myself in terms of theory and technique—rather than interpret the veiled as well as undisguised attempts at personal assassination—might relax the opposing forces sufficiently to engage mutually and thoughtfully. Here was an opportunity to clarify misapprehensions, exchange ideas, and expand the network of participation. People could weigh in with their opinions and emotional reactions. We could agree or not, but, one hopes, we would maintain a respectful interest in each other, and all learn by our discourse.

Refusal. For Sydney and Wilma most conspicuously, an experiential large group, or, possibly, my method of leading it, was unappealing and not acceptable as a vehicle for learning. When they failed to sow anarchy (a destructive form of rebellion; see Tubert-Oklander, 2010), they withdrew and refused to engage. We could not establish productive links, and, perhaps responding to their adamancy, no other group member even attempted to bridge to them directly and sympathetically. Wilma's refusal was all the more fearsome for being cloaked. I could not clarify or answer any query to her satisfaction. "Sometimes questions are not questions," I had retorted, pointedly confronting the reality of her unyielding criticality. I invited her to continue, but did not pursue the matter further. Our refusal was mutual, our impasse recognised, and, while not resolved, it was available as an emotional experience for the whole group to think about.

Oratory and pragmatics of the presenter

The presenter—group leader or therapist—may vary not only the content of his or her remarks according to group context and process, but also its manner of expression. Bion (1987) noted that "the analyst has to be an artist – he has to make constructions of what is going on" (p. 76). Apropos is Nietzsche's aphorism, "We have art so that we shall not be destroyed by the truth" (in Schneider, 2010, p. 521). This suggests the importance of mastery of oratory and pragmatics (Watzlawick, Bavelas, & Jackson, 1967), that, in the context of psychotherapy, are artistic devices utilised to represent painful truth. As one must distinguish art from artifice, likewise oratory from mere rhetoric, and pragmatic play and humour from manic defence.

While the overarching objective remains to encourage thoughtful discourse, the group leader's specific tactics differ according to the pathway of group process—resistance, rebellion, or refusal. In my opinion, whether functioning as presenter or therapist, one needs to speak in down-to-earth vernacular, convey compassion, and avoid sounding omniscient or oracular. A judicious use of humour communicates a broadened view: "a way of accepting oneself and the world with neither undue guardedness nor pretentious standing on high places" (Poland, 1990, p. 198).[44] Ideally, what the presenter says, and how it is said, should represent personal risk, and open the way for mutual discovery.

In opting for a discussion rather than formal lecture with "PowerPoint" or printed hand-out, I strove to introduce myself as a playful thinker rather than a knower, to allow for spontaneity and interaction, and to encourage the large group to think with me and on their own, and for us to learn together. However, during the afternoon's large group, I discovered that some individuals had found it provocative that my responses and rejoinders were not always direct and conclusive. But, questions are not only questions: they may open up, close, or foreclose channels of communication.

So, even my introduction created controversy and perhaps began to stimulate outrage. However, it succeeded in establishing the presenter as approachable, and volunteers rushed to join the fishbowl. Without much explicit prompting, they began to reveal, take risks, and explore relationships. For example, Shari opened by claiming to be a "rebel", but she did not follow the pathway of rebellion, as I use the term, as she did not challenge the nature of the group or my methods. Although Enid and Gabe rebelled against my request to stay seated, they adhered to the therapeutic directive to put their actions into emotionally meaningful language. Ari's words, that he joined the fishbowl "to save the situation" were patently false; their import was in what the words did not say, but revealed—intentionally and unintentionally—about his psychology.

Constructive processes of resistance were in gear. While not always obediently following my directives, the participants were co-operating by symbolising: thinking about and deepening their experience. We engaged in metaphor, irony, and verbal and enactive play,[45] all of which served to generate and articulate multiple levels of meaning, personal, interpersonal, historical, and transferential–countertransferential.

In a new group, particularly, the participants might not immediately understand the intended meanings of the leader's interventions, but the discourse goals must be perceived as caring and helpful. Incongruities and discontinuities should be interesting, relevant, and sufficiently safe to the observers to be enjoyable and stimulate curiosity. I used a variety of communicative devices, including indirection, emphasis, humour, sarcasm, and irony, to call attention to multiple and contradictory meanings and motivations. These interventions were in the service of generating a group culture attuned to verbal, paraverbal (e.g., tone, pitch, pacing, sighs, and other utterances), and non-verbal (e.g., posture and gesture) expressions of meaning: to the nuances of self-presentation and self–other recognition, to the metapsychology of what is said and what might be meant.

My intent was to attack (deconstruct) a thought, not the thinker, and to call attention to, and stimulate, deeper connections. For instance, gently mocking[46] Ari's professed reason for joining the group—"I like the way you come in to 'save the situation'"—I "duelled" with Ari on his own symbolically oedipal terms, which both explained his aggression and made it safe. My dubious "Are you?" to Enid's protestation of being "totally confused" suggested also the opposite—that she was not. It freed her to express other thoughts. Her clear if timorous exposition of our perplexing fishbowl situation served as an educative nuclear idea describing key qualities of both the small and large group. When teasingly cautioned against limiting herself as "group translator", Carol vowed with relief, "to resign from that role". And, finally, ironic humour may reflect sympathy with the thinker struggling with a difficult thought, as did my "Yeah, 'maybe'," when Ari acknowledged the possibility of possessing a "bullheaded" personality.

Ambiguity, indirection, and self/group-referential metapsychological play have limits, however. When the demonstration group communications threatened to lose "as if" qualities, I worked to ensure safe boundaries, resolute but still with a playful attitude when possible. So, when Shari continued to pursue the reddening Robert, I gestured to him and said "Back up", and relaxed both combatants (and presumably others) by humorously turning the aggression on to me: "Whoever acts like a therapist is going to get killed." Jimmy confirmed that I had made it feel "safe . . . I was scared that you would let things get out of control" and he felt secure enough to attack me for my seeming preference for Robert.

More than occasionally I made whole- and sub-group references (as in the group's wish to "kill" anyone acting as therapist) and directed group interactions ("Connect to another person directly"; "Let's get other people involved"; "Try to hold on to your seats") and also, tentative, partial interpretations to individual members, for example, Enid's confidence issues, Carol's role as care-taker, and Ari's adversarial intellectualisations. My interventions were not intended to concentrate on particular nuclear ideas, but the opportunities were there, if the group chose to develop any of them further.

The criticisms that emerged in the large group—that my humour precluded other group interactions, of being unclear in my thinking, unreceptive to feedback, and a questionable group leader—did not jibe with my own evaluation or the feedback from the fishbowl volunteers. I waited to discover where the criticisms would take us, and to assess whether they related to personal and/or philosophical differences, and to dynamics emerging from the large group as well.

"A jest's prosperity lies in the ear / Of him that hears it, never in the tongue / Of him that makes it" (Shakespeare, 1961, *Love's Labour's Lost*, V, ii). Apparently, not every observer understood or liked the rationales for indirect, incongruous, or playful oratory, or at least my use of it. Some seemed outraged by my illuminations of group leadership, no matter the group context in which they were delivered and how they seemed to be received by others.

I have quoted Nietzsche's aphorism earlier in this volume: "every profound spirit needs a mask" (in Trilling, 1971, p. 119). Presenters and volunteers (similarly to therapist and group members) wear masks: that is, roles that are social and mutually contracted, and which allow the potentiality for profound discourse not otherwise possible. Within their respective roles, the participants may bear and bear witness to the struggle to develop and communicate truth.

In my judgement, a comedic mask—which did not preclude other therapeutic masks as well—provided entry into the fishbowl to operate quickly and effectively in establishing trust and safety, and to encourage group processes that involved uncovering and exploring the symbolic processes and defensive manoeuvres that define resistance. I took authorisation to bring to awareness some of what would otherwise stay inhibited, suppressed, repressed, or dissociated.

In the large group, in which processes of rebellion and refusal became prominent, strategies using play and humour would probably be perceived as self-protective and inauthentic. Different oratorical skills were called for. The group centred on a consideration of my qualities as leader and my modes of pursuing the goals of the group conference, as well as of the demonstration and large group. I had to speak with a voice of authority—not to represent "establishment" Truth—but to discover, clarify, and present my own truths, without being polemical, unduly defensive, or unreceptive in the face of dissension or even outright rejection.

I attempted to deal with criticisms, disapproval, even attacks, by encouraging their expression, and discussing them seriously, and certainly, not interpret them as projections or manifestations of anxiety. Still, I had limits in what I was willing to tolerate as legitimate challenge. Certain communications, particularly from Wilma and Sidney, had anarchic goals: annihilating any truth-value of my ideas, sowing doubts about my moral fibre, and, ultimately, undermining the morale of all participants.

In the demonstration group, the symbolic processes, derivatives of resistance, were salient and could be productively brought forth: Ari's criticisms of the leader seemed playful and merely metaphorically murderous, and I responded in kind. He expressed that which exists in every member's mind: would the leader be a safe enough figure to duel with? Could I withstand criticism and contain aggression that potentially could be directed towards other members?

In contrast, I found no way to temper Wilma's outrage, to quell her subterranean assaults, and enter into a constructive dialogue or group discourse. To accomplish the containing function and to protect the integrity of the whole group as well as myself, I felt I had to meet Wilma's aggression with my own. Sidney's attacks—cloaked in moral righteousness—seemed to be met adequately by other members, including the subgroup of the formerly quiet who spoke up and were able to express aspects of their own psychology. Via oratory and pragmatics, the nuclear idea of "me" had extended discourse across the *experiential, symbolic, affective,* and *metapsychological* domains, increasing participation and bringing vitality and depth to the group process.

Diplomatic uses of humour

My oratory, interspersed with indirect speech acts marked by play and humour, served to establish leadership, make manifest and deal with struggles for power, status, dominance, and submission, and to reach specific goals: discovering and transmitting emotional knowledge publicly and safely. I had the ambition also to deconstruct certain polemic ideas and "establishment" tendencies. Meredith (1892, p. 89) wrote in his ode "To the Comic Spirit", humour serves to "darest probe / Old Institutions and Establishments, . . . / For what their worth; and questionly prod / for why they stand upon a racing globe".

In the large group as well as in the fishbowl, I needed to work with and encourage the participants to trust going beyond rules of logic and conventionality that hamper emotional "truthing". A judicious use of humour could stimulate a "bisociation" (Koestler, 1964) of ideas, forming links and associations among anxiety-producing concepts.[46]

Nuclear ideas often arise from and produce thoughts and feelings often judged as irrational, "not nice", and socially unacceptable. As Freud (1905c) explained, humour's power derives at least partially from the revelation of often unpleasant and disavowed contents. As an indirect or sublimated mode of expressing sexuality and aggression, warded-off libidinal and destructive impulses to reach conscious awareness with force and momentary pleasure (Christie, 1994).

Humor expresses a kindly aspect of the superego, comforting an intimidated ego by repudiating reality with illusion (Freud, 1927d). In facilitating the overcoming of social inhibitions and prohibitions, humour is potentially relieving and soothing, fostering both psychic integration and group bonding. The "comic spirit" creates "the sacred chain / Of man to man" (Meredith, 1892, p. 69). Indeed, in the fishbowl specifically, humour fostered the playful "as if", yet truthful nature of our interactions that mirror the illusionary quality of the therapeutic process.

Humour serves as an information-gathering device, for laughter— or its absence—provides feedback. Given that laughter is predominantly an involuntary response, eliciting laughter allows the leader to "mindread" mental states of other individuals and determines "cooperator value" (Jung, 2003): that is, their status as group members (Hewitt, 2002). To quote the playwright, Tom Stoppard, "I think of laughter as the sound of comprehension" (in Singer, 2011, p. 27). Many of the communications during the morning's lecture/discussion and fishbowl were greeted with laughter and reciprocated, and I concluded these interactions were not merely amusing, but contributing to achieving metapsychological as well as diplomatic goals, synchronising social knowledge and identifying those who share in it.

However, the afternoon's large group painfully demonstrated how laughter in itself is not a marker of humour's success or failure. Humour can exist without laughter, and *vice versa*, since laughter can be triggered by nervousness, discomfort, or deference to a speaker (Giles & Oxford, 1970), or even as a default response (Zemach, 1959).

Humour can be double-edged: at once group forming and group excluding (Meyer, 2000). Likewise, it can both trigger outrage and disarm it. Humour identifies those amused as sharing the linked knowledge set. More ambiguous are those who laugh but who might not be amused. My oratory contributed to group organisation, allegiance to the presenter, and to the symbolic play and moving enactments displayed in the fishbowl. It also stimulated a dissenting outgroup—those who did not wish to submit to me as the leader: my methods of pursuing interactional meaning, or to consider the ideas that I came to represent.

The idea of the leader may trump the leader's ideas

I have described a presentation to a professional organisation of group psychotherapists. I offered "me", my way of thinking and clinical functioning, to this pre-existing community that had its own culture, methods, and myths. Any time a culture, and guardians of that culture, are challenged to think and experience in new ways, the challenger, outrageous or not, may be met with outrage.

The use of indirect speech acts, including humour, changes group context and process. Some perceived my oratory as positive, and perhaps outrageous, but it provoked outrage in others. It might be that my way as the invited presenter, my playful style specifically, further infuriated the disgruntled. Perhaps they felt they were not being taken seriously; certainly, we had difficulty meeting on mutually acceptable terms. In being "me", I became a primary focus, invigorating but, for some, fogging with outrage, the overarching nuclear ideas of the conference's topic—loving, hating, and curiosity: group processes of resistance, rebellion, and refusal.

CHAPTER ELEVEN

The group therapist is "that guy": organising speech

In the development of new group, and as an element of any self-reflecting group, the leader employs and encourages the use of language to move process from its underlying basic assumptiveness to the symbolised and articulated emotional experience from which develops nuclear ideas. The therapist stirs up and restructures mental space, disrupting the members in their fantasy relationship to the group as an encompassing maternal object. Hence, the therapist asserts a "third", or oedipal, vertex, expressed through initiating and inviting verbal intercourse. Equipped with a powerful organ of speech, he or she necessarily obtrudes, serving as a "phallus" (Lacan),[48] whether or not sexualised explicitly in images and verbalisations of the group members.

The group situation

The training group—consisting of professionals from different disciples attached to a private hospital, along with non-affiliated individuals—had been working together for nearly two years in a series of two-day weekday formats, with a rotating local staff and the occasional consultant. For this series of lectures, experiential groups, and supervisory workshops, seventeen individuals—twelve women and five men—were in attendance. Although I did not know it at the workshop's initiation, a subset had just returned from a European group conference where they had attended small, median, and large groups.

I was introduced by the hospital's director, a vibrant and erudite woman, older than I, who also served as director of the programme, core instructor, and supervisor. My task was to explicate and demonstrate principles from my writings, and, specifically, devote attention to the model of combined psychotherapy (Billow, 2009, 2010a). The director was concerned that the programme's candidates were failing to introduce group treatment into their practices. "They don't want to separate from their role as students."

After a preliminary lecture, I raised issue with the placement of the director, her seat currently adjoining mine. The room became silent, until she declared that she would position herself outside the circle for the weekend's duration. That did not go over well with the candidates: "You would still be in the group." "I would feel watched and uncomfortable." "I would not know what you were thinking."

"Sometimes when there are more attendees and we break up into two groups, I join one, so I'll stay," she offered. I said that this did not solve our problem: "You remain 'the director', even in a member role." She responded in good spirit, "Listen, this is your weekend; I will do whatever you want. I will leave the room." "That's not fair either," I demurred, "You wanted to attend and get something too."

"Don't worry about me!" I could not help but worry, and told her so, ". . . and besides, we'd miss you."

"I'm a big girl, I'll stay and we'll work it out." That seemed the best option, and we marked the start of the first of three ninety-minute process groups and one case conference, all of which I abbreviate.

Experiential session 1

A hiccup broke an interval of silence, which was ignored, followed by meandering comments about how to begin. I said that we had begun, and had assumed the hiccup to be a commentary about what had transpired, as well as what might. "No, I'm sorry, my stomach, go on." The speaker, Theresa, was a noticeably anxious figure, seated in a chair pulled back from the circle. After a few minutes, she bolted from the room.

"Theresa does that often at our meetings, she comes in and out," a member informed me. "She keeps her seat back, answers her phone."

"Yes, but she's a very good writer and thinker," the director interjected.

Theresa returned and the former discussion of how to proceed resumed.

I addressed Theresa: "Are you OK?" She seemed surprised when I informed her that her absence had been the subject of concern. "I had another endo [endoscopy]—almost couldn't make it, GERD [gastro-oesophageal reflux disease] acts up bad."

Apparently Theresa's news of the cause of her spasmodic gastric distress was a revelation to other members. "I've been uneasy about initiating a dialogue with you." Now they enquired about her seating position and phone behaviour.

"Well, my ex-husband threatens me—I have an order of protection. One of my kids still has a need to see him—but they're all [her children] big successes. So it is not all bad. I'm going to shut up now."

The director attempted to support Theresa by encouraging her to talk further, about what was positive. I reassured the director that Theresa and I were doing fine and did not need her help.

"I'm expressing my opinion," she protested.

"No therapeutic opinions, just your feelings," I chastised.

"Not if I don't want to," she replied.

I said, "That goes for all of us," which received a warm laugh from her and others.

Group members spoke of "digesting difficult material" and the danger of "ruminating." Carola said that in the group she was conducting, she had no choice but to ruminate. Out of frustration with her co-therapist, she withdrew into her own thoughts. She did not want to ruminate or withdraw here. I commented, alluding to the director: "I don't think the issue of co-therapy is settled in our group," which brought laughter. "You're the boss," the director exclaimed, and I nodded dubiously.

Several interesting issues were raised as the participants caught up with each other and related to me, and then, Lukas broke in:

"I need to talk about feelings related to something sexual. Something happened during the [recent European] Conference. I felt invaded. I have a lot of important feelings relating to sexuality to talk about in this group."

Michael and Carola encouraged him to go on. I said I was not comfortable with talking about sexual feelings so early in our workshop. Some members concurred, but Michael was disappointed: "I guess we will talk about something else if you want." I clarified that we could talk about sex, but that first I wanted to talk about talking about sex. I wanted to understand more about "why now?" and if the topic felt sufficiently safe for other members. No one would benefit if Lukas became the target of voyeuristic curiosity.

> Lukas: "Yes, that's how I felt in the other group [at the Conference], like I was being abused, almost like a rape. I felt I was unprotected and could not find my voice."
>
> Pierra, trembling: "I was in your group. I had a terrible headache the next day, didn't know why. Could not talk. I did not know what happened [in that group] until now." She began to cry, and as did Lukas and Rebecca. The director asked Theresa to get the tissues, which were near her, and then began to address Pierra. "No co-leading," I interjected, "let's give Pierra a chance to talk."
>
> Pierra protested: "No, I can't." I maintained focus on her, encouraging her to take her time. "I grew up alone. My parents worked hard and we did not have time to talk, too afraid, too, of my father." She thanked us and gathered herself together, while Rebecca recounted a similar story of her family life.

Lukas declared that he felt clarified and supported by the members who had spoken up. When he persisted in revisiting the Conference group and began once more to describe how upset he was by "a guy's actions", I redirected him to consider how he was connecting to "this group" and to me particularly. This was the first time had Lukas mentioned the gender of the individual, and it remained unclear whether the man was a group member or the leader. But, I speculated to the group: "Sooner or later, I will become 'that guy'."

Afternoon case conference

Sarah, a social worker on the hospital's staff, had been requested by the clergy from a nearby fundamentalist community to work with a female youth group sent from their villages for education. There were, however, severe strictures on her leadership. Only a female co-therapist from the sect was permitted to talk to the teenagers directly, and, further, a male clerical representative had to be present. "Any hint of challenge to their authority or point of view and I will be dismissed."

The director helpfully turned our attention to the mores of the religious community, with which she had expertise, but which left Sarah out of the relational equation. After a while, I redirected, suggesting that, for now, we focus on the psychology and therapeutic options of Sarah, the appointed leader.

Sarah reported feeling confused, worried, even frightened: how could she function effectively and have a voice without being dismissed? She had established quasi-therapeutic relationships with each of the potential group members and with the co-therapist, who seemed to share her dread of the students' re-entry into their respective communities, which were known for female oppression and violence.

So, non-verbal, but articulated bonds existed, I suggested. Sarah's protruding presence, being a mature woman from the "outside" world, modelled and conveyed an enduring—although unspoken—message of female empowerment. Under the Elder's watchful eyes, Sarah could function as a "double agent", covertly containing her constituents, nurturing them while also stimulating their cognitive–sexual development.

I thought to myself: a better allegory for our workshop could not be scripted. Like Sarah, I was an outsider invited to educate and influence. To function with *integrity*, both of us had to be willing to enter in the physical and mental space of our respective group cultures, stirring up the constituents in purview of their administrators. It was late in the day, there were other concepts to review, and I decided that it was not the time to make it all about "me". Introducing that nuclear idea via an examination of parallel process between two ostensible leaders and our respective groups could wait, to be tested later.

Experiential session 2

Theresa reported that she had stayed the night in town, "at an expensive hotel, and slept like a baby." She reassured us: "That's not all I'm getting." She had been taking extensive notes the day before and gestured to them.

> Lea: "I found your lectures yesterday very helpful . . . but I can't understand your books." People laughed, and she became embarrassed and apologetic. "I don't feel very smart."

A swell of members attested to similar "baby" reactions, which I took as efforts to assuage Lea's (and their own) discomfort and also as an invitation for growth: "Back off, she doesn't need protection."

This was the first time Lea had spoken, and another new voice then cried out, "How do you know?" Hilde led a foray of protests and reassurances, and, when Lea began to cry, Hilde said I was "very nervy!" I registered Hilde's disapproval but maintained my enquiry.

> Lea (to me): "Thank you for saving me, giving me a place to talk. I was quiet because I was afraid of hurting your feelings. I might be dyslexic, that's why I might have trouble reading you." I reflected that a fear of hurting could make one quiet and dyslexic. Other members extended the conversation with Lea and some spoke for the first time.

> At one point, Lukas turned to Michael:

> "You've been unusually quiet."

> "Have I? I've been watching and learning. [To me] I like the way you operate."

> Lukas concurred: "I had a weak father and it is great to see a man handle a powerful woman, my father never could deal with my mother."

I wondered to myself if he was talking only about the Director, or also about some or all of the women who had or had yet to come forth. The theme of fathers, strong, weak, feared, or inadequate had intense currency among the members, and personal histories unfolded and absorbed our interest.

> Lea spoke up again: "I miss [the director]. I was the only child, in the middle; both parents were powerful. I didn't want either to be hurt."

> "I'm here, doing fine. I'm enjoying this a great deal. I speak when I want to," the director reassured her.

Several members expanded on Lea's theme of being "stuck" in the middle in their families, past and present, and not wanting to "cause trouble". Now was the time, I thought, to recall yesterday's case conference, and Sarah's predicament: how to cope with the Elders while preserving her own mind and asserting her own voice (even if nonverbally conveyed). I reintroduced the dynamic between the director and "me", but while people seemed to understand the analogy, the nuclear idea that it represented—or my way of presenting it—did not have verbal traction.

People remained fearful of "hurt", "troubling" reactions—internal as well as interpersonal—in verbally approaching their fantasies and ideas relating to our unavoidable coupling. Still, while they refused to openly consider such complexities, the participants were observing and interfacing with "me". Models of the container–contained were being played out on varying oedipal and pre-oedipal symbolic levels, and I had no doubt that the attendees were forming opinions and coming to tentative conclusions regarding their leader.

During the lunch break, the director reminded me to review the concept of combined individual–group psychotherapy, which I did during the lecture–discussion. A coffee break preceded the final process group, with an exchange that I found fortuitous, but not as I had anticipated.

Experiential session 3

Almost all the members had spoken and I invited Max to join in. He haltingly complied:

> "Maybe the group is too big, and I like it if there is a smaller group. But I have been listening and getting a lot from this."

> "Yes, but you have more to say," I pursued.

"Let the fellow be!" Hilde cried out, playful but also serious. I noted that she seemed comfortable in taking me on. Since she talked to me directly, I did likewise. I explained—as if to her alone—that during the coffee break, Max and I had spoken, and I had asked him if I could reference us to model how integrating dyadic communication into the group situation might work.

> Max interjected: "I told Richard that I felt inhibited. I'm not a regular therapist yet. I'm in group therapy. But I get a lot from these meetings. I pay attention and have been very involved."

This seemed to satisfy the members and Max, and the subject of combined psychotherapy was dropped. Lukas returned to the topic of his conference group and the lingering effects of the sexually aggressive man. Other voices joined in. Hilde: "I was there too. I didn't speak up yesterday, which made me feel like I was [again] being a co-conspirator." The director volunteered that she was puzzled, since the conference has a fine reputation and she did not hear from her colleagues about anything unusual or traumatic transpiring.

I, too, remained confused about the European conference group, but which, despite being stimulated and curious, I did not want to make our focus. What was happening in our group was of greater concern. I persisted, but my enquiry met with silence that became uncomfortably long, and when I asked about it, longer still. The group seemed frozen and I seemed to have no options but to wait it out.

Lea, who yesterday had expressed a belief in her learning disability, finally and tentatively came forth.

> "Maybe people are frightened by how you approached Max during the coffee break and pressured him."
>
> Hilde (to Max, concerned and quite angry): "He was picking on you!"
>
> Max: "No, it was fine, really, not at all. I need to be brought out."
>
> Lea: "But the way he did it!"
>
> Michael (as if forgiving me, and explaining): "We do things differently here."

While I did not comprehend Lea and Michael's perception of my "way" of conducting, Max did:

> "No, *he* didn't! *I* approached *him*."

Apparently, many people had shared a petrifying misapprehension of my "doing" Max, that is, of accosting him in the vestibule and pressuring him to verbally expose himself.

> Hilde (to Max, with relief): "Did you!"

Max then divulged more than I would have ever relayed regarding his "social anxiety" and insomnia.

> "That's why I always yawn in these sessions . . . I apologised and explained to Richard, and he just asked if he could invite me to say something—anything. I needed him to bring me in and I have done it! I won't leave without having spoken up!"

Another silence had descended on the group, now one of relief and relaxation. A fantasy of sexual abuse (by forced verbal intercourse) had been covertly transmitted among the members—felt, believed, responded to with an intimidated silence, and now, dissipated. And I could say confidently and with satisfaction, "So, I have become 'that guy'."

Hilde: "I wasn't going to be a co-conspirator and stay quiet when some-one gets treated badly. I did that in my family and in the other [confer-ence] group—not with you."

I took her remarks as a compliment to us both, told her so, and she agreed. Several others thanked Lea and Hilde for speaking up, and Lukas refocused on Max.

"I've noticed your yawning—not only during this workshop, and wondered if we threatened you."

Lea: "I wondered if you were like me, feeling that you weren't able to understand."

The experiential group was ending the way it began: attending to a member whose paraverbal behaviour—yawning—begged for naming and group reference.

The use of language establishes "me"

Lacan (1977[1958], pp. 43–44) held that the psychoanalyst

knows better than anyone else . . . [to take] an everyday event for a fable addressed to whoever hath ears to hear . . . even the sigh of a momentary silence [may stand] for the whole lyrical development it replaces.

To the extent that this is true, the group leader must use such knowledge—relying on training, empathic intuition, and reverie—to listen for and unpack into discursive language the "lyric" of silent glances, hiccups, yawns, and the copious indications of covert and submerged relationships, sexual and pre-sexual, particularly as they involve the leader.

I was not imported for, or interested in, presenting a model of co-therapy, yet next to me—in physical and emotional proximity—was the esteemed director of the hospital and its group programme, to boot, a gracious host. In assessing the situation, I concluded that an immediate and ongoing leadership task was to loosen, without severing, the powerful non-verbal bonds between the director and each of us. Exposing our predicament to language, and front and centre (the *double entendres* are intended), I would also be asserting an independent presence.

Having an affectionate and respectful rapport with the director gave me verbal and also enactive leverage. Also, I have worked on *diplomatic* (Chapter Four) skills—expressing power and preference— with a certain class of problematic participants. I am referring to people like us: practitioners and students of group psychotherapy.

Calling attention to our relationship could be used to advantage, providing understanding and enhancing meaning. To free members sufficiently to "name", that is, to put words to an authentic experience, diplomatic limit setting was required, along with an implicit invitation for challenge and dissent. When I playfully chastised the director for "helping" me with Theresa: "No therapeutic opinions, just your feel- ings," she spiritedly retorted, "Not if I don't want to." She would surrender gamely, but not masochistically submit (Ghent, 1990).

In directing and, at times, quieting our feisty director, I believe that we were both aware that there would be consequences, anticipated as well as unforeseen. Her influence on the group's history and culture could not be disentangled from whatever would eventuate. It had been the custom for her to attend and participate in previous work- shops; voluntary absence or exile would only amplify her presence in fantasy. I thought that the best option was to call attention to, and verbally inspect, the elephant in the room: the director's relationship to the group, and, specifically, to its invited presenter and designated, if temporary, leader.

Theresa's hiccup expressed but could not discharge, disgorge, or expel the discomfort with which we began. Neither could the hiccup be ignored, or treated as if localised solely in the body of the member. Certainly, the paraverbalisation marked my quandary, and, given their involvement in the discussion regarding the placement of the director, had saliency for all group members. I was an unfamiliar leader, coupled with the symbiotic figure of maternal and basic assumptive dependency—the director. (She had informed me that certain capable students could stay with her "forever" without progressing into being group therapists.) The anticipated and ongoing process of any experiential group has hiccups: upsetting intervals of confusion, ambivalence, and pain. Our situation, while intriguing and challeng- ing, was particularly unsettling and with risk, for it added an unusu- ally intense Oedipal dimension to the work as the invited presenter.

While hiccups cannot be eliminated, they can be relieved by empathic actions, thoughts, and words. Naming Theresa's hiccup as a commentary on my leadership, applicable to what had, as well as what might, transpire, normalised the speaker and localised her speech act as a group event. "Are you OK?" provided further opportunity for Theresa to demystify her spasmodic group behaviour.

Seemingly for the first time, she became a dialogic figure of compassion and identification. Others associated to the problem of "digesting difficult material". I could not wonder to myself if all present wanted to be babies of the director (I included myself). Remaining naïve, ruminating, or withdrawing, such as in the presence of a difficult peer or co-therapist (Carola's predicament in her group, and, by extension, in ours), remained defensive options. While the director labelled me as "boss", the matter of co-therapy—how I would negotiate our pairing—could not be easily or fully assimilated.

Indeed, it was the non-conscious that reigned as boss (Giraldo, 2012), speaking through bodily reactions, paraverbalisations, symbols and enactments, and stimulating unexpected associations and ideas. However far we seemed to stray from the topic, I remained aware that probably all of us remained "unsettled" by the presence of two leaders, and the sexual and pre-sexual fantasies that the pairing stimulated (Bion, 1961). As always, I attempted to remain alert for derivatives of a nuclear idea of "me", which would need to be developed in language and referenced across its four domains (experiential, affective, symbolic, and metapsychological).

I surmised that Lukas was unconsciously talking about this idea—the leadership pair and my role specifically—when he interjected: "I need to talk about feelings related to something sexual. Something happened during the [European] conference. I felt invaded." This session being paramount, I was concerned that he—and others—had been invaded by my presence, and that also, like Theresa and Carola, Lukas naïvely might be sacrificially offering himself up. Volunteering for another abusive exposure—a regressive group enactment—would not aid Lukas, or others, in finding the multi-toned "lyric" (Lacan) of non-conscious.

Earlier in the first experiential session, and prior to it, we had talked about talking. We agreed to limit the Director's options: "No therapeutic opinions, just your feelings," I had iterated. Her good-naturedly rebellious response, "Not if I don't want to", and my rejoinder, "That goes for all of us", demonstrated and provided a message of safety to the whole group. Premature or imposed talk could reinforce rather than resolve trauma, being an enactment and not effective naming. As a containing leader, I had to locate and localise sexuality (Nitsun, 2006; Nitzgen, 2009), that is, to discover its relevance to the members in the here-and-now group context. But to reinforce a message of safety, I insisted that first we needed "to talk about talking about sex."[49]

Lukas reported having felt, in the antecedent conference group, "abused, almost like a rape . . . unprotected and could not find my voice." For Pierra, symbolic expression had remained silent, expressed in the symptom of her trembling body: "I had a terrible headache the next day, didn't know why." The web of communication expanded from the unarticulated and bodily, referring to both this group and the conference group, to the verbally symbolised—familial, projective, and transferential levels of discourse (Foulkes, 1971, p. 212). Pierra: "We did not have time to talk, too afraid, too, of my father." Pierra and Lea each expressed gratitude for "giving me a place to talk".

I took Lukas's reinsertion of the theme of the sexually abusive man as an inducement to relocate the discourse to our group's "frame of reference" (Foulkes), specifically to "me", its designated leader. "Sooner or later," I suggested playfully, "I will become 'that guy'." On the intersubjective register, I already had.

The afternoon's supervisory session illustrated how the naming process requires delicacy and integrity: awareness of the historical and current group context, delimited by cultural and social constraints. The despotic Elders—the fundamentalist clergymen—served allegorically as malevolent representatives of "that guy", reintroducing trauma by imposing severe verbal restraints on speaking and speakers.

I was encouraged when the associative web closed in around me during the second morning's experiential group, in which I and the director became the necessary metaphoric figures for the members' histories, memories, and fantasies of "being in the middle" with powerful but misattuned parents, for those "very nervy" fathers who came on too strong, or not strong enough, and for wished-for fathers who could "handle a powerful woman".

As oedipal partner to the director, and a multi-dimensional displacement figure in the members' transferences (and in my countertransference), I served as an idealised/demonised part object. But, despite my invitation to be considered otherwise, I remained, in public discourse, ideal and avoided. The third experiential session— punctuated by the report on my coffee-break interlude with Max— providentially stimulated and exposed the reverse.

The members had idealised my leadership, making it a "pillar of the faith" (Lacan, 1977[1953], p. 219). But the group's lengthy silence, despite multiple invitations for discourse, insinuated that I had broken the social pact and was being exiled from the verbal community of others. "We do things differently," Michael declaimed. I was "that guy". For a fearful and exciting, speechless interlude, a primitive and perverse version of "infantile sexuality in interaction" (Foulkes, 1990[1972], p. 243) preoccupied the members' mental space.

The therapist talks as a sexual being

The individual and group are continually and repetitively drawn to trauma (Freud's repetition compulsion), to that which stimulates fear and a pre-linguistic hunger for symbiotic union/dissolution.[50] The group leader bears the tension of serving as the preverbal vehicle for such traumatogenic expectations and regressive wishes—for what is at "the same time within language and outside of it" (Lacan, 1975, p. 174)—for stirring up and also for shattering by placing them firmly within the language system.

Authentic group experience entails the therapist repetitively taking on the multiple roles in regressive and often pathogenic infantile sexual scenes, now attributed causally to him or her. The therapist's subjectivity co-determines how he or she enters in (Richarz, 2008) and linguistically disentangles him or herself from the basic assumptive concreteness of such situations.

Max's clarification could not absolve me from being the "doer", and all the participants the "done to". The Director had advised that the candidates did not "want to separate from their role as students. They could talk theory with me forever!" In the leadership role, I disrupted the workshop participants' maternal relationship with the Director (and by extension, with "me" as her symbiotic representative), which had condemned them to joyfully reside "forever" within a dependency group.

The hiccup and much that preceded and followed remained symptomatic, to the extent that discourse represented "theory", "ruminations" rather than transformative "digestions". Locating pre-oedipal and oedipal trauma in the group—Theresa, Carola, Lukas, Sarah, Lea, Hilde, and Max were the prominent spokespersons—exposed my role as the problematic but obligatory "that guy". In calling verbal attention to "me", to how I functioned and whom I came to represent as group leader, we could move away from "theory" and from re-enacting and reinforcing trauma, and toward appreciating language as "nervy" and anxiety-producing but ultimately a humanising dimension of intersubjective living.

Concluding remarks

"Naming"—the therapeutic approach of limit-setting, inviting, and embracing in language—is effective to the extent to which verbal communication can be trusted and appreciated. At various moments, a group or some of its members will attempt to form, reform, or deform the leader's necessarily powerful organ of speech. If the leader is seen as losing skill, or is "deskilled" by the group—he or she is effectively castrated, or made perverse, and cannot successfully carry out the paternal aspect of the containing function and psychoanalytic law: "put it into words".

The therapist's very use of language is "sexy talk". As "that guy", we speak words that are experienced as both dangerously seductive and potentially creative and procreative. For, there is "something fascinating about the analytic intercourse . . . [which seems] to give birth to an idea" (Bion, 2005, p. 22).

Bion's (1965) symbolic representation of the meaning-making container–contained relationship ($\female\male$) ideographically evokes female–male interdependence. To "organise" a group and make it transformative, the leader must be both woman enough to establish pre-verbal bonding (Billow, 2003b) and man enough to enter into, and fascinate with, language. An essential aspect of the professional/personal "me" involves, then, existing in one's own mind as this complex, procreative partner and exposing this self in words and behaviour.

Lukas had not been alone and is not unique in a need to give voice to sexual trauma, past, anticipated, and ongoing. To some extent, all of us suffer and appreciate the unsettling exposure to naked experience that psychodynamic group leaders invite and that nuclear ideas attempt to capture.

NOTES

1. Throughout this volume, I use the term "non-conscious" rather than "unconscious", to avoid structure metaphors and to accommodate theories that have expanded upon the repression-based model of mental organisation (e.g., Bion, 1965; Bromberg, 2011; Bucci, 1997; Stern, 2009). As Strachey (1957, p. 165) reminds us, the word "unconscious" does not have a German equivalent, and is best understood as a passive participle. The apposite translation of Freud's *bewusst* and *unbewusst* are, respectively, "consciously known" and "not consciously known".

2. Grice (1989) introduced the technical term implicate for indirect speech acts (Searle, 1975), where what is said is distinct from what is meant, implied, or suggested (see also Lakoff, 1977): for example, by use of figures of speech (metaphor, irony, sarcasm, exaggeration, understatement ("litote")), or intonation and emphasis.

3. A group localises itself by enacting "equivalences" (Hopper, 2003a). People bring sociopolitical configurations existing outside the group and enact them in the group. The resulting interactive relationships—intrapsychic, interpersonal and immediate—are also historic, cultural, and involve the larger socio-political setting in which the group (including the therapist) is embedded.

4. That is, the nuclear idea contained and made sense of anxiety and energised bonding and symbolic (symbiotic and commensal) learning links. See note 7.

5. Bion (1962) outlined three prototypes of object relationships that support or interfere with the individuals' drive to think, and therefore, to fantasise and to play. The three prototypes are relational models (images and unconscious fantasies) of early care-taker experiences involving containing and being contained. Bion labelled the models, respectively, *symbiotic, commensal*, and *parasitic*. For clarity, these prototypes may be denoted as *bonding, symbolic*, and *antilinking* mental and social interactions.

   Reciprocal interaction (Billow, 2003a)—a reversible, nesting process— is involved, as the container at one transformational level serves as the contained at another. Being held and also contained at the pre-verbal level of basic trust (bonding) stimulates self-reflection, the psychic freedom to think and develop independent thoughts. The group and leader become the contained, thought about as collective and individual ideas (symbolically).

   On the level of self, then, the individual comes to serve as the container of one's mentality, a function provided by a foundation of healthy dependence (bonding) on others. On the level of the structure of thought, an idea comes to serves as the container of the individual and group's developing thoughts and emotions, which are the contained (and held symbolically by the participants).

6. In Lacanian theory and technique, the therapist, as *Savoir*, informed by knowledge of the unconscious drives (*jouissance*) and desire, and maintainer of the Symbolic Order, interprets the metaphoric or metonymic messages contained in the members' communications. Certain members may participate with the therapist in shifting discourse from "in" to "of" the group (Giraldo, 2012, p. 76).

7. Lyon, Berly, and Klassen (2012) apply to the group situation Allen, Fonagy, and Bateman's (2008) concept of the "mentalizing stance". They describe how the therapist attempts to hold in mind both the members of the group and the group itself, and simultaneously track his or her own shifts in self-states as well.

8. As in Milton:

   > Shine inward, and the mind through all her powers
   > Irradiate, there plant eyes, all mist dispel from thence
   > Purge and disperse, that I may see and tell
   > Of things invisible to mortal sight
   >
   > (Milton, *Paradise Lost*, Book 3, ll. 52–55)

9. Disputes involving the legitimacy and extensiveness of scrutiny occupy the front pages of our newspapers: for example, racial and ethnic profiling, "don't ask, don't tell", invasion of privacy, and due process. The

following headlines appeared in one week's *New York Times* (March, 2010): "With Scrutiny, Vatican Faces Test of 'Moral Credibility'"; "Watchdog Group Seeks Justice Dept. Scrutiny of Ex-Georgia Congressman"; "New E.P.A. Scrutiny Is Set for a Chemical in Plastics"; "Hedge Fund Networkers Under Scrutiny".

In the USA, three distinct "levels of scrutiny" define and limit the extent to which acts of scrutiny are reasonable means to an end that may be legitimately pursued by the government (Breyer, 2005).

10. Garments that once served as protection against desert winds for both genders have become the traditional Islamic burkha, cloaking the woman's entire body to avoid scrutiny. Serving similar functions are the nun's habit, and the wigs and conservative attire of Orthodox Jewish women.

Feminist literary and art theorists have called attention to how the very act of "seeing" might represent an enactment of male objectification and domination, via a syntax of "gendered vision". In Henry James' *Portrait of a Lady*, for example, Ralph Touchett maintained a sado-erotic, "perverse gaze of sympathy", objectifying his cousin, Isabel (Hinton, 1999). In examining the genre of portrait painting in fifteenth-century Florence, Simons (1992) argued that presenting the female sitter with "an averted eye and a face available to scrutiny" (p. 41) symbolised how a strongly male-dominated society objectified brides and wives as visible emblems of status and property exchange.

11. A recent controversy involved whether Pope Benedict's tepid response to pederast priests should have been scrutinised. As Cardinal Ratzinger, he was nicknamed "God's Rottweiler", the scrutinising enforcer on matters of faith and sin (Dowd, 2010a). However, before resigning, he served as the "First See", and "is judged by no one" (Canon 1404, in Dowd, 2010b).

12. The roots of "peer" include "look closely", "look narrowly", and "pry" (www.wordnik.com/words/peer/etymologies).

13. *Passion* involves self-scrutiny—closely tracking the release and transformation of one's own basic affects and attendant fantasies and thoughts, on the path of reaching heightened self–other awareness (Billow, 2002).

14. An idea can incite scrutiny in such a way that the social or psychological outcome is negative, or even catastrophic. As a society, we debate whether certain explorations in the realm of nuclear physics or genetic biology represent a search for truth that far exceeds our moral capabilities of using it. The philosopher of science, Nicholas Rescher (1987, p. 9), questioned whether "there are things we ought not to know on moral grounds".

15. As noted in the previous chapter, a nuclear idea may have prominence without becoming an immediate or even explicit focus of group activity.

16. In a Special Issue of *The International Journal of Group Psychotherapy*, edited by Gantt and Cox (2010), the contributors applied biological and psychological perspectives to group therapy. See also Aron and Anderson (2000), on relational perspectives, Brownell (2010) on Gestalt therapy, Cohen (2011) in reference to somatic psychotherapy, and Eldridge and Cole (2008) and Ogden, Kekuni, and Pain (2006) on trauma-based treatment.

17. According to Piaget (1969), a hallmark of mature thinking involves mental manipulation without actual physical objects or images (as in metapsychology, music, or mathematics). Still, even in maturity, the right brain (Schore, 2003) continues to stimulate our symbols and metaphoric expression, modulates non-verbal communication, and constructs non-conscious internal working models of interpersonal experience. It remains the hypothetical location of unconscious-to-unconscious communication, the clinician's dream-like reverie (Grotstein, 2007, p. 82). However, researchers continue to question and debate localisation and modality specialisation; some suggest that brain areas are highly inter-connected and process information in a distributed manner (Caramazza & Coltheart, 2006).

18. "Properly speaking, the unconscious is the real psychic; its inner nature is just as unknown to us as the reality of the external world, and it is just as imperfectly reported to us through the data of consciousness as is the external world through the indications of our sensory organs" (Freud, 1900a, p. 456).

19. Even if the infant does not yet have a mind discriminated from the body, it relates to the mother and begins to build models of self and other (De Bianchedi, 2001).

20. In Bion's theory, transformations refer to psychic reality. While potentially infinite, transformations contain the constant (sensory, affective, ideational) and variable (the series of abstractions and generalisations). Transformations take place also non-linguistically, as in art, music, or in dream imagery. For example, the image of a woman—in "her infinite variety" (Shakespeare, 1961, *Anthony and Cleopatra*, II, 2, line 272)—undergoes diverse "takes" by Reubens, Renoir, Picasso, and DeKooning.

21. In "reversible perspective", the therapist might assume wrongly that the other shares the same sensory basis. Both individuals may refer to a picture; the therapist assumes a shared perception of two faces, while the other clandestinely insists on the vase (Bion, 1962).

22. The founder of group analysis, Foulkes (1964, p. 163), seemed less doctrinaire: for example, "an interpretation does not become a 'group interpretation' because it is given in the form 'we,' 'all of us,' 'the group this' or 'the group that.' Neither does it become an individual interpretation

because it is directed to and concerned with any particular individual." He also carried out regularly scheduled individual consultations, presumably to get a better understanding of each group member.

23. Efforts to assess character, personality, and even predict behaviour based on physical characteristics extend from historical cultures to today. While Sheldon's (1940) tripartite partition of temperament based on somotype (ecto, meso, and endomoph) is of recent vogue, the ancient Chinese art of face reading mapped out more than 100 distinct regions and their links to specific traits, illnesses, and fate (Grady, 2011). Ayurvedic medicine, used in India since 3000 bc, determines personality by assessing three main metabolic body types (*doshas*)—Vata, Pita, and Kapha.

   Perceived physical difference and cultural notions of preferred types continue to assert influence on subgroup formation and social process, with consequences to human welfare, fuelling xenophobia, racism, even genocide.

24. Bion (1961) emphasised the contrary principle of valency, the regressive, collective tendency for immediate and persistent reliance on shifting, basic assumption defences. I believe that progression and regression co-exist and interact.

25. As many readers already know, "basic assumptions" refers to three types or constellations of primitive object relations, fantasies, and affects that groups enact to avoid struggling with thinking about and organising emotional thoughts. These are, respectively, group configurations based on fight/flight, pairing, and dependency basic assumptions.

26. There are very few places without Internet access—people communicate and share information instantly. The computer and mobile phone are power equalisers, modes through which the disenfranchised may band together and find strength in numbers (as per the "Arab Spring" movement spurred by Middle Eastern youth).

27. Epstein (2011, p. 62) provides an interesting clue:

   'The version of ourselves we present to the world,' wrote the English writer William Donaldson . . . 'bears no resemblance to the truth. If we knew the truth about each other, we could take not one seriously. There isn't one of us could afford to get caught. That's all life is. Trying not to be found out.' Gossip, of course, tries to find out.

28. I use "bipolar" not in the *DSM* diagnostic sense, but as a description of a primitive type of mentation characterised by splits between opposing elements, with no middle ground.

29. Freud's (1921c, p. 123) comments remain apropos:

> The psychology of the group is the oldest human psychology; what we have isolated as individual psychology, by neglecting all traces of the group, has only since come into prominence out of the old group psychology.

Bion (1961, p. 133) emphasised, "there are characteristics in the individual whose real significance cannot be understood unless it is realized that they are part of his equipment as a herd animal".

30. Gramsci's ideas have been adopted by political thinkers across the political spectrum, as in the leftist notion of "co-optation by the bourgeoisie" or the conservative thinker, Patrick Buchanan's term, "culture war" (introduced during the 1992 Republican Convention), to describe the political and social struggle in the USA, which could be conceived as between competing sets of polemic ideas.

31. Being deprived of power and recognition generates fantasies of being bullied, and retaliation, as in Eminem's rap: "I'd like to be the strangler / Of this punk ass little pussy's puny neck . . . / he just displays complete lack of respect" ("Bully", 2006).

32. The major rating agencies (Moody's and Standard and Poor's) inveigled governments, clients, and themselves into believing that the mortgage securities Wall Street was selling should be rated triple A, when they were not even of junk quality. This led to the nearly world-wide economic crisis beginning in 2008.

33. From Old French *avogler*: to blind, deceive; from Medieval Latin *ab oculis*: without eyes (*Collins English Dictionary*, 2009).

34. "An L relationship clearly cannot be regarded as excluding K either in logic or reality" (Bion, 1965, p. 70). Racker (1968, p. 174) concluded similarly, "to understand, to unite with another, and hence, also to love, prove to be basically one and the same. Love includes love of truth".

35. Still, Freud (1921c, p. 37) defined libido as "the energy of those instincts to do with all that may be comprised under the word 'love'". In a letter to Jung, he also described psychoanalysis as "in essence a cure through love" (McGuire, 1974, pp. 12–13), although he was referring to the patient's relationship to the doctor and not a process of mutuality.

36. In his revolutionary text, Racker (1968) described the analyst as a conflicted individual, vulnerable to unconscious influence despite training and personal psychotherapy. The therapist's "'internal and external dependencies, anxieties, and pathological defences . . . [respond] to every event of the analytic situation" (Racker, 1968, p. 132).

37. "There is a need for awareness of an emotional experience, similar to the need for an awareness of concrete objects that is achieved through the

sense impressions, because lack of such awareness implies a deprivation of truth and truth seems to be essential for psychic health. The effect on the personality of such deprivation is analogous to the effect of physical starvation on the physique" (Bion, 1962, p. 56).

38. I utilise Girard's (1965, 2004) ideas in regard to mimesis, contagious violence, and scapegoating. In Girard's interpretation of the Oedipus myth, the plague of infertility that affected Thebes was caused—in part—by Oedipus's mimetic desire: to become the Other and acquire the Other's objects of desire. Oedipus comes to recognise that he has projected blame on the Other (Laius) for his own desire and that he has responsibility for the disorder in the group. But others also had contributed to the contagion of antagonism: Laius, the Sphinx, the oracle, the prophet, Tiresias, and so forth.

39. Girard (2004, p. 28) clarifies, "Existence is not given but constructed. . . . To choose to be *oneself* is to choose to be the *Other*: And the Other here is the father and, at first, he alone". In my view, "father" represents desirable leadership qualities that are culturally paternal but not gender specific, and which do not negate the primacy of pre-oedipal, "maternal" influences, as in bonding. Initially, the infant conceptualises and responds (mimetically and otherwise) to a unitary parental function, later differentiated maternally and paternally, but not necessarily tied to the gender of the Other. The effective leader must be man and woman enough to set off desire, or else another leader is chosen from the group (see also, Chapter Eleven).

40. Bion (1965, pp. 73–74) stated that "meaning, or its lack . . . must be regarded as functions of L, H and K links of the self with the self". In effect, H and K (associated with the various group members) had remained "unfriendly", that is, hyperbolic "things in themselves" ("beta elements"), greedily "competing" to dominate my personality (see Billow, 2003a). It became difficult to contain myself.

41. To refresh the reader, Bion (1970) refocused group theory, supplementing intra- and interpsychic perspectives with socio-political analysis. He asserted that psychic evasiveness (*psi*) is an ineliminable dimension of thought, communication, and social organisation. To some extent, the psychotherapy group exists as a political "establishment", and so corresponds to *psi* and promulgates polemic ideas (this volume, Part II).

42. For example: "Does your heart believe your head? Ask your heart" (Semrad, 2003, p. 24).

43. Ogden (1997, p. 12) asserted that the therapist's words should "upset (unsettle, decenter, disturb, perturb) the given". The therapist's language should aspire to a "particular form of evocative, sometimes maddening, almost always disturbing vagueness" (Ogden, 1997, p. 11).

44. Winnicott (1971, p. 46) insisted on the importance of play in adult treatment, linking it to humour: "[Playing] manifests itself, for instance, in the choice of words, in the inflections of the voice and indeed in the sense of humour".

45. Grice (1989) introduced the technical term implicate for indirect speech acts (Searle, 1975), where what is said is distinct from what is meant, implied, or suggested, for example, by use of figures of speech (metaphor, irony, sarcasm, exaggeration, understatement ("litote")), or intonation and emphasis (see also Lakoff, 1977). Matte Blanco (1988) traced the roots of such symbolic expression to the "symmetrical" logic of the unconscious, which equates the concrete with the abstract.

46. In "games of the person" (Trevarthen, 1980), the participants, as with mother and infant, develop play routines, communicating via teasing, imitation, and gentle mockery.

47. The eighteenth century Scottish philosopher, James Beattie (1778), defined humour as

    the view of two or more inconsistent, unsuitable, or incongruous parts or circumstances, considered as united in one complex object or assemblage, or as acquiring a sort of mutual relation from the peculiar manner in which the mind takes notice of them. (quoted in Ritchie, 2004, p. 48).

48. Lacan (1977[1953]) reframed and extended Klein's (1928, 1952) theory of the early stages of the oedipal complex in terms of the language system. He conceptualised an essential paternal function that obtrudes by demanding verbal communication. The linguistic "no" frustrates the child's desire to satisfy the preverbal mother by being all-in-all to her (Silverman, 1992, p. 101). Lacan's pun, "*nom-du-pere*", stands equally as "the father's name", or "the father's no". Being a semiotic concept, the "father-who-names" (by saying "no" to symbiosis) is defined with or against the "preverbal mother", without relation to the gender of the individual parent (Silverman, 1999, p. 346).

49. In reading an earlier version of this chapter, Macario Giraldo noted that I attempted to integrate Lukas into the group by prohibiting fulfilling his and the group's underlying voyeuristic wish (Lacan's drive-driven *jouissance*) and naming it. Lukas (and others) desired to become the object of my desire.

50. Kristeva (1982, p. 9) refers to this drive-driven state of *jouissance* as "*abjection*": "One does not know it, one does not desire it, one joys in it. Violently and painfully".

REFERENCES

Adams, R. (2000). Loving mimesis and Girard's *Scapegoat of the Text*: a creative reassessment of mimetic desire. In: W. M. Swartley (Ed.), *Violence Renounced: René Girard, Biblical Studies, and Peacemaking* (pp. 277–307). Telford, PA: Pandora Press.

Agazarian, Y. M. (1997). *Systems-Centered Therapy for Groups*. New York: Guilford Press.

Agazarian, Y. M. (2012). Systems-centered[(r)] group psychotherapy: putting theory into practice. *International Journal of Group Psychotherapy, 62*: 171–195.

Alford, C. F. (1994). *Group Psychology & Political Theory*. New Haven, CT: Yale University Press.

Alford, C. F. (1995). The group as a whole or acting out the missing leader? *International Journal of Group Psychotherapy, 4*: 125–141.

Allen, J. (2006). *Hostages and Hostage-taking in the Roman Empire*. Cambridge: Cambridge University Press.

Allen, J., Fonagy, P., & Bateman, A. (2008). *Mentalizing in Clinical Practice*. Washington, DC: American Psychiatric Association.

Anspach, M. R. (2004). Editor's introduction: Imitating Oedipus. In: Girard, R. (2004), *Oedipus Unbound: Selected Writings on Rivalry and Desire* (pp. vii–liv), M. R. Anspach (Ed. & Trans.). Stanford: Stanford University Press.

Aristotle (1998). *The Metaphysics*, H. Lawson-Tancred (Trans.). London: Penguin Classics.

Aron, L. (1996). *A Meeting of Minds: Mutuality in Psychoanalysis*. Hillsdale, NJ: Analytic Press.

Aron, L., & Anderson, F. S. (Eds.) (2000). *Relational Perspectives on the Body*. London: Routledge.

Ashuach, S. (2012). Am I my brother's keeper? The analytic group as a space for re-enacting and treating sibling trauma. *Group Analysis, 45*: 155–167.

Austin, H. (1962). *How To Do Things With Words*. Oxford: Clarendon Press.

Baars, B. J. (1992). Divided consciousness or divided self. *Consciousness and Cognition, 1*: 59–60.

Beebe, B., & Lachmann, F. (2002). *Infant Research and Adult Treatment: Co-constructing Interactions*. Hillsdale, NJ: Analytic Press.

Beebe, B., & Stern, D. N. (1977). Engagement–disengagement and early object experiences. In: N. Freedman & S. Grand (Eds.), *Communicative Structures and Psychic Structures* (pp. 35–55). New York: Plenum Press.

Benjamin, J. (1988). The *Bonds of Love*. New York: Pantheon.

Bennis, W. (2007). The challenges of leadership in the modern world: introduction to the Special Issue. *American Psychologist, 62*: 2–5.

Bennis, W. T., & Shepard, H. A. (1956). A theory of group development. *Human Relations, 9*: 415–437.

Benveniste, D. (1998). Play and the metaphors of the body. *Psychoanalytic Study of the Child, 53*: 65–83.

Berk, T. J. C. (2011). *The Group Focal Conflict Theory Revisited*. Herault, France: Berk.

Billow, R. M. (1975). A cognitive developmental study of metaphor comprehension. *Developmental Psychology, 11*: 415–423.

Billow, R. M. (1977). Metaphor: a review of the psychological literature. *Psychological Bulletin, 84*: 81–92.

Billow, R. M. (1981). Observing spontaneous metaphor in children. *Journal of Experimental Child Psychology, 31*: 430–445. Reprinted in: M. B. Franklin & S. S. Barten (Eds.), *Child Language: A Reader*. New York: Oxford University Press, 1988.

Billow, R. M. (2001). The therapist's anxiety and resistance to group. *International Journal of Group Psychotherapy, 51*: 225–242.

Billow, R. M. (2002). Passion in group: thinking about loving, hating, and knowing. *International Journal of Group Psychotherapy, 52*: 355–372.

Billow, R. M. (2003a). *Relational Group Psychotherapy: From Basic Assumptions to Passion*. London: Jessica Kingsley.

Billow, R. M. (2003b). Bonding in group: the therapist's contribution. *International Journal of Group Psychotherapy, 53*: 83–110.

Billow, R. M. (2003c). Relational variations of the container–contained. *Contemporary Psychoanalysis, 39*: 27–50.

Billow, R. M. (2004). Truth and falsity in group. *International Journal of Group Psychotherapy, 54*: 321–345.

Billow, R. M. (2005). The two faces of the group therapist. *International Journal of Group Psychotherapy, 55*: 167–187.

Billow, R. M. (2009). The radical nature of combined psychotherapy. *International Journal of Group Psychotherapy, 59*: 1–28.

Billow, R. M. (2010a). *Resistance, Rebellion and Refusal in Groups: The 3 Rs.* London: Karnac.

Billow, R. M. (2010b). Modes of therapeutic engagement: Part I: Diplomacy and integrity. *International Journal of Group Psychotherapy, 60*: 1–28.

Billow, R. M. (2010c). Modes of therapeutic engagement: Part II: Sincerity and authenticity. *International Journal of Group Psychotherapy, 60*: 29–58.

Billow, R. M. (2012). It's all about me: introduction to relational group psychotherapy. In: J. L. Kleinberg (Ed.), *The Wiley–Blackwell Handbook of Group Psychotherapy* (pp. 169–185). Chichester: John Wiley.

Billow, R. M. (2013). The invited presenter: outrageousness and outrage. *International Journal of Group Psychotherapy, 63*: 317–345.

Bion, W. R. (1961). *Experiences in Groups.* London: Tavistock.

Bion, W. R. (1962). *Learning from Experience.* London: Heinemann. Reprinted in: *Seven Servants: Four Works by Wilfred R. Bion.* New York: Aronson, 1977.

Bion, W. R. (1963). *Elements of Psycho-analysis.* London: Heinemann. Reprinted in: *Seven Servants: Four Works by Wilfred R. Bion.* New York: Aronson, 1977.

Bion, W. R. (1965). *Transformations.* London: Heinemann. Reprinted in: *Seven Servants: Four Works by Wilfred R. Bion.* New York: Aronson, 1977.

Bion, W. R. (1966). Book review: Medical orthodoxy and the future of psychoanalysis, by K. R. Eissler. *International Journal of Psychoanalysis, 47*: 575–579.

Bion, W. R. (1967). *Second Thoughts.* London: Heinemann.

Bion, W. R. (1970). *Attention and Interpretation.* London: Tavistock. Reprinted in: *Seven Servants: Four Works by Wilfred R. Bion.* New York: Aronson, 1977.

Bion, W. R. (1975). *Bion's Brazilian Lectures 2: Rio/Sao Paulo, 1974.* Rio de Janeiro, Brazil: Imago Editoria.

Bion, W. R. (1987). *Clinical Seminars and Four Papers*, F. Bion (Ed.). Abingdon: Fleetwood Press.

Bion, W. R. (1997). *Taming Wild Thoughts*, F. Bion (Ed.). London: Karnac.

Bion, W. R. (2005). *The Tavistock Seminars*. London: Karnac.

Blake, W. (1977). Auguries of Innocence (Poems from the Pickering manuscript). In: *The Complete Poems*, A. Ostriker (Ed.). London: Penguin Classics.

Blake, W. (2008). *The Complete Poetry and Prose of William Blake*, D. Erdman (Ed.). Berkeley: University of California Press.

Boesky, D. (2000). Affect, language, and communication. *International Journal of Psychoanalysis, 81*: 257–262.

Bollas, C. (1987). *The Shadow of the Object: Psychoanalysis of the Unthought Known*. London: Free Association Books.

Bollas, C. (1989). *Forces of Destiny. Psychoanalysis and the Human Idiom*. Northvale, NJ: Jason Aronson.

Brenner, C. (2002). Conflict, compromise formation, and structural theory. *Psychoanalytic Quarterly, 70*: 397–417.

Breuer, J., & Freud, S. (1893–1895). *S.E.*, 2. London: Hogarth.

Breyer, S. (2005). *Active Liberty: Interpreting Our Democratic Constitution*. New York: Knopf.

Britton, R. (1998). Book review. *Taming Wild Thoughts*, by W. R. Bion. Edited by Francesca Bion. London: Karnac Books, 1997. *International Journal of Psychoanalysis, 79*: 817–819.

Britton, R., & Steiner, J. (1994). Interpretation: selected fact or overvalued idea. *International Journal of Psychoanalysis, 75*: 1069–1078.

Bromberg, P. (2009) Multiple self states, the relational mind, and dissociation: a psychoanalytic perspective. In: P. F. Dell & J. A. O'Neill (Eds.), *Dissociation and the Dissociative Disorders: DSM and Beyond* (pp. 637–652). New York: Routledge.

Bromberg, P. M. (2011). *The Shadow of the Tsunami: And the Growth of the Relational Mind*. New York: Routledge.

Brownell, P. (2010). *Gestalt Therapy: A Guide to Contemporary Practice*. New York: Springer.

Bucci, W. (1997). *Psychoanalysis and Cognitive Science: A Multiple Code Theory*. New York: Guilford Press.

Calef, V., & Weinshel, E. (1981). Some clinical consequences of introjection: gaslighting. *Psychoanalytic Quarterly, 50*: 44–67.

Caper, R. (1999). Group psychology and psychoanalytic group. Published on the Internet by the International Psychoanalytic Association, Committee on Interregional Conferences (www.ipa.org.uk/CIRC/Caper-m1.htm).

Caramazza, A., & Coltheart, M. (2006). Cognitive neuropsychology twenty years on. *Cognitive Neuropsychology, 23*: 3–12.

Chekhov, A. (2006). *Note-book of Anton Chekhov*, S. Koteliansky & L. Woolf (Trans.). Middlesex: Echo Library.

Christie, L. (1994). Some psychological aspects of humor. *International Journal of Psychoanalysis, 75*: 479–489.

Chused, J. (1991). The evocative power of enactments. *Journal of the American Psychoanalytic Association, 39*: 615–640.

Chused, J. (1992). The patient's perception of the analyst. *Psychoanalytic Quarterly, 63*: 161–184.

Cohen, S. (2011). Coming to our senses: the application of somatic psychology to group psychotherapy. *International Journal of Group Psychotherapy, 63*: 397–413.

Collins English Dictionary (2009). 10th edn. New York: HarperCollins.

Cunningham, V. (1994). *In the Reading Gaol: Postmodernity, Texts and History*. London: Blackwell.

Dalal, F. (2000). *Taking the Group Seriously*. London: Jessica Kingsley.

Dali, S. (2007). *Diary of a Genius*. Washington, DC: Solar Books.

Davies, J. (1999). Dissociation, therapeutic enactment and transference–countertransference process. *Gender and Psychoanalysis, 2*: 241–259.

Davies, S. (1991). *Milton*. New York: St Martin's Press.

de Bianchedi, E. T. (2001). The passionate psychoanalyst or learning from the emotional experience. *Fort Da, 7*: 19–28.

de Tocqueville, A. (2003). *Democracy in America*, I. Kramnick (Ed.), G. Bevan (Trans.). London: Penguin Classics.

Derrida, J. (2002). Des tours de Babel. In: *Acts of Religion*, G. Anidjar (Ed.). London: Routledge.

Dickinson, E. (1960). *The Complete Poems of Emily Dickinson*, T. H. Johnson (Ed.). Boston: Little, Brown.

Douglas, M. (1982). *Natural Symbols: Explorations in Cosmology*. New York: Pantheon.

Dowd, M. (2010a). A nope for Pope. *The New York Times*, March 28, p. A11.

Dowd, M. (2010b). Should there be an inquisition for the Pope? *The New York Times*, March 31, p. A23.

Dundes, A. (1992). *Evil Eye: Folklore Casebook*. Madison, WI: University of Wisconsin Press.

Durkheim, E. (1982). What is a social fact? In: *The Rules of the Sociological Method* (pp. 50–59), S. Lukes (Ed.), W. D. Halls (Trans.). New York: Basic Books.

Edgar, A. (2002). Mauss, Marcel (1872–1950). In: A. Edgar and P. Sedgwick (Eds.), *Cultural Theory: The Key Thinkers* (pp. 156–158). New York: Routledge.

Eibl-Eibesfeldt, I. (2007). *Human Ethology*. New Brunswick, NJ: Aldline Transaction.

Eldridge, C., & Cole, G. (2008). Learning from work with individuals with a history of trauma: integrating body-oriented techniques and relational psychoanalysis. In: F. S. Anderson (Ed.), *Bodies in Treatment* (pp. 79–102). New York: Analytic Press.

Epstein, J. (2011). *Gossip. The Untrivial Pursuit*. Boston, MA: Houghton Mifflin Harcourt.

Ettin, M. (1999). *Foundations and Applications of Group Psychotherapy*. London: Jessica Kingsley.

Ezquerro, A. (2010). Cohesion and coherency in group analysis. *Group Analysis, 43*: 496–504.

Ezriel, H. (1950). A psycho-analytic approach to the treatment of patients in groups. *British Journal of Psychiatry, 96*: 774–779.

Ferenczi, S. (1956). Stages in the development of the sense of reality. In: *Sex in Psycho-Analysis* (pp. 213–239). New York: Dover.

Ferro, A., & Basile, R. (2009). *The Analytic Field. A Clinical Concept*. London: Karnac.

Fonagy, P., & Target, M. (1998). Mentalization and the changing aims of child psychoanalysis. *Psychoanalytic Dialogues, 8*: 87–114.

Foucault, M. (1975). *Birth of the Clinic, An Archaeology of Medical Perception*, A. M. Sheridan Smith (Trans.). New York: Vintage.

Foucault, M. (1995). Panopticism. In: A. Sheridan (Trans.), *Discipline and Punish: The Birth of the Prison* (pp. 195–228). New York: Vintage.

Foulkes, S. H. (1964). *Therapeutic Group Analysis*. London: George Allen & Unwin.

Foulkes, S. H. (1971). The group as the matrix of the individual's mental life. In: E. Foulkes (Ed.), *Selected Papers of S. H. Foulkes*. London: Karnac, 1990.

Foulkes, S. H. (1975). *Group Analytic Psychotherapy: Methods and Principles*. London: Gordon and Breech.

Foulkes, S. H. (1990[1972]). Oedipus conflict and regression. In: *Selected Papers: Psychoanalysis and Group Analysis* (pp. 235–248). London: Karnac.

Foulkes, S. H., & Anthony, E. (1965). *Group Psychotherapy: The Psychoanalytic Approach*. Baltimore, MD: Penguin.

Frank, K. (1997). The role of the analyst's inadvertent self-revelations. *Psychoanalytic Dialogues, 7*: 281–314.

Franklin, A., & White, T. (1968). "Think" (lyrics), *Aretha Now*. Atlantic Records.

Freud, S. (1900a). The *Interpretation of Dreams*. *S.E.*, *4–5*. London: Hogarth.

Freud, S. (1905c). *Jokes and their Relation to the Unconscious*. *S.E.*, *8*. London: Hogarth.

Freud, S. (1905d). *Three Essays on the Theory of Sexuality*. *S.E.*, *7*: 125–245. London: Hogarth.

Freud, S. (1911b). Formulations regarding the two principles in mental functioning. *S.E.*, *12*: 213–226. London: Hogarth.

Freud, S. (1912b). The dynamics of transference. *S.E.*, *12*: 97–108. London: Hogarth.

Freud, S. (1912e). Recommendations to physicians practising psycho-analysis. *S.E.*, *12*: 109–120. London: Hogarth.

Freud, S. (1912–1913). *Totem and Taboo*. *S.E.*, *13*: 1–161. London: Hogarth.

Freud, S. (1914d). On the history of the psycho-analytic movement. *S.E.*, *14*: 3–66. London: Hogarth.

Freud, S. (1916d). Some character types met with in psycho-analytic work. *S.E.*, *14*: 309–334. London: Hogarth.

Freud, S. (1920g). *Beyond the Pleasure Principle*. *S.E.*, *18*: 7–64. London: Hogarth.

Freud, S. (1921c). *Group Psychology and the Analysis of the Ego*. *S.E.*, *18*: 67–143. London: Hogarth.

Freud, S. (1923b). *The Ego and the Id*. *S.E.*, *19*: 3–66. London: Hogarth.

Freud, S. (1927d). Humour. *S.E.*, *21*: 159–166. London: Hogarth.

Friedman, T. (2011). Who's the decider? *The New York Times*, Wednesday, November 16, p. A35.

Gans, J., Rutan, S., & Lape, E. (2002). The demonstration group: a tool for observing group process and leadership style. *International Journal of Group Psychotherapy*, *52*: 233–252.

Gans, J. S. (2010). *Difficult Topics in Group Psychotherapy. My Journey from Shame to Courage*. London: Karnac.

Gantt, S., & Cox, P. (Eds.) (2010). Neurobiology and building interpersonal systems: groups, couples, and beyond. *International Journal of Group Psychotherapy* (Special Issue), *60*(4).

Garrels, S. (2006). Imitation, mirror neurons, and mimetic desire: convergences between the mimetic theory of Rene Girard and empirical research on imitation. *Contagion: Journal of Violence, Mimesis, and Culture*, *12–13*: 47–86.

Gayle, R. (2009). Co-creating meaningful structures within long-term psychotherapy group culture. *International Journal of Group Psychotherapy*, *59*: 311–333.

Gerson, S. (1996). Neutrality, resistance, self-disclosure. *Psychoanalytic Dialogues*, *6*: 623–645.

Ghent, M. (1990). Masochism, submission, surrender: masochism as a perversion of surrender. *Contemporary Psychoanalysis, 26*: 108–136.

Giles, H., & Oxford, G. (1970). Towards a multidimensional theory of laughter causation and its social implications. *Bulletin of the British Psychological Society, 23*: 97–105.

Gill, M. M. (1994). *Psychoanalysis in Transition*. Hillsdale, NJ: Analytic Press.

Giraldo, M. (2012). *The Dialogues In and Of The Group*. London: Karnac.

Girard, R. (1965). *Deceit, Desire, and the Novel: Self and Other in Literary Structure*, Y. Freccero (Trans.). Baltimore, MD: Johns Hopkins University Press.

Girard, R. (2004). *Oedipus Unbound: Selected Writings on Rivalry and Desire*, M. R. Anspach (Ed. & Trans.). Stanford, CA: Stanford University Press.

Goffman, E. (1959). *Presentation of Self in Everyday Life*. New York: Anchor Book.

Goldberg, A. (2001). Postmodern psychoanalysis. *International Journal of Psychoanalysis, 82*: 123–128.

Grady, D. (2011). What's in a face at 50? *The New York Times*, July 31, p. SR4.

Gramsci, A. (1971). *Selections from the Prison Notebooks*, Q. Hoare & G. Nowell Smith (Eds. & Trans.). New York: International.

Gramsci, A. (1992). *Prison Notebooks*, J. Buttigieg (Ed.). New York: Columbia University Press.

Green, A. (2000). The central phobic position. *International Journal of Psychoanalysis, 81*: 429–451.

Greenberg, J. (1995). Self-disclosure: is it psychoanalytic? *Contemporary Psychoanalysis, 31*: 193–205.

Greenson, R. (1967). *The Technique and Practice of Psychoanalysis*. New York: International Universities Press.

Grice, H. P. (1989). *Studies in the Way of Words*. Cambridge, MA: Harvard University Press.

Grosskurth, P. (1991). *The Secret Ring: Freud's Inner Circle and the Politics of Psychoanalysis*. New York: Addison-Wesley.

Grossman, W. (1995). Psychological vicissitudes of theory in the clinical work. *International Journal of Psychoanalysis, 76*: 885–889.

Grossmark, R. (2007). The edge of chaos: enactment, disruption, and emergence in group psychotherapy. *Psychoanalytic Dialogues, 17*: 479–499.

Grotstein, J. (2000). *Who is the Dreamer Who Dreams the Dream: A Study of Psychic Presences*. Hillsdale, NJ: Analytic Press.

Grotstein, J. (2007). *A Beam of Intense Darkness*. London: Karnac.

Grotstein, J. (2009). *But At the Same Time and On Another Level: Vol. 1. Psychoanalytic Theory and Technique in the Kleinian/Bioinion Mode*. London: Karnac.

Grotstein, J. S. (2004). The seventh servant: the implications of a truth drive in Bion's theory of 'O'. *International Journal of Psychoanalysis, 85*: 1081–1101.

Gurewitz, B. (2007). Scrutiny (lyrics). Bad Religion, *New Maps of Hell*. Epitaph Records.

Haidt, J. (2012). The *Righteous Mind*. New York: Pantheon Books.

Hand, L. (1927). The preservation of personality. In: I. Dilliard (Ed.), *The Spirit of Liberty* (enlarged 3rd edn). New York: Knopf, 1974.

Hewitt, J. (2002). *The Architecture of Thought: A New Look at Human Evolution*. Salisbury: Holmhurst House Press.

Hinton, L. (1999). *The Perverse Gaze of Sympathy: Sadomasochistic Sentiments from Clarissa to Rescue 911*. New York: State University of New York Press.

Hobbes, T. (1996). *Leviathan, Volume I*. Oxford: Oxford University Press.

Hobdell, R. (1991). Individual and group therapy combined. In: J. Roberts and M. Pines (Eds.), *The Practice of Group Analysis*. London: Tavistock/ Routledge.

Hoffman, I. Z. (1992). Expressive participation and psychoanalytic discipline. *Contemporary Psychoanalysis, 2*: 1–14.

Hoffman, I. Z. (1996). The intimate and ironic authority of the psychoanalyst's presence. *Psychoanalytic Quarterly, 65*: 102–136.

Hoffman, I. Z. (2009). Therapeutic passion in the countertransference. *Psychoanalytic Dialogues, 19*: 617–637.

Hoggett, P. (1998). The internal establishment. In: P. B. Talamo, F. Borgogno, & S. A. Merciai (Eds.), *Bion's Legacy to Groups* (pp. 9–24). London: Karnac.

Homer (1996). *The Odyssey*, R. Falges (Trans.). New York: Viking.

Hopper, E. (2003a). *The Social Unconscious: Selected Papers*. London: Jessica Kingsley.

Hopper, E. (2003b). *Traumatic Experience in the Unconscious Life of Groups: The Fourth Basic Assumption: Incohesion: Aggregation/Massification or (ba) I:A/M*. London: Jessica Kingsley

Hopper, E. (2013). Consulting in/to organizations/societies as traumatized living human social systems. *International Journal of Group Psychotherapy, 63*(2): 267–272.

Hopper, E., & Weinberg, H. (Eds.) (2011). *The Social Unconscious in Persons, Groups, and Societies: Volume I: Mainly Theory*. London: Karnac.

Horowitz, L. (1983). Projective identification in dyads and groups. *International Journal of Group Psychotherapy, 33*: 259–279.

Ivey, G. (2008). Enactment controversies: a critical review of current debates. *International Journal of Psychoanalysis, 89*: 19–38.

Jacobs, T. (2001). On misreading and misleading patients. *International Journal of Psychoanalysis, 82*: 653–669.

Jastrow, M. (1898). *The Religion of Babylonia and Assyria*. Charleston, SC: Nabu Press.

Johnson, S. (1759/1985). *The History of Rasselas, Prince of Abissinia*. England: Penguin Classics.

Jonsen, A., & Toulmin, S. (1988). *The Abuse of Casuistry: A History of Moral Reasoning*. Berkeley, CA: University of California.

Jung W. E. (2003). The inner eye theory of laughter: mindreader signals cooperator value. *Evolutionary Psychology, 1*: 214–253.

Kernberg, O. (2000). A concerned critique of psychoanalytic education. *International Journal of Psychoanalysis, 81*: 97–120.

Kieffer, C. (2007). Emergence and the analytic third: working at the edge of chaos. *Psychoanalytic Dialogues, 17*: 683–703.

Kieffer, C. (2010). Richard Billow's "Modes of therapeutic engagement: Part I: Diplomacy and integrity and Part II: Sincerity and authenticity". *International Journal of Group Psychotherapy, 60*: 307–312.

Kite, J. (2008). Ideas of influence: the impact of the analyst's character on the analysis. *Psychoanalytic Quarterly, 77*: 1075–1104.

Klein, M. (1928). Early stages of the Oedipus complex. In: *Love, Guilt and Reparation and Other Works* (pp. 186–198). New York: Delacorte, 1975.

Klein, M. (1952). Some theoretical conclusions regarding the emotional life of the infant. In: *Envy and Gratitude* (pp. 61–93). New York: Delacorte Press, 1975.

Koestler, A. (1964). *The Act of Creation*. London: Hutchinson.

Kohut, H. (1984). *How Does Analysis Cure?* A. Goldberg & P. Stepansky (Eds.). Chicago, IL: University of Chicago Press.

Kristeva, J. (1982). *Powers of Horror: An Essay on Abjection*, L. Roudiez (Trans.). New York: Columbia University Press.

Lacan, J. (1975[1991]). *The Seminar of Jacques Lacan: Freud's Papers on Technique (Book I)*, J.-A. Miller (Ed.), J. Forrester (Trans.). London: W. W. Norton.

Lacan, J. (1977[1953]). The function and field of speech and language in psychoanalysis. In: *Ecrits* (pp. 179–225), A. Sheridan (Trans.). New York: Norton.

Lacan, J. (1977[1958]). On a question preliminary to any possible treatment of psychosis. In: *Ecrits* (pp. 30–113), A. Sheridan (Trans.). New York: Norton.

Lacan, J. (1978). Of the gaze as objet petit a. In: *The Four Fundamental Concepts of Psychoanalysis* (pp. 67–123), A. Sheridan (Trans.) New York: Norton.

Lakoff, R. (1977). What you can do with words: politeness, pragmatics and performatives. In: R. Rogers, R. Wall, & J. Murphy (Eds.), *Proceedings of the Texas Conference on Performatives, Presuppositions and Implicatures* (pp. 79–106). Arlington, VA: Center for Applied Linguistics,

Lampl-de Groot, J. (1981). Notes on "multiple personality". *Psychoanalytic Quarterly, 50*: 614–624.

Langs, R. (1978). Some communicative properties of the bipersonal field. *International Journal of Psychoanalytic Psychotherapy, 7*: 87–135.

Le Bon, G. (2002). *The Crowd. A Study of the Popular Mind.* Mineola, NY: Dover.

Levine, H. (2012). The analyst's theory in the analyst's mind. *Psychoanalytic Inquiry, 32*: 18–32.

Lipin, T. (1992). Dr. Otto Isakower's analyzing instrument: reflections three decades later. *Journal of Clinical Psychoanalysis, 1*: 227–228.

Lloyd Webber, A., & Rice, T. (1976). "Rainbow High", *Evita*. Lyrics@Universal Music.

Lyon, K. B., Berley, R., & Klassen, K. (2012). Unbearable sates of mind in group psychotherapy: dissociation, metallization, and the clinician's stance. *Group, 36*(4): 267–282.

Mankell, H. (2005). *Before the Frost.* New York: The New Press.

Matte-Blanco, I. (1988). *Thinking, Feeling and Being.* London: Routledge.

Maugham, S. (1915). *Of Human Bondage.* London: Vintage Classics, 2000.

Mauss, M. (1990). *The Gift: Forms and Functions of Exchange in Archaic Societies.* London: Routledge.

Mazer, H. (2003). Introduction. In: S. Rako & H. Mazer (Eds.), *Semrad: The Heart of a Therapist.* Lincoln, NE: iUniverse.

McGuire, W. (Ed.) (1974). *The Freud–Jung Letters: The Correspondence between Sigmund Freud and C. G. Jung,* R. Manheim (Trans.). Princeton, NJ: Princeton University Press.

McLaughlin, J. (1991). Clinical and theoretical aspects of enactment. *Journal of the American Psychoanalytic Association, 29*: 595–614.

Menzies Lyth, I. (1988). A psychoanalytic perspective on social institutions. In: E. Spillius (Ed.), *Melanie Klein Today, Vol. 2* (pp. 284–299). London: Routledge.

Meredith, G. (1892). To the Comic Spirit. In: *Poems* (pp. 69–91). London: Macmillan.

Merleau-Ponty, M. (1964). *Signs.* Evanston, IL: Northwestern University Press.

Meyer, J. (2000). Humor as a double-edged sword: four functions of humor in communication. *Communication Theory, 10*: 310–331.

Michels, R. (1988). The psychology of rights. In: V. D. Volkan & T. C. Rodgers (Eds.), *Attitudes of Entitlement: Theoretical and Clinical Issues* (pp. 53–62). Charlottesville, VA: University Press of Virginia.

Migliorati, P. (1989). The image in group relationships. *Group Analysis, 22*: 189–199.

Milton, J. (1971). *Paradise Lost. The Complete Poetry of John Milton* (pp. 249–517), J. Shawcross (Ed.). New York: Doubleday.

Moeller, M. L. (2002). Love in the group. *Group Analysis, 35*: 484–498.

Nietzsche, F. (1980). *Sämtliche Werke: Kritische Studienausgabe*, Vol. 6 [*Twilight of the Idols*, "Maxims and Arrows," section 26], G. Colli & M. Montinari (Eds.). Berlin: de Gruyter.

Nitsun, M. (2006). *The Group as an Object of Desire: Exploring Sexuality in Group Therapy*. London: Routledge.

Nitzgen, D. (2009). The location of sexuality in group analysis. *Group Analysis, 42*(3): 215–228.

Ogden, P., Kekuni, M., & Pain, C. (2006). *Trauma and the Body: A Sensorimotor Approach to Psychotherapy*. New York: Norton.

Ogden, T. (1997). Some thoughts on the use of language in psychoanalysis. *Psychoanalytic Dialogues, 7*: 1–21.

Ogden, T. (2004). The analytic third: implications for psychoanalytic theory and technique. *Psychoanalytic Quarterly, 73*: 167–195.

Ogden, T. (2011). Reading Susan Isaacs: toward a radically revised theory of thinking. *International Journal of Psychoanalysis, 92*: 925–942.

O'Leary, J., & Wright, F. (2005). Social constructivism and the group-as-a-whole. *Group, 29*: 257–276.

Ormont, L. (1992). *The Group Therapy Experience*. New York: St. Martins.

Ormont, L. (2001). The use of the group in resolving the subjective countertransference. In: L. B. Furgeri (Ed.), *The Technique of Group Treatment* (pp. 191–205). Madison, CT: Psychosocial Press.

Piaget, J. (1969). The *Language and Thought of the Child*. Cleveland, OH: Meridian Books.

Plato (1973). *The Republic and Other Works*, Book VII, B. Jowett (Trans.). New York: Anchor Books.

Poland, W. (1990). The gift of laughter: on the development of a sense of humor in clinical analysis. *Psychoanalytic Quarterly, 49*: 197–225.

Poulton, J. L. (2013). *Object Relations and Relationality in Couple Therapy*. Lanham, MD: Jason Aronson.

Racker, H. (1968). *Transference and Countertransference*. Madison, CT: International Universities Press.

Rako, S. (2003). Introduction. In: S. Rako & H. Mazer (Eds.), *Semrad: The Heart of a Therapist* (pp. 11–18). Lincoln, NE: iUniverse.

Redl, F. (1980). Group emotion and leadership. In: S. Scheidlinger (Ed.), *Psychoanalytic Group Dynamics: Basic Readings* (pp. 15–68). New York: International Universities Press.

Reik, T. (1983). *Listening with the Third Ear.* New York: Farrar, Straus and Giroux.

Renik, O. (1993). Analytic interaction: conceptualizing technique in light of the analyst's irreducible subjectivity. *Psychoanalytic Quarterly, 62*: 553–571.

Renik, O. (1995). The ideal of the anonymous analyst and the problem of self-disclosure. *Psychoanalytic Quarterly, 64*: 466–495.

Rescher, N. (1987). *Forbidden Knowledge and Other Essays on the Philosophy of Cognition.* Dordrecht: Reidel.

Richarz, B. (2008). Group process and the therapist's subjectivity: interactive transference in analytical group psychotherapy. *Int. J. Group Psychotherapy, 58*(2): 141–161.

Ritchie, G. (2004). *The Linguistic Analysis of Jokes.* London: Routledge.

Rosenfeld, H. (1988). A clinical approach to the psychoanalytic theory of the life and death instincts: an investigation into the aggressive aspects of narcissism. In: E. Spillius (Ed.), *Melanie Klein Today, Vol. 1* (pp. 239–255). London: Routledge.

Rutan, J. S., & Stone, W. (2001). *Psychodynamic Group Therapy* (3rd edn). New York: Guilford Press.

Scheidlinger, S. (1974). On the concept of the "mother group". *International Journal of Group Psychotherapy, 24*: 417–428.

Schermer, V. (2012). Group-as-a-whole and complexity theories: areas of convergence. Part II: Application to group relations, group analysis, and systems centered therapy. *Group Analysis, 45*: 481–497.

Schermer, V., & Rice, C. (2012). Towards an integrative intersubjective and relational group psychotherapy. In: J. L. Kleinberg (Ed.), *The Wiley–Blackwell Handbook of Group Psychotherapy* (pp. 59–88). Chichester: John Wiley.

Schiller, H. (1989). *Culture, Inc. The Corporate Takeover of Public Expression.* New York: Oxford University Press.

Schlapobersky, J. (1994). The language of the group: monologue, dialogue and discourse in group analysis. In: D. Brown & L. Zinkin (Eds.), *The Psyche and the Social World.* London: Jessica Kingsley.

Schneider, J. (2010). From Freud's dream-work to Bion's work of dreaming: the changing conception of dreaming in psychoanalytic theory. *International Journal of Psychoanalysis, 91*: 521–540.

Schore, A. N. (2003). *Affect Regulation and the Repair of the Self.* New York: Norton.

Schwartz, H. (2012). Intersubjectivity and dialecticism. *International Journal of Psychoanalysis, 93*: 401–425.

Searle, J. (1975). Indirect speech acts. In: P. Cole & J. L. Morgan (Eds.), *Syntax and Semantics, 3: Speech Acts* (pp. 59–82). New York: Academic Press. Reprinted in S. Davis (Ed.), *Pragmatics: A Reader* (pp. 265–277). Oxford: Oxford University Press, 1991.

Searles, H. (1979). *Countertransference and Related Subjects*. New York: International Universities Press.

Segal, H. (1957). Notes on symbol formation. *International Journal of Psychoanalysis, 78*: 43–52.

Semrad, E. (2003). *The Heart of a Therapist*, S. Rako & H. Mazer (Eds.). Lincoln, NE: iUniverse.

Shakespeare, W. (1961). *The Complete Works*. New York: Harcourt, Brace.

Shapiro, E., & Ginzberg, R. (2001). The persistently neglected sibling relationship and its applicability to group therapy. *International Journal of Group Psychotherapy, 51*: 327–341.

Sheldon, W. (1940). The *Varieties of Human Physique: An Introduction to Constitutional Psychology*. New York: Harper.

Shklar, J. (1989). The liberalism of fear. In: N. Rosenblum (Ed.), *Liberalism and the Moral Life* (pp. 21–39). Cambridge, MA: Harvard University Press.

Silverman, K. (1992). *Male Subjectivity at the Margins*. New York: Routledge.

Silverman, K. (1999). The subject. In: J. Evans & S. Hall (Eds.), *Visual Culture: The Reader* (pp. 340–355). London: Sage.

Simons, P. (1992). Women in frames: the gaze, the eye, the profile in renaissance portraiture. In: N. Broude & M. D. Garrard (Eds.), *The Expanding Discourse: Feminism and Art History* (pp. 39–57). Boulder, CO: Westview Press.

Singer, M. (2011). Revivals: pacing it. *The New Yorker*, 11 March, pp. 24–27.

Slavson, S. R. (1992). Are there "group dynamics" in therapy groups? In: K. R. Mackenzie (Ed.), *Classics in Group Psychotherapy* (pp. 166–182). New York: Guilford Press.

Smith, H. F. (2008). Vicious circles of punishment: a reading of Melanie Klein's *Envy and Gratitude*. *Psychoanalytic Quarterly, 77*: 199–218.

Spezzano, C. (1996). The three faces of two-person psychology: Development, ontology, and epistemology. *Psychoanalytic Dialogues, 6*: 599–621.

Srivastva, S., & Barrett, F. (1988). The transforming nature of metaphors in group development: a study in group theory. *Human Relations, 4*: 31–64.

Sterba, R. (1934). The fate of the ego in analytic therapy. *International Journal of Psychoanalysis, 15*: 117–126. Reprinted in R. Langs (Ed.), *Classics in Psycho-Analytic Technique* (pp. 304–310). New York: Aronson, 1981.

Stern, D. B. (2009). *Partners in Thought: Working with Unformulated Experience, Dissociation, and Enactment.* New York: Routledge.

Stern, D. N. (1971). A microanalysis of mother–infant interaction. *Journal of the American Academy of Child Psychiatry, 10*: 501–517.

Stolorow, R. D. (1997). Principles of dynamic systems, intersubjectivity, and the obsolete distinction between one-person and two-person psychologies. *Psychoanalytic Dialogues, 7*: 859–868.

Strachey, J. (1957). Editor's note. *S.E., 14*: 161–165. London: Hogarth.

Thoma, H., & Kachele, H. (1994). *Psychoanalytic Practice: Volume 1, Principles.* Northvale, NJ: Jason Aronson.

Thomas, D. (1954). *A Child's Christmas in Wales.* New York: New Directions.

Trevarthen, C. (1980). The foundations of intersubjectivity: development of interpersonal and cooperative understanding in infants. In: D. K. Alson (Ed.), *The Social Foundations of Language and Thought* (pp. 316–342). New York: Norton.

Trevino, J. (2003). *Goffman's Legacy.* Lanham, MD: Rowman & Littlefield.

Tricaud, F. (1977). *L'accusation: Recherche Sur les Figures de L'agression Ethique.* Paris: Dalloz.

Trilling, L. (1971). *Sincerity and Authenticity.* Cambridge, MA: Harvard University Press.

Tronick, E. (1989). Emotions and emotional communication in infants. *American Psychologist, 44*: 112–119.

Tubert-Oklander, J. (2006). I, Thou, and Us: relationality and the interpretative process in clinical practice. *Psychoanalytic Dialogues, 16*: 199–216.

Tubert-Oklander, J. (2010). The safety net: postscript to 'Anarchy' by Richard M. Billow and the March 2010 issue of Group Analysis. *Group Analysis, 43*: 197–201.

Visser, M. (2009). *The Gift of Thanks: The Roots and Rituals of Gratitude.* Boston, MA: Houghton Mifflin Harcourt.

Volkan, V. (1985). The need to have enemies and allies: a developmental approach. *Political Psychology, 6*: 219–247.

Vygotsky, L. S. (1962). *Thought and Language.* Cambridge, MA: MIT Press.

Wallerstein, R. (1988). One psychoanalysis or many? *International Journal of Psychoanalysis, 12*: 60–70.

Warner, S. T. (1985). The Scapegoat (II. 1–4). In: *Selected Poems.* Manchester: Carcanet Press.

Watzlawick, P., Bavelas, J., & Jackson, D. (1967). *Pragmatics of Human Communication. A Study of Interactional Patterns, Pathologies, and Paradoxes*. New York: Norton.

Whitaker, C. A., & Bumberry, W. A. (1988). *Dancing With the Family: A Symbolic-experiential Approach*. New York: Brunner/Mazel.

Whitaker, D. (1989). Group focal conflict theory: Description, illustration and evaluation. *Group, 13*, 225–251.

Whitaker, D., & Lieberman, M. (1964). *Psychotherapy Through the Group Process*. Chicago, IL: Aldine.

Winnicott, D. W. (1971). *Playing and Reality*. London: Tavistock.

Wordsworth, W. (1839). *The Poetical Works of William Wordsworth, Vol. VIII*, W. Knight (Ed.). London: Macmillan, 1896.

Wright, F. (2004). Being seen, moved, disrupted and reconfigured: group leadership from a relational perspective. *International Journal of Group Psychotherapy, 54*: 235–250.

Yalom, I. (1995). *The Theory and Practice of Group Psychotherapy* (4th edn). New York: Basic Books.

Zacarro, S. J. (2007). Triad-based perspectives of leadership. *American Psychologist, 62*: 6–16.

Zemach, S. (1959). A theory of laughter. *Journal of Aesthetics and Art Criticism, 17*: 311–329.

INDEX

Adams, R., 182
affect(ive), xxiii, xxv, 5, 8, 18–22,
    24, 28, 41–45, 56–57, 59, 63,
    68, 70, 78, 88, 103, 154,
    157–159, 183, 201, 207, 221,
    228–229
    basic, 169, 227
    charge, 44
    depression/depressive, 44
    dimension, 6, 40, 52, 54, 161
    elements, 68
    links, 53
    openness, 185
    outburst, 42
    painful, 20
    process, 160
    reactions, 41
    resonance, 23
    response, 66
    saliency, 23
    sensory-, 8, 53–54, 62, 66
    significance, 56
Agazarian, Y. M., 18, 63, 157

aggression, xxii, 20, 28, 83, 89–90, 93,
    103–104, 109, 121–122, 126, 128,
    133, 135, 150, 154, 166–167,
    175–176, 179, 199, 205–208
    see also: sexual(ly)
Alford, C. F., 83, 184
Allen, J., 69, 226
American Group Psychotherapy
    Association (AGPA), xvii,
    147
Anderson, F. S., 228
anger, 9, 12–13, 18, 30, 33, 51, 58,
    60, 65–66, 70, 77–78, 82, 85, 106,
    110, 113, 116–117, 128–129, 131,
    154, 168, 175, 181, 188, 196, 202,
    218
Anspach, M. R., 180
Anthony, E., 18, 157
anxiety, xxiii, xxv, 12, 17, 20, 22,
    36–37, 44, 50, 52, 59, 66, 70, 75,
    77–78, 83–84, 102–103, 107, 110,
    113, 117–118, 126, 132, 135, 137,
    145, 148, 152, 154–155, 158, 161,